High Intermediate Course

i

NEW EDITION
TOEFL® iBT
SPEAKING

LinguaForum

New Edition TOEFL *i*BT i-Speaking

지은이	링구아포럼 리서치센터
선임연구원	Daniel K. Paxitzis
감수	William Winchester, Brantley Smith, Jamie Marr.
본문디자인	주보민
표지디자인	구수연
편집인	최선주
발행인	이길호
발행처	링구아포럼

1판 2쇄	2010. 10. 22			
교재문의	02) 3480-6627	대표전화 02) 3480-6614		
등록번호	제2000-000335호	등록일자 2000. 5. 17	ISBN 978-89-5563-533-9 (94740)	가격 17,000원

Copyright © 2009-2010 by LinguaForum
No unauthorized photocopying.
All rights reserved. No part of this book may be reproduced or transmitted in any form or by any means, electronic or mechanical, including photocopying, recording, or any other information storage and retrieval system without the written permission of the publisher.

이 책은 링구아포럼이 독창적으로 개발하였습니다. 이 책의 내용, 사진 등 일부 혹은 전체 내용을 어떠한 방법으로도 무단 복사, 복제, 전재하는 것은 저작권법에 의해 금지되어 있습니다.
Printed in the Republic of Korea

R/N (CRneiTFSG): 12280940KB/03191040KB/10221040KB

Foreword /머리말/

토플 Speaking은 대체 어떻게 공부해야 고득점을 얻을 수 있을까? 토플을 치러야 하는 모든 학생들이 한번쯤은 해본 질문이었을 것이다. 한국인들에게 Speaking은 토플 시험에서 가장 어려운 영역 중에 하나이다. 그렇기 때문에 토플 Speaking이 요구하는 능력이 무엇인지 정확하게 집고 넘어갈 필요가 있는 것이다.

토플 Speaking 영역에서는 대화능력을 테스트하고 있지 않다. 주어진 주제에 대해, 본인의 생각을 정리하여 혼자 말하는 능력을 테스트한다. 즉, 쌍방향 대화가 아닌 일방적으로 나의 생각을 말하는 것이다. 짧은 인터뷰나 프리즌테이션을 하는 것과 흡사하다. 그렇기 때문에 문제를 대할 때 최대한 나의 생각을 빨리 정리해서 조리 있게 말하는 데 초점을 두고 답을 준비해야 한다.

그렇다면 나의 생각을 빨리 정리해서 조리 있게 말할 수 있는 방법은 무엇일까? 무엇보다 토플 Speaking에서 다루는 주제를 정확하게 알아야 한다. 어떤 질문이 주어졌다 하더라도 그 질문에 대해 답을 하기 위해서는 생각을 해야 한다. 즉, 한국어로든 영어로든, 질문을 받았을 때 생각 없이 조리 있게 말을 하기는 어렵다. 만약 질문이 어렵다면 한국어로 답을 한다 할지라도 답하는 과정이 쉽지만은 않을 것이다. 이 때문에 토플러들은 무엇보다 먼저 각 Speaking tesk에서 다뤄지는 많은 문제 유형들을 비교분석하며 공부해야 한다. 문제에서 요구하는 것이 무엇인지 알면 각 문제를 어떻게 대해야 하는지 또한 알 수 있다. 문제에 답하는데 필요한 능력이 무엇인지 알 수 있다면 누구보다 효과적으로 TOEFL iBT를 준비할 수 있을 것이다.

TOEFL iBT Speaking을 치를 때 가장 중요한 능력은 요령이 아닌 기본기다. 아무리 시험을 치르는 기술이 훌륭해도 기본이 없이 토플 고득점을 획득하기란 거의 불가능하다고 봐야 한다. 여기서 말하는 기본기는 어휘가 50%, 문장 구성 능력 10%, 듣기 능력 10%, 그리고 말하기 능력 30% 정도로 구분할 수 있다. 시험을 준비함과 동시에 어휘를 공부해야 한다. 언어를 공부하는데 있어 어휘보다 더 중요한 것은 없다고 봐도 된다. 그만큼 어휘를 많이 알면 알수록 도움이 된다. 어휘를 공부하는 방법은 사람마다 다를 수 있다. 특별히 한가지 방법이 옳다고 말할 수는 없지만 어휘 암기에서 반복은 아주 중요하다. 무작정 쓰면서 암기하는 것 보다 의미나 분야별로 나눠진 어휘들을 반복해서 학습하다 보면 어휘를 자연스럽게 익힐 수 있다. 그리고 prefixes나 suffixes를 공부해서 정확한 어휘의 뜻은 모를 지라도 어휘의 뜻을 대략적으로 이해하면서 어휘 지식의 폭을 넓혀야 한다. 조금씩 아는 어휘가 많아지면 이때부터 독서를 통해 Context안에서 어휘를 이해하고 자연스럽게 받아드리는 연습을 하면 된다.

독서를 하면 어휘 능력뿐 아니라 문장 구성 능력이 높아진다. 여기서 말하는 문장 구성 능력은 쉽게 말하면 읽기 능력이다. 짧고 긴 문장들을 꾸준히 읽으면서 문장 구성 요소들을 살피며 문장 구성 이해와 함께 독해력을 높이는 것이다. 기초적으로 주어+동사의 구조를 바탕으로 문장이 어떻게 길게 만들어 지는지를 관찰하고 파악하는 연습이다. 이 연습을 통해서 어렵고 복잡한 문장도 아주 간단한 문장 구조임을 알 수 있게 된다. 물론 많이 읽는 것도 중요하지만 TOEFL에서 다루는 내용들을 읽는 것이 훨씬 더 중요하기 때문에 읽기 자료로는 Lingua TOEFL iBT Core Topic Guide v. 1-4권을 강력하게 추천한다. 이 4권의 책들을 통해 문장 구성 능력과 독해력을 높일 뿐 아니라 우리에게는 생소한 미국문화를 주제별로 아주 간단 명료하게 잘 설명해 놓았기 때문에 미국문화에 대해 깊이 있게 이해할 수 있게 될 것이다. Core Topic Guide는 토플을 준비하는 모든 수업생뿐 아니라 미국문화를 이해 하기 원하는 모든 이에게 큰 유익을 줄 것이다.

듣기 연습은 대학 강의를 추천한다. 미국의 많은 아이비리그 대학과 상위권 사립대학들은 인터넷 상에서 무료로 대학 강의를 들을 수 있도록 여러 많은 강의들을 제공하고 있다. 꾸준히 대학 수업을 듣다 보면 Integrated Tasks에서 다루는 대학 강의에 관한 문제들을 대하는 데도 많은 도움을 받을 수 있을 것이다.

그리고 마지막으로 말하기 능력이다. 말하기 능력은 하루 아침에 좋아지기는 힘들다. 많은 사람들이 원어민처럼 말하려고 노력한다. 원어민처럼 영어를 구사하면 좋겠지만 토플 Speaking 고득점을 위해서 꼭 원어민처럼 말해야 하는 것은 아니다. 영어를 모국어로 사용하지 않는 사람들을 위해 TOEFL Speaking이 제작 되었다는 것을 인지하고 질문에 대답을 할 때 외국인의 발음을 똑같이 흉내 내려고 하기 보다는 최대한 정확하게 발음해서 듣는 자가 내가 말하는 내용을 최대한 쉽게 이해할 수 있도록 일정한 속도로 분명하게 발음하며 말하는 연습을 거듭해야 한다. 실제로 토플 Speaking 수험생 중 발음은 원어민과 사뭇 다르지만 본인의 생각을 조리 있고 분명하게 발음하는 이들이 고득점이 많이 나온다. 무엇보다 자신 있고 당당하게 본인의 생각을 말할 수 있도록 꾸준히 연습하자.

LinguaForum TOEFL iBT i-Speaking New Edition은 수업생들이 무엇보다 TOEFL에 필요한 능력을 습득하는데 초점을 맞추고 제작되었다. 시험을 치르는데 가장 중요한 Skill을 선별하여 수험생이 직접 응용해서 사용하며 체계적으로 말하기 학습을 할 수 있도록 교재를 구성하였다. 그 외 시험에 필요한 모든 Skill들은 Workbook에 포함시켜 고득점을 노리는 학습자들을 위해 충분한 연습 문제를 제공하였다. 무엇보다 TOEFL을 공부할 때는 효율적으로 공부할 필요가 있다. 많은 내용을 공부하기 보다 선별된 자료를 체계적으로 공부해야 실질적인 도움을 받을 수 있다. 이 책의 안내에 따라 꼼꼼히, 그리고 충실히 문제를 풀어나가다 보면 어느덧 주어진 문제에 자신있게 영어로 답하는 자신의 모습을 발견하게 될 것이다.

LinguaForum Research Center
TOEFL iBT Speaking 연구팀

Structure /이 책의 구성과 특징/

PART A Independent Tasks

각 Task의 전반적인 설명과 Sample Q&A를 통해서 모든 문제를 정확하게 이해할 수 있도록 하였다. 그리고 Outlining → Speaking Grammar → Delivery의 단계적인 말하기 학습법을 통해 체계적으로 Independent Task를 대할 수 있도록 하였다.

■ Outlining

Brainstorming단계를 통해 여러 가지 주제에 대해 폭넓게 생각해 보는 연습을 하고, Outlining을 통해 구체적으로 본인이 말하고자 하는 요점들을 정리하는 연습을 제공하였다.

■ Speaking Grammar

Outlining 단계에서 정해진 Key words를 사용하여 가장 기초적이고 효율적인 문법을 사용하여 시험에서 즉시 사용할 수 있는 문장을 만드는 방법을 제시하였다. 그와 함께 Template을 사용하여 자연스럽게 문장을 말할 수 있도록 기본 틀을 제공하였다.

■ Delivery

완성된 답을 알맞게 끊어 읽는 연습을 함으로써, 질문에 자연스럽게 답할 수 있는 연습문제를 제공하였다. 또한 자세하게 분류된 Evaluation Sheet을 사용해서 본인 스스로, 혹은 친구나 선생님과 함께 수험생 자신의 답변을 채점할 수 있도록 하였다.

PART B Integrated Tasks

각 Task에 대한 전반적인 설명과 Sample Q&A를 통해서 모든 문제를 정확하게 이해할 수 있도록 하였다. 그리고 Outlining → Speaking Grammar → Delivery의 단계적인 말하기 학습법을 통해 체계적으로 Integrated Tasks를 연습할 수 있도록 하였다.

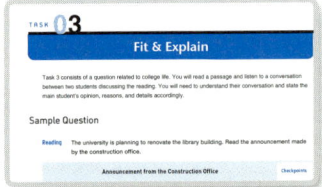

■ **Outlining**

Task 3 & 5는 대학 생활에 관한 주제를 다룬다. 먼저 Task 3에서는 지문을 읽고 대화를 들은 후 Note-taking을 하며, Task 5에서는 대화만 듣고 Note-taking하는 연습을 한다. 그리고 Task 4 & 6는 대학 강의에 관한 주제에 다루며 Task 4에서는 지문을 읽고, 강의를 들은 후 Note-taking을 하고, Task 6에서는 강의만 듣고 Note-taking하는 연습을 한다.

■ **Speaking Grammar**

Outlining 단계에서 Note-taking에서 쓴 Key words와 가장 효율적인 문법을 사용하여 시험에서 즉시 사용할 수 있는 문장을 만드는 방법을 제시하였다. 그와 함께 Template을 사용하여 자연스럽게 문장을 말할 수 있도록 기본 틀을 제공하였다.

■ **Delivery**

완성된 답을 알맞게 끊어 읽는 연습을 함으로써 질문에 자연스럽게 답할 수 있는 연습문제를 제공하였다. 또한 자세하게 분류된 Evaluation Sheet을 사용해서 본인 스스로, 혹은 친구나 선생님과 함께 수험생 자신의 답변을 채점할 수 있도록 하였다.

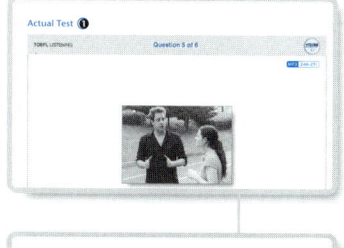

PART C Actual Test

2회분의 Actual Test를 수록하여, 실전에서의 자신의 예상 점수를 가늠해 보고 실전 적응력을 높일 수 있도록 하였다.

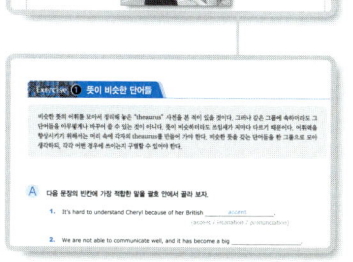

Workbook & Answer Key

시험에 필요한 모든 skill을 체계적으로 배울 수 있게 TOEFL에 필요한 skill관련 문제를 다량 수록하였다. 또한 Answer Key에는 Campus Tip를 제공하여 미국의 대학 생활에 대한 이해를 도울 수 있도록 하였다.

Contents

PART A **Independent Tasks**

Task 1. Personal Preference — 18

Task 2. Paired Choice — 32

PART B **Integrated Tasks**

Task 3. Fit & Explain — 60

Task 4. General / Specific — 74

Task 5. Problem / Solution — 88

Task 6. Summary — 102

PART C Actual Test

Actual Test 1   **119**

Actual Test 2   **127**

Workbook

1. Independent Task Skills   137
2. Integrated Task Skills   163
3. Pronunciation   189
4. Grammar   197

Orientation   220

Answer Key & Explanations

http://test.linguaforum.com 자료실에서 다양한 학습 자료를 볼 수 있습니다.

PART *A*

Independent Tasks

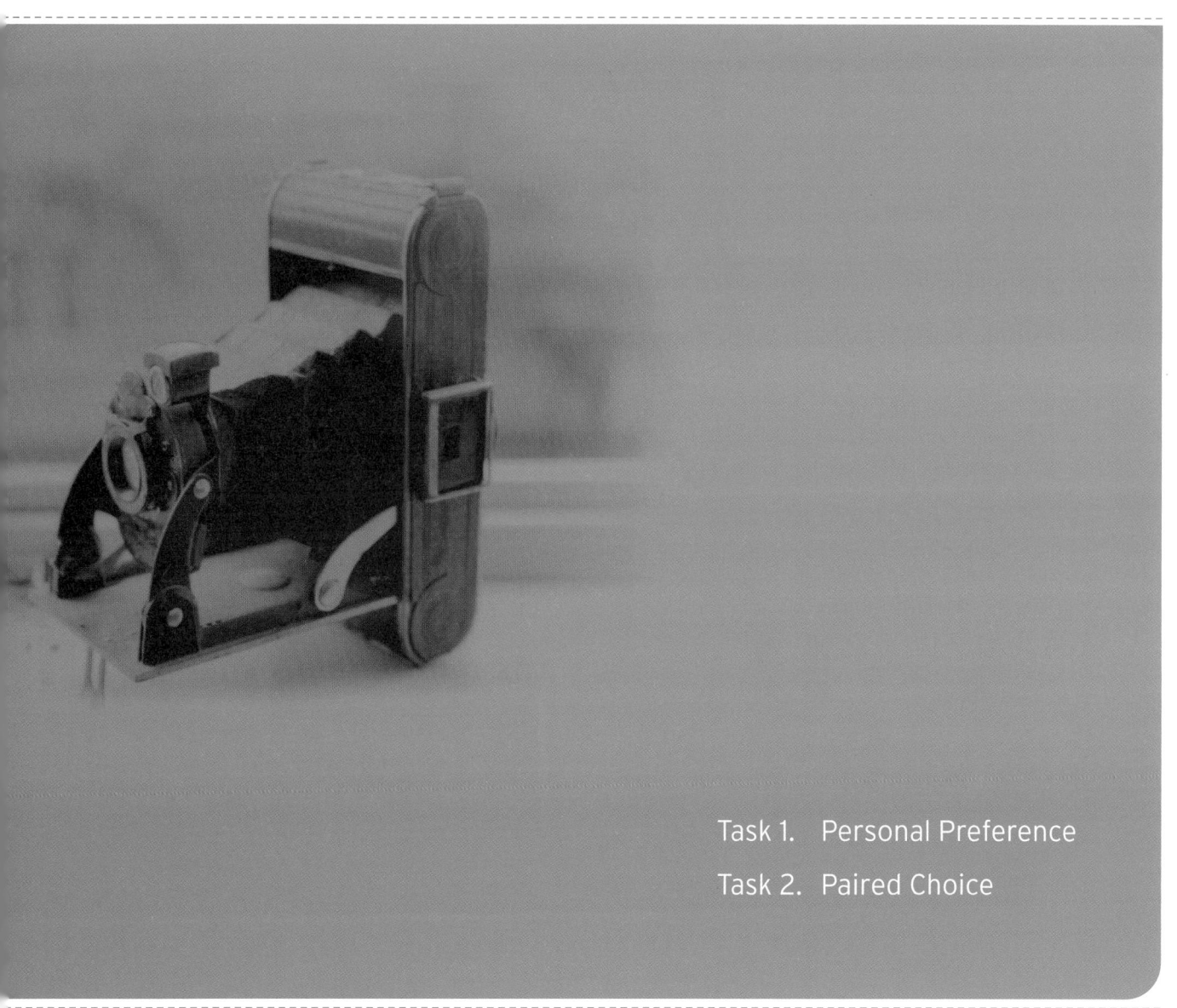

Task 1. Personal Preference
Task 2. Paired Choice

Independent Speaking Tasks

In this section, you will demonstrate your ability to discuss a variety of topics. You will provide speaking responses for Tasks 1 and 2 in the Independent Speaking section, and you will not be required to read a passage or listen to anything in order to answer the questions. Rather, you will base your responses on your own experiences and opinions.

Task 1

What does the question ask?

: It asks you to talk about your personal hobbies, choices, interests, or events.

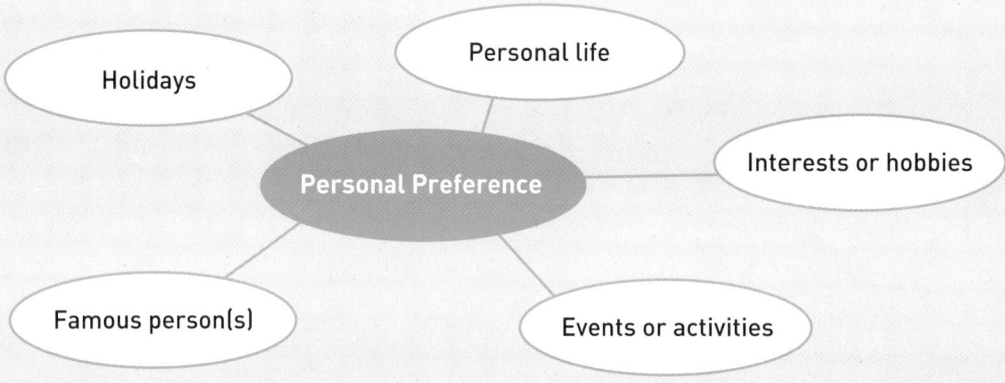

How much time do I have?

: 60 seconds

Question Types for Task 1

- If you could only take one entertainment item with you on vacation, what would it be and why would you take it? Include details and examples in your response.

- Describe your favorite mode of transportation and why it is your favorite. Please include details and examples in your response.

- If you could change one policy at your school, what policy would you change and why would you change it? Include examples and details to support your explanation.

- Describe an interesting person you know and explain why you find that person interesting. Please include examples and details in your response.

Responding Process of Task 1

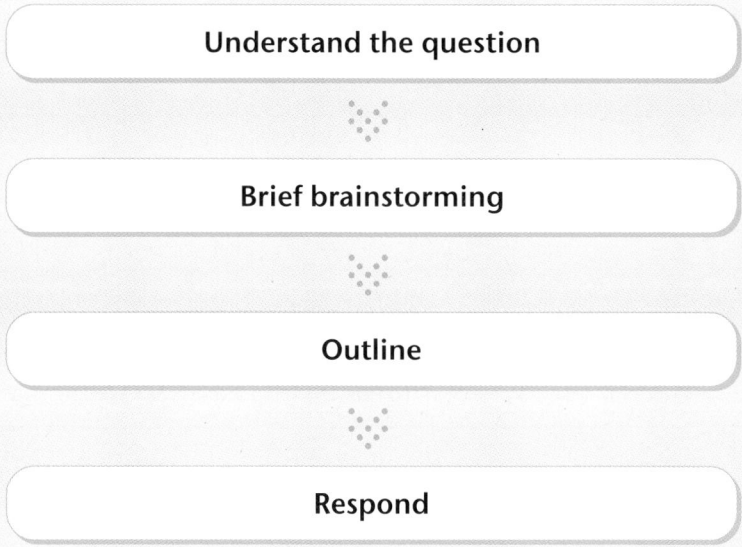

Strategies for Task 1

- Quickly understand what the question asks you to do
- (Produce many ideas through a brainstorming process)
- Organize the ideas in an outline
- Practice expressing key ideas in complete sentences
- Relax and speak clearly and confidently
- Do not hesitate or mumble, even when you make mistakes
- Remember, your time is limited

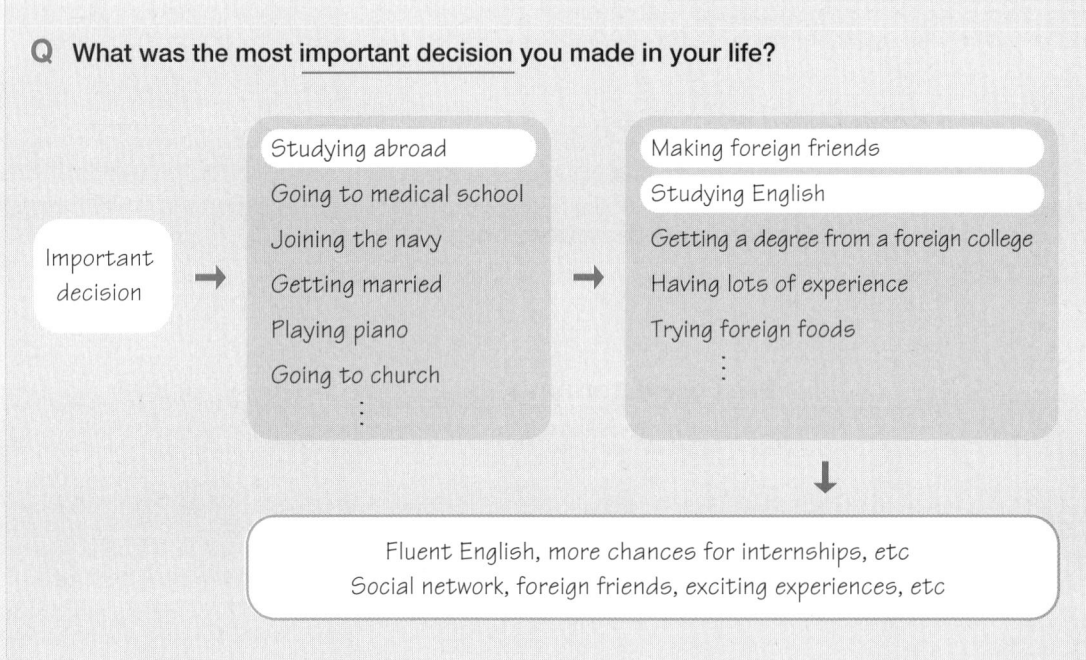

Q What was the most important decision you made in your life?

Important decision →
- Studying abroad
- Going to medical school
- Joining the navy
- Getting married
- Playing piano
- Going to church
⋮

→
- Making foreign friends
- Studying English
- Getting a degree from a foreign college
- Having lots of experience
- Trying foreign foods
⋮

↓

Fluent English, more chances for internships, etc
Social network, foreign friends, exciting experiences, etc

Task 2

What does the question ask?

: It asks you to choose one of two perspectives on an issue or one of two ways of doing something.

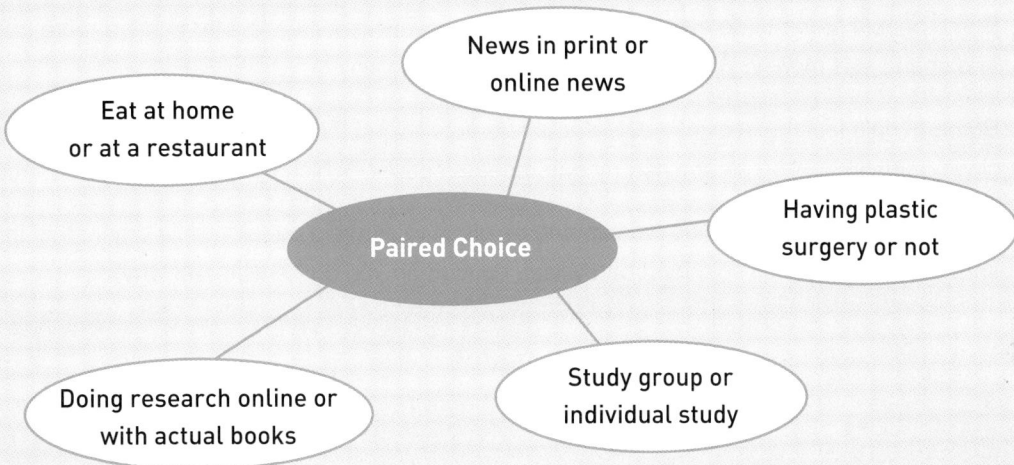

How much time do I have?

: 60 seconds

Part A. Independent Tasks • 15

Question Types for Task 2

- Some people like to do activities (e.g. a picnic, a walk, a short trip, a game) during a holiday. Other people prefer to stay home and relax. Which way do you prefer and why?

- Some students prefer living with a roommate, while others prefer to live alone. Which do you prefer and why?

- Some people prefer to do extra work for more money, while others prefer to have more free time and spend less money. Which option do you prefer and why?

- Some people feel that a class grade should be determined by several tests, while others feel that a class grade should be determined by one research paper. Which opinion do you prefer and why?

- Some people feel that surplus food should be given to starving people, while others feel that surplus food should be sold for profit. Which opinion do you agree with and why?

Responding Process of Task 2

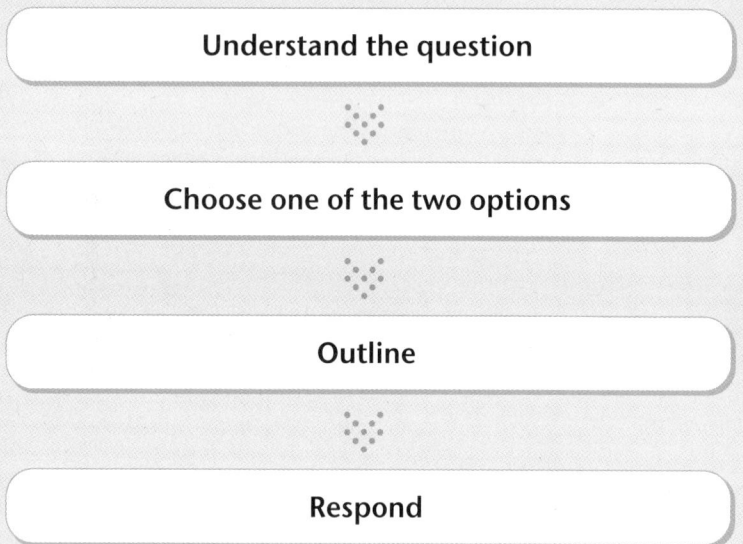

Understand the question

↓

Choose one of the two options

↓

Outline

↓

Respond

Strategies for Task 2

- Quickly understand what the question asks you to do
- Choose one of the two options as quickly as you can
- (Produce many ideas through a brainstorming process)
- Organize the ideas in an outline
- Practice expressing key ideas in complete sentences
- Relax and speak clearly and confidently
- Do not hesitate or mumble, even when you make mistakes
- Remember, your time is limited

Q Some people want to go to the mall with friends and others by themselves. <u>Which of the two ways of shopping</u> do you prefer and why?

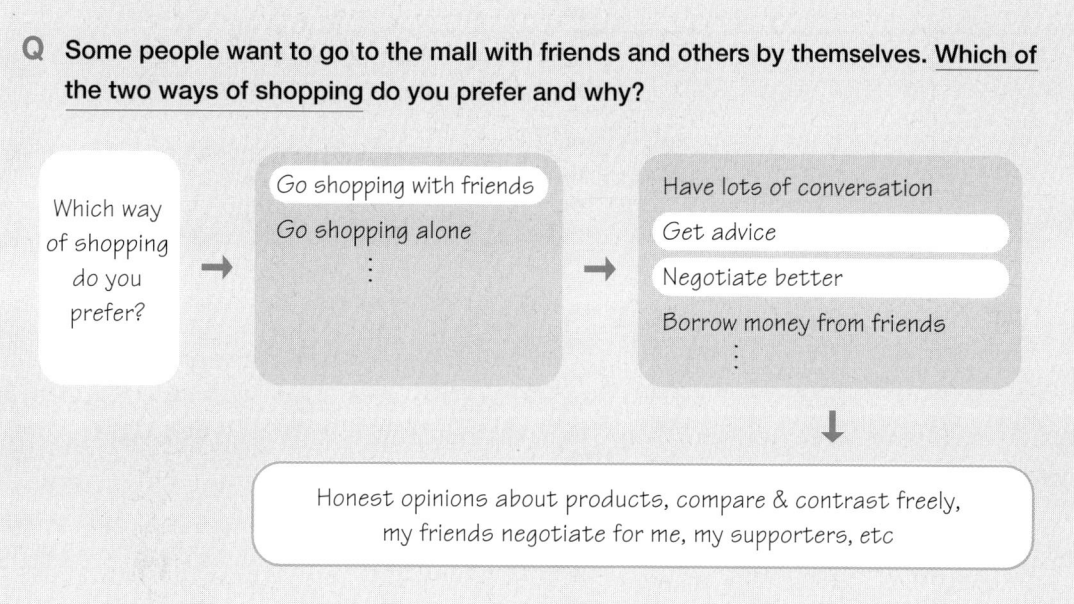

Which way of shopping do you prefer? → Go shopping with friends / Go shopping alone → Have lots of conversation / Get advice / Negotiate better / Borrow money from friends

↓

Honest opinions about products, compare & contrast freely, my friends negotiate for me, my supporters, etc

TASK 01

Personal Preference

Task 1 will ask you to describe your personal life, choices, or interests. You need to discuss an issue, a place, a holiday, a person, etc. The topics for Task 1 will vary, but you will always be asked to base your response on your personal opinions or experiences. When you respond, you need to provide you main topic along with reasons and supporting details.

Sample Question MP3 2

Q   What is your favorite city in the world and why? Please include details and examples in your response.

Preparation time : 15 seconds
Response time   : 45 seconds

| Responding process of Task 1 |

| Topic | Reason 1 & Details | Reason 2 & Details |

1. Personal Preference

Make an outline

Topic	New York	
Reason 1		**Reason 2**
Diversity		Convenience
Details		**Details**
- Various kinds of ethnic foods - Lots of people from all around the world		- A good transportation system - Many shopping malls

Sample Response

New York
→ My favorite city in the world is New York.

Diversity – Various kinds of ethnic foods – Lots of people from all around the world
→ First, I like New York because of its diversity. Meeting lots of people from all around the world and tasting various kinds of ethnic foods are what I love about New York.

Convenience – A good transportation system – Many shopping malls
→ Second, to live in New York is to live among many conveniences. That I can live my life with a good transportation system and many shopping malls around is one of the greatest merits of living in New York.

It is very important that you practice making key ideas into complete sentences. As you practice more, you will gain confidence to respond to the questions of Task 1.

1 Outlining

>> Read the questions and develop your ideas.

1 What is the most fascinating place you have ever visited and what made it so interesting? Please include specific details and examples in your response.

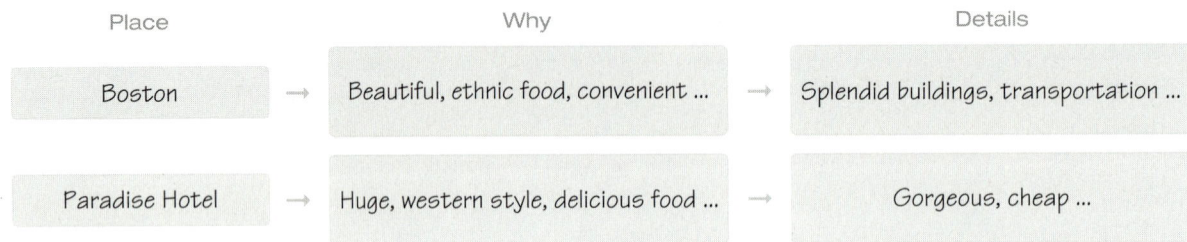

Place	Why	Details
Boston	Beautiful, ethnic food, convenient ...	Splendid buildings, transportation ...
Paradise Hotel	Huge, western style, delicious food ...	Gorgeous, cheap ...

2 Describe an activity you would like to do on weekends and explain why. Include details and examples to support your explanation.

Activity	Why	Details

3 If you could do one thing to improve your community, what would you do and why? Please include specific details and examples in your response.

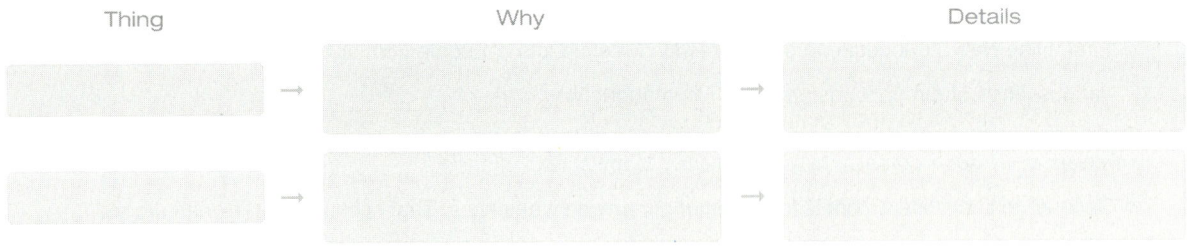

Thing	Why	Details

4 What do you think is the most helpful device ever invented and why do you think so? Include details and examples to support your explanation.

Device	Why	Details

1. Personal Preference

≫ Read the questions and fill in the blanks with key ideas.

1 What is the most fascinating place you have ever visited and what made it so interesting? Please include specific details and examples in your response.

Topic	Boston
Reason 1 Beautiful	**Reason 2** Convenient
Details Streets are filled with splendid buildings	**Details** A well-organized transportation system

2 Describe an activity you would like to do on weekends and explain why. Include details and examples to support your explanation.

Topic	
Reason 1	**Reason 2**
Details	**Details**

3 If you could do one thing to improve your community, what would you do and why? Please include specific details and examples in your response.

Topic	
Reason 1	**Reason 2**
Details	**Details**

4 What do you think is the most helpful device ever invented and why do you think so? Include details and examples to support your explanation.

Topic	
Reason 1	**Reason 2**
Details	**Details**

2 Speaking Grammar

■ **Sentence Structure:** Subject + Predicate

Noun + Verb	My favorite activity **is** to play soccer.
To infinitive + Verb	To play soccer in front of thousands of fans **would be** my dream come true.
Gerund + Verb	Playing soccer **is** my favorite activity during weekends.
Noun clause + Verb	That playing soccer is my favorite activity **is known** to all my friends.

■ **Templates**

- Templates for Topic Sentences

As far as I'm concerned	**As far as I'm concerned,** my favorite activity is to play soccer.
In my opinion,	**In my opinion,** there is no better way to spend one's weekend than playing soccer.

- Templates for Reason Sentences

One reason is that...	**One reason is that** soccer is exciting.
The other reason is that...	**The other reason is that** playing soccer is a great way to enjoy spending my time.

- Templates for Detail Sentences

What I'm saying is that...	**What I'm saying is that** soccer is so fun that I even forget to eat while playing it.
In other words,	**In other words,** soccer is an excellent activity that I can enjoy with my friends.

1. Personal Preference

≫ **Complete and speak your answers.**

1 What is the most fascinating place you have ever visited and what made it so interesting? Please include specific details and examples in your response.

- **Topic** As far as I'm concerned, Boston is the most fascinating place in the world.
  - **Reason 1** One reason is that Boston is very beautiful.
    - **Details** What I am saying is that the streets in Boston are filled with splendid buildings.
  - **Reason 2** The other reason is that Boston is very convenient.
    - **Details** In other words, Boston has a good transportation system. So, it's very convenient to commute in Boston.

2 Describe an activity you would like to do on weekends and explain why. Include details and examples to support your explanation.

- **Topic** In my opinion,
  - **Reason 1** One reason is that
    - **Details** What I am saying is that
  - **Reason 2** The other reason is that
    - **Details** In other words,

Speaking Grammar

3 If you could do one thing to improve your community, what would you do and why? Please include specific details and examples in your response.

- **Topic** As far as I'm concerned, _____
  - **Reason 1** One reason is that _____
    - **Details** What I am saying is that _____
    _____
    _____
  - **Reason 2** The other reason is that _____
    - **Details** In other words, _____
    _____
    _____

4 What do you think is the most helpful device ever invented and why do you think so? Include details and examples to support your explanation.

- **Topic** In my opinion, _____
  - **Reason 1** One reason is that _____
    - **Details** What I am saying is that _____
    _____
    _____
  - **Reason 2** The other reason is that _____
    - **Details** In other words, _____
    _____
    _____

③ Delivery

— 1. Personal Preference

1 Put a slash ("/") where you want to pause (before commas, prepositions, conjunctions, etc.) and respond slowly.

> As far as I'm concerned, / Boston is the most fascinating place for me. / One reason is that / Boston is very beautiful. / What I am saying is that / the streets in Boston are filled with splendid buildings. / The other reason is that / Boston is very convenient. / In other words, / Boston has a good transportation system. / So, / it's very convenient to commute in Boston.

* As shown above, practice the delivery with your answers for Q2, Q3, & Q4.

Read the evaluation questions and check the level of your delivery. On a scale from 1 to 5 (1=very poor, 2=poor, 3=OK, 4=good, 5=very good), rank your delivery accordingly.

Could you complete your response?	1	2	3	4	5
Is your answer coherent and unified?	1	2	3	4	5
Do you find a sequence in your response?	1	2	3	4	5
How is the use of vocabulary?	1	2	3	4	5
Does your response show grammatical structures?	1	2	3	4	5
How is the use of idiomatic expressions?	1	2	3	4	5
Is your response fluent and smooth?	1	2	3	4	5
Is your pronunciation clear?	1	2	3	4	5
How is the use of stress and intonation?	1	2	3	4	5

* Use the extra evaluation sheets provided at the end of the main textbook (p.227) and evaluate your deliveries for Q2, Q3, & Q4.

Practice Questions

» Read the questions and speak your answers.

1 If you could only take one entertainment item with you on vacation, what would it be and why would you take it? Include details and examples in your response.

Preparation time : 15 seconds | Response time : 45 seconds

2 Describe your favorite mode of transportation and why it is your favorite. Please include details and examples in your response.

Preparation time : 15 seconds | Response time : 45 seconds

| 1. Personal Preference |

3 What was your proudest moment in school and why are you proud of that moment? Use specific examples and details in your response.

Preparation time : 15 seconds | **Response time :** 45 seconds

4 If you could change one policy at your school, what policy would you change and why would you change it? Include examples and details to support your explanation.

Preparation time : 15 seconds | **Response time :** 45 seconds

Practice Questions

5 Describe an interesting person you know and explain why you find that person interesting. Please include examples and details in your response.

Preparation time : 15 seconds | **Response time :** 45 seconds

6 Describe a musical instrument that you would like to learn to play and explain why you want to learn it. Use specific details and examples in your response.

Preparation time : 15 seconds | **Response time :** 45 seconds

| 1. Personal Preference

7 Describe an event that was historically important for your country and explain why. Please include specific details and examples in your response.

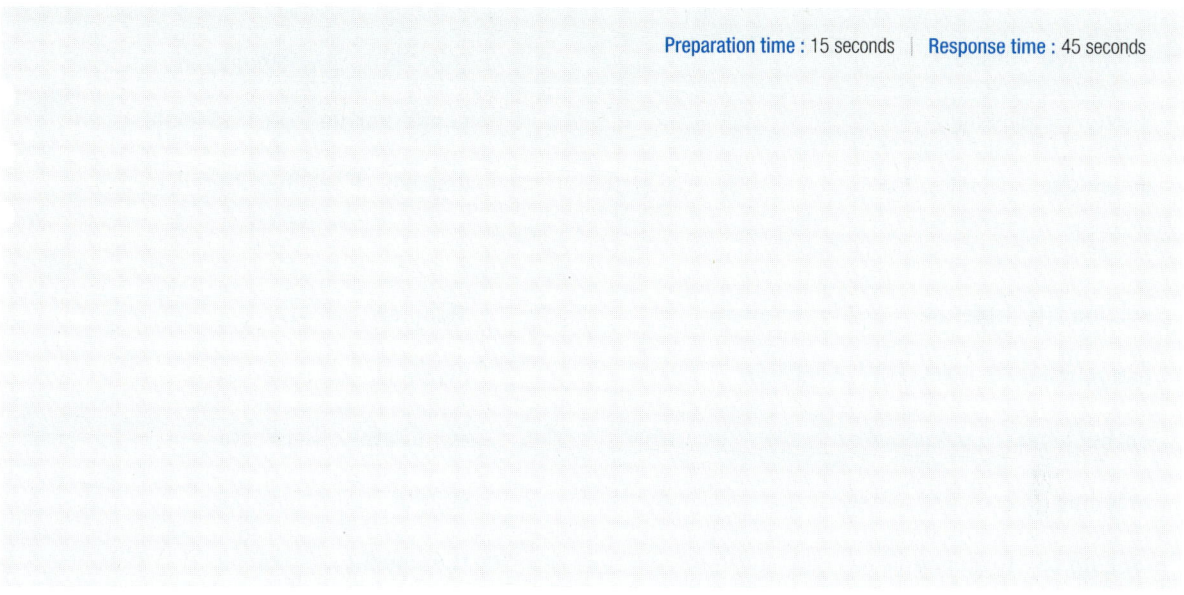

Preparation time : 15 seconds | Response time : 45 seconds

8 Describe a person that you think has a great influence on people's lives today. Include specific details and examples in your response.

Preparation time : 15 seconds | Response time : 45 seconds

Vocabulary Study — Daily Expressions

- **spare time**   free time
- **talent**   *n.* ability, gift
- **dream job**   desirable job
- **hiking**   *n.* climbing
- **genealogy**   *n.* family tree

- **surfing the Internet**   using the Internet
- **babysitting**   *n.* taking care of children
- **enthusiasm**   *n.* passion, zeal
- **attempt**   *n.* try
- **look up to**   to admire

- **a lifetime friend**   a close friend
- **study abroad**   study in a foreign county
- **go to the theater**   watch a movie
- **hang out**   spend time socially
- **egocentric**   *adj.* selfish

- **ambitious**   *adj.* aspiring
- **determined**   *adj.* strong minded
- **hilarious**   *adj.* very funny
- **hasty decisions**   quick decisions
- **coincidence**   *n.* accidental happening

- **kind-hearted**   *adj.* compassionate
- **self-assured**   *adj.* confident
- **reluctant**   *adj.* unwilling
- **conservative**   *adj.* traditional
- **discern**   *v.* tell the difference

- **sluggish**   *adj.* lazy
- **insolent**   *adj.* rude
- **stimulate**   *v.* motivate
- **skillful**   *adj.* having skills
- **thoughtful**   *adj.* caring

- **vigorous**   *adj.* strong
- **pleasant**   *adj.* pleasing
- **adorable**   *adj.* lovable
- **chore**   *n.* everyday jobs
- **beware**   *v.* be careful

- **vulnerable**   *adj.* weak
- **tardy**   *adj.* late
- **urgent**   *adj.* needing immediate attention
- **feel at home**   feel comfortable
- **stressed out**   exhausted

A Choose the word which is closest in meaning to the vocabulary listed below.

1. Genealogy
2. Determined
3. Vigorous
4. Discern
5. Self-assured
6. Sluggish
7. Vulnerable
8. Insolent
9. Pleasant
10. Tardy

(a) Confident
(b) Tell the difference
(c) Rude
(d) Strong minded
(e) Family tree
(f) Lazy
(g) Strong
(h) Weak
(i) Late
(j) Pleasing

B Complete the sentences by filling in the blanks.

| hilarious | reluctant | enthusiasm | kind-hearted | looked up to |
| egocentric | genealogy | conservative | pleasant | chores |

1. People who have _____ are very diligent and passionate in whatever they do.

2. The _____ party did not want him to be the president of the U.S.A.

3. The Indians were _____ to eat the pizza because they didn't like instant food.

4. Most students in the class _____ their teacher.

5. An _____ person rarely cares about the thoughts and feelings of others.

TASK 02

Paired Choice

Task 2 asks you to choose one of two perspectives on a given issue or one of two alternative ways of doing something. Choose one point of view as quickly as you can and prepare your response. When you respond, you need to provide your main topic along with reasons and supporting details.

Sample Question MP3 3

Q Some course grades are largely based on students' individual projects, while other courses put great importance on team projects. Which way of grading do you prefer and why? Please include details and examples in your response.

| Preparation time : 15 seconds |
| Response time   : 45 seconds |

| Responding process of Task 2 |

Topic → **Reason 1 & Details** → **Reason 2 & Details**

| 2. Paired Choice |

Make an outline

Topic: Individual Projects

Reason 1	Reason 2
Fairer way to grade students	Better results
Details	**Details**
- Team project: only 1 or 2 stud. work hard. - Everyone gets the same grade: Not fair!	- Ind. proj. motivate stud. to study harder - Team papers tend to be short & superficial

Sample Response

Individual projects
→ In my opinion, individual projects should be considered more important than team projects when grading students' performances.

Fairer way to grade students - Team project: only 1 or 2 stud. work hard. - Everyone gets the same grade: Not fair!
→ This is because I believe the grading system based on individual work is a fairer way to grade students. Nine times out of ten, only one or two students really work hard on a team project. So, it is not fair if every member of a team gets the same grade regardless of their contribution.

Better results - Ind. proj. motivate stud. to study harder - Team papers tend to be short & superficial
→ Another reason is that focusing on individual projects can derive better results from students. Individual projects give students motivation to study harder, since students are aware that they're going to be graded based on their own work, while team papers tend to be relatively short and superficial.

It is very important that you practice making key ideas into complete sentences. As you practice more, you will gain confidence to respond to the questions of Task 2.

1 Outlining

>> Read the questions and develop your ideas.

1 Some people like listening to music while they study, and others would rather not listen to music while studying. Which do you prefer and why?

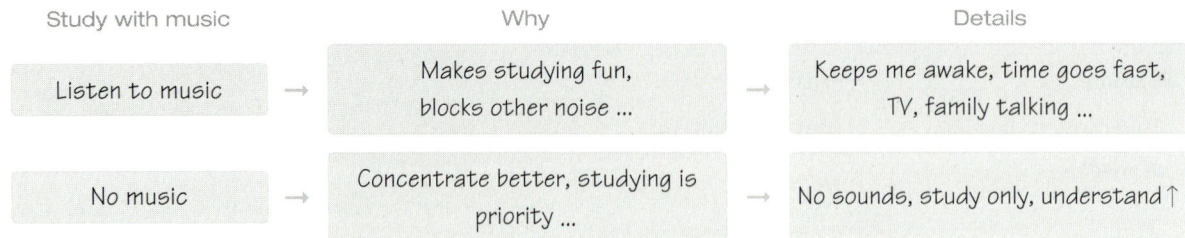

Study with music	Why	Details
Listen to music →	Makes studying fun, blocks other noise ... →	Keeps me awake, time goes fast, TV, family talking ...
No music →	Concentrate better, studying is priority ... →	No sounds, study only, understand ↑

2 Some people like eating dinner at home on their birthdays, while others like going out to nice restaurants for their birthdays. Which do you prefer and why?

Where to eat	Why	Details
→	→	
→	→	

3 Some people would like one four-month summer vacation from school, while other people would like separate, shorter vacations. Which option do you prefer and why?

Kind of vacation	Why	Details
→	→	
→	→	

4 Some people prefer to work during the day, while others prefer to work at night. Which way do you prefer and why?

When to work	Why	Details
→	→	
→	→	

2. Paired Choice

» Read the questions and fill in the blanks with key ideas.

1 Some people like listening to music while they study, and others would rather not listen to music while studying. Which do you prefer and why?

Topic	Listen to music
Reason 1 Makes studying fun	**Reason 2** Blocks other noise
Details - Keeps me awake - Time goes fast	**Details** - TV - Family talking

2 Some people like eating dinner at home on their birthdays, while others like going out to nice restaurants for their birthdays. Which do you prefer and why?

Topic	
Reason 1	**Reason 2**
Details	**Details**

3 Some people would like one four-month summer vacation from school, while other people would like separate, shorter vacations. Which option do you prefer and why?

Topic	
Reason 1	**Reason 2**
Details	**Details**

4 Some people prefer to work during the day, while others prefer to work at night. Which way do you prefer and why?

Topic	
Reason 1	**Reason 2**
Details	**Details**

2 Speaking Grammar

■ **Sentence Structure: Comparatives**

1 & 2 syllables: **adj. + -er**	Living in a small town is **wis**er than living in a big city.
3 syllables: **more + adj.**	People who live in a small town feel more **comfortable** than people who live in a big city.
Descriptive adj. (awake, alike, alone): **more + adj.**	People living in a small town are more **aware** of the quality of living than people living in a big city are.

■ **Templates**

- Templates for Topic Sentences

I would say that	**I would say that** people living in a small town are wiser than people living in a big city.
I believe that...	**I believe that** people living in a small town feel more comfortable than people living in a big city.

- Templates for Reason Sentences

That's because...	**That's because** it's especially better to raise kids in a small town.
Furthermore,	**Furthermore,** people who live in a small town feel more comfortable than people who live in a big city.

- Templates for Detail Sentences

I mean...	**I mean** our kids can benefit from a safe environment and a friendly neighborhood.
Especially,	**Especially,** clean air and pure water can help maintain good health.

2. Paired Choice

≫ **Complete and speak your answers.**

1 Some people like listening to music while they study, and others would rather not listen to music while studying. Which do you prefer and why?

Topic I would say that listening to music while I study is more helpful than not listening to music.

Reason 1 That's because music makes studying fun.

Details I mean I can stay awake while studying if I listen to music that I love. Besides, I feel that time flies when I listen to my favorite music while studying.

Reason 2 Furthermore, I won't be disturbed by noise if I listen to music when I study.

Details Especially, my family and relatives often gather together to watch TV and have talks. If I listen to music while studying, I won't be annoyed by noise outside my room.

2 Some people like eating dinner at home on their birthdays, while others like going out to nice restaurants for their birthdays. Which do you prefer and why?

Topic I believe that

Reason 1 That's because

Details I mean

Reason 2 Furthermore,

Details Especially,

Speaking Grammar

3 Some people would like one four-month summer vacation from school, while other people would like separate, shorter vacations. Which option do you prefer and why?

- **Topic** I would say that _____
  - **Reason 1** That's because _____
    - **Details** I mean _____
      _____
      _____
  - **Reason 2** Furthermore, _____
    - **Details** Especially, _____
      _____
      _____

4 Some people prefer to work during the day, while others prefer to work at night. Which way do you prefer and why?

- **Topic** I believe that _____
  - **Reason 1** That's because _____
    - **Details** I mean _____
      _____
      _____
  - **Reason 2** Furthermore, _____
    - **Details** Especially, _____
      _____
      _____

③ Delivery

---| 2. Paired Choice |

1 Put a slash ("/") where you want to pause (before commas, prepositions, conjunctions, etc.) and respond slowly.

> I would say that listening to music / while I study is more helpful than not listening to music. / That's because / music makes studying fun. / I mean / I can stay awake while studying / if I listen to music that I love. / Besides, / I feel that time flies / as I listen to my favorite music while studying. / Furthermore, / I won't be disturbed by noise / if I listen to music when I study. / Especially, / my family and relatives often gather together to watch TV / and have talks. / If I listen to music while studying, / I won't be annoyed by noise / outside my room.

* As shown above, practice the delivery with your answers for Q2, Q3, & Q4.

Read the evaluation questions and check the level of your delivery. On a scale from 1 to 5 (1=very poor, 2=poor, 3=OK, 4=good, 5=very good), rank your delivery accordingly.

Could you complete your response?	1	2	3	4	5
Is your answer coherent and unified?	1	2	3	4	5
Do you find a sequence in your response?	1	2	3	4	5
How is the use of vocabulary?	1	2	3	4	5
Does your response show grammatical structures?	1	2	3	4	5
How is the use of idiomatic expressions?	1	2	3	4	5
Is your response fluent and smooth?	1	2	3	4	5
Is your pronunciation clear?	1	2	3	4	5
How is the use of stress and intonation?	1	2	3	4	5

* Use the extra evaluation sheets provided at the end of the main textbook (p.227) and evaluate your deliveries for Q2, Q3, & Q4.

Practice Questions

>> Read the questions and speak your answers.

1 Some students prefer living with a roommate, while others prefer to live alone. Which do you prefer and why?

Preparation time : 15 seconds | Response time : 45 seconds

2 Some people like to do activities (e.g. a picnic, a walk, a short trip, playing a game) on a holiday. Other people prefer to stay home and relax. Which way do you prefer and why?

Preparation time : 15 seconds | Response time : 45 seconds

2. Paired choice

3 Some people think that schools should emphasize the learning of art, while others think that the learning of science is more important. Which opinion do you agree with and why?

Preparation time : 15 seconds | Response time : 45 seconds

4 Some people prefer to do extra work for more money, while others prefer to have more free time and spend less money. Which option do you prefer and why?

Preparation time : 15 seconds | Response time : 45 seconds

Practice Questions

5 Some people think that colleges should not keep students for more than five years, while others think colleges should allow students to attend as long as necessary. Which opinion do you agree with and why?

Preparation time : 15 seconds | Response time : 45 seconds

6 Some people feel that a class grade should be determined by several tests, while others feel that a class grade should be determined by one research paper. Which opinion do you prefer and why?

Preparation time : 15 seconds | Response time : 45 seconds

2. Paired Choice

7 Some people like riding in carpools, while others like riding alone. Which option do you prefer and why?

Preparation time : 15 seconds | Response time : 45 seconds

8 Some people feel that surplus food should be given to starving people, while others feel that surplus food should be sold for profit. Which opinion do you agree with and why?

Preparation time : 15 seconds | Response time : 45 seconds

Vocabulary Study — Daily Expressions

- **eat out** having meals at a restaurant
- **trivial** *adj.* insignificant
- **go through** undergo
- **preference** *n.* liking
- **appreciation** *n.* thanks

- **convenience** *n.* easy
- **intelligence** *n.* cleverness
- **cost-effective** *adj.* cheap
- **vice versa** *adv.* conversely
- **hold your horses** be patient

- **pick up your ears** listen carefully
- **judgmental** *adj.* critical
- **expectant** *adj.* expecting for something good
- **awesome** *adj.* very amazing
- **skeptical** *adj.* doubtful

- **self-centered** *adj.* selfish
- **high-spirited** *adj.* full of joy
- **anxious** *adj.* worried
- **tip of the iceberg** a small visible part
- **to make a long story short** to simplify

- **prejudiced** *adj.* biased
- **outdated** *adj.* old-fashioned
- **endurance** *n.* patience
- **magnificent** *adj.* very good
- **educated** *adj.* having gained knowledge at school

- **opinionated** *adj.* expressing one's opinion strongly
- **passionate** *adj.* having strong zeal
- **optimistic** *adj.* positive
- **hesitation** *n.* pause due to uncertainty or fear
- **idealistic** *adj.* believing in something good

- **outgoing** *adj.* sociable
- **pathetic** *adj.* causing sadness or sympathy
- **gifted** *adj.* outstanding
- **termination** *n.* end, stop
- **modify** *v.* change

- **intervene** *v.* intentionally get involved
- **give it a try** attempt
- **come up with** suggest
- **at the end of the day** in the long run
- **long for** desire

A Choose the word which is closest in meaning to the vocabulary listed below.

1. Prejudiced
2. Outgoing
3. Trivial
4. Give it a try
5. Self-centered
6. Termination
7. Magnificent
8. Judgmental
9. Come up with
10. Endurance

(a) Very good
(b) Attempt
(c) Sociable
(d) Insignificant
(e) End
(f) Critical
(g) Biased
(h) Suggest
(i) Patience
(j) Selfish

B Complete the sentences by filling in the blanks.

| pathetic | anxious | skeptical | optimistic | outdated |
| awesome | come up with | long for | convenience | educated |

1. The _____ man was so knowledgeable that he could answer all the questions asked.

2. Though he did very poorly on his mid-term test, he was _____ about the result of the test.

3. I couldn't _____ any solution to handle that situation because I was completely lost at that time.

4. I am so lucky that a(n) _____ store is located right next to my house.

5. The concert ticket was very expensive, but the performance was _____ last night.

PART B

Integrated Tasks

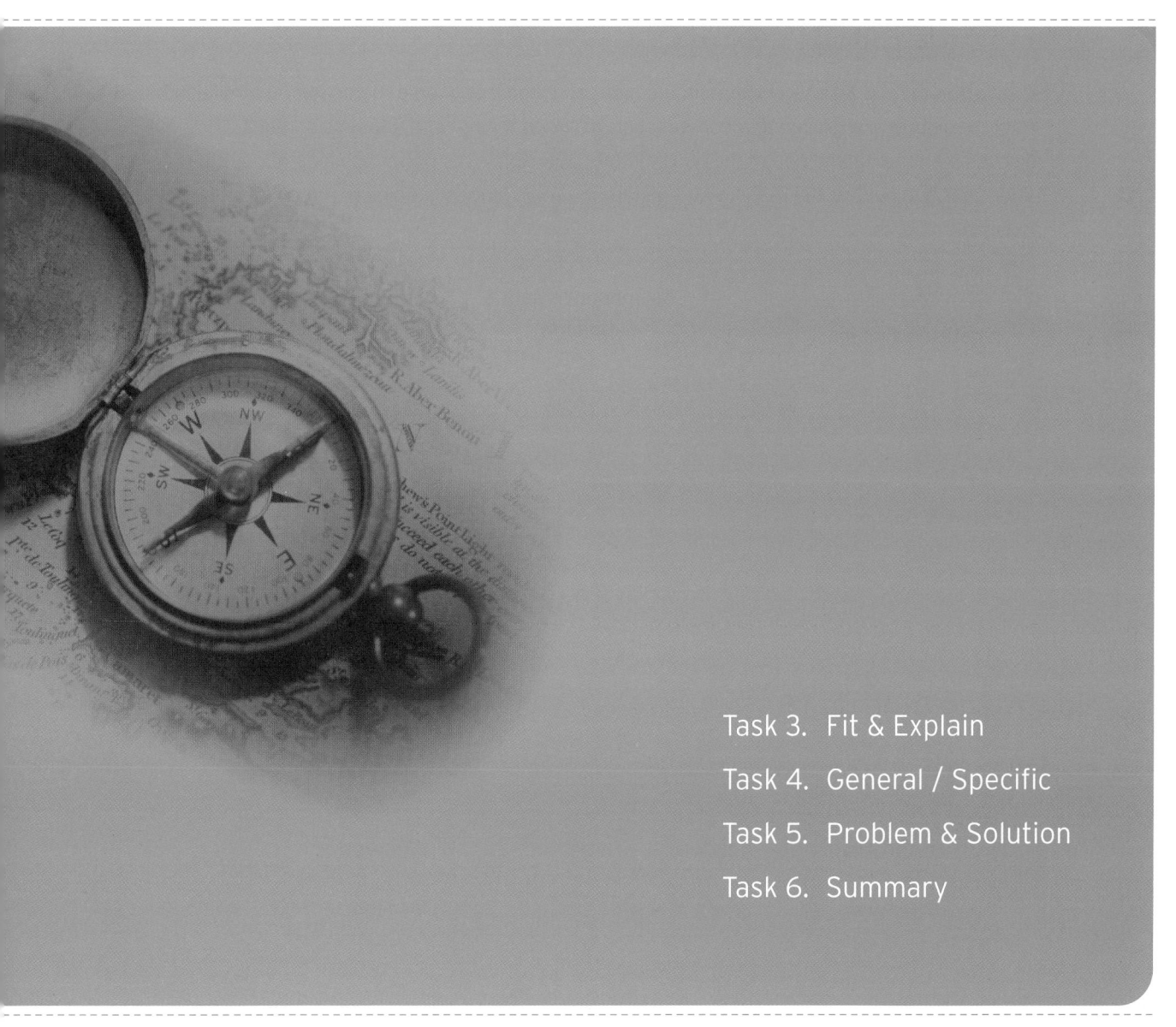

Task 3. Fit & Explain
Task 4. General / Specific
Task 5. Problem & Solution
Task 6. Summary

Integrated Speaking Tasks

In this section, you will demonstrate your ability to synthesize and paraphrase the listening and/or reading passages. In the Integrated Speaking section you will respond to tasks 3, 4, 5, and 6. Tasks 3 and 4 contain both reading and listening passages, and tasks 5 and 6 contain listening passages only. Tasks 3 & 5 ask questions related to campus life, and tasks 4 and 6 ask questions related lectures. With the exception of Task 5, you are not basing your responses on your personal opinions or experiences but solely on information from the listening and/or reading passages.

Task 3

What does the question ask?

: It asks you to read an announcement, a notice, an E-mail, or even a memo left on a bulletin board. After reading, you will listen to a conversation between a male and a female student. They will discuss the reading and one of the two students will explain his or her opinions about the reading. Your task is to explain the reading and restate the main student's opinion, providing sufficient reasons and details.

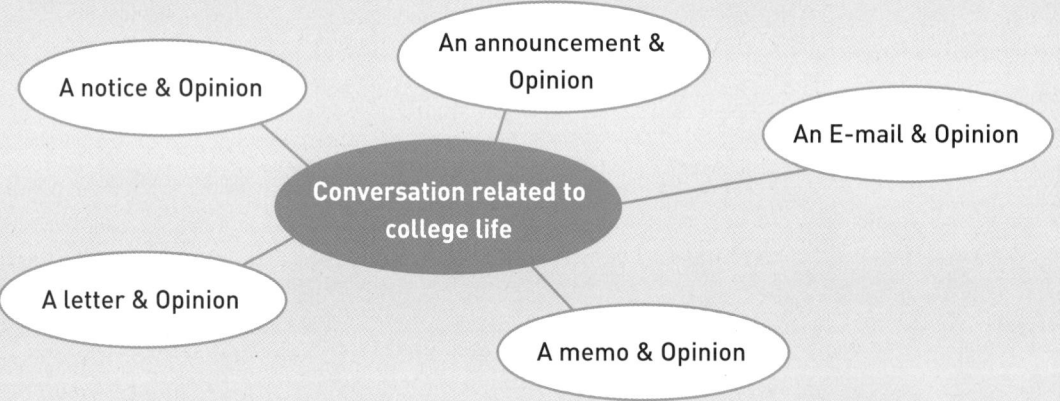

How much time do I have?

: 90 seconds

Question Types for Task 3

- The man expresses his opinion of the announcement made by the Athletics Office. State his opinion and explain the reasons he gives for holding that opinion.

- The woman expresses her opinion of the school's plan for the book sale. State her opinion and explain the reasons she gives for holding that opinion.

- The woman expresses her opinion of the announcement made by the university library. State her opinion and explain the reasons she gives for holding that opinion.

- The man expresses his opinion of the announcement about the car ban for freshmen. State his opinion and explain the reasons he gives for holding that opinion.

Responding Process of Task 3

Understand the question

Read the passage & Take notes

Listen to the conversation & Take notes

Respond

Strategies for Task 3

- Quickly understand what the question asks you to do
- Find the main student when listening to the conversation
- As you read and listen, organize the major ideas in an outline
- Practice expressing key ideas in complete sentences
- Relax and speak clearly and confidently
- Do not hesitate or mumble, even when you make mistakes
- Remember, your time is limited

Q The man expresses his opinion of the university's policy on academic probation. State his opinion and explain the reasons he gives for holding that opinion.

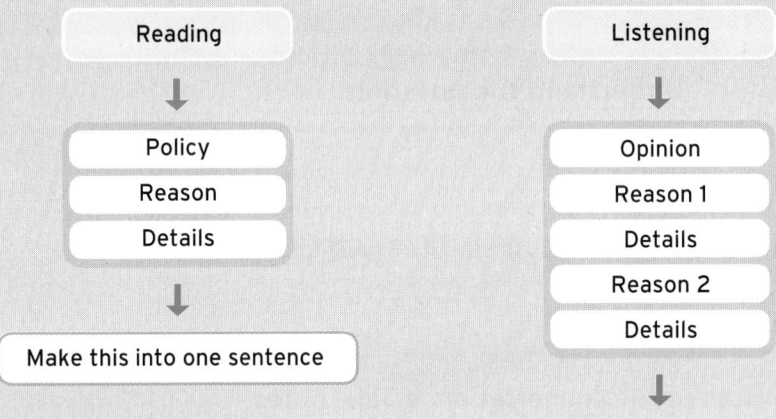

Tip When reading, try to understand the main idea of a policy change, a student's writing, etc. Then, jot down an opinion, reasons, and supporting details of the main student when you listen to the conversation between the two students.

Task 4

What does the question ask?

: It asks you to read an article, a textbook, or a journal. After reading, you will listen to part of a lecture. Your task is to understand the main idea of the reading passage and listen to the lecture that provides two examples of the main idea. The question will ask you to integrate the reading and listening passages and explain how the lecture is related to the reading.

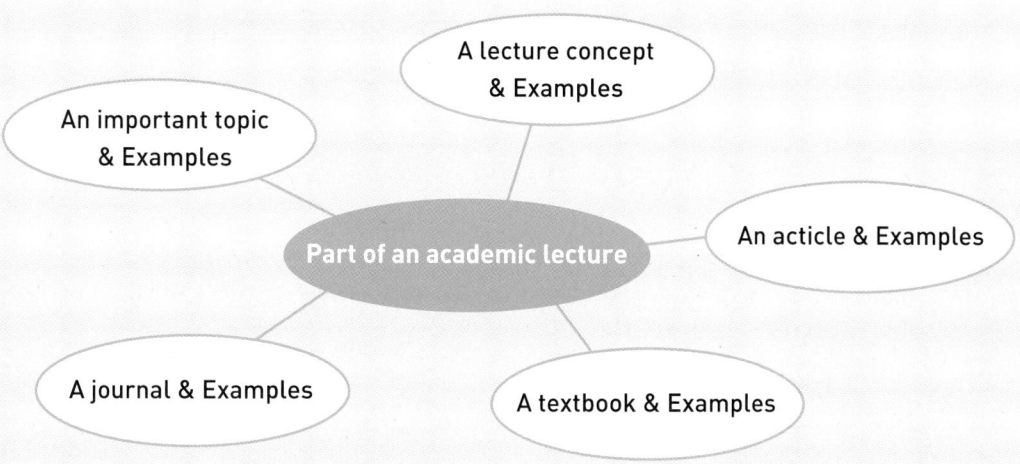

How much time do I have?

: 90 seconds

Question Types for Task 4

- The professor explains the principle of mountain-building through folding by giving examples. Explain how the examples illustrate the concept of mountain-building through folding.

- The professor talks about why entrepreneurs study public demand for certain goods. Explain how this relates to the concept of opportunity costs.

- The professor talks about voluntary and involuntary organic functions in humans. Explain how this demonstrates the functioning of the nervous system.

- The professor describes the halo effect by providing two examples. Explain how these examples demonstrate how the halo effect works and how it is applied.

Responding Process of Task 4

Understand the question

↓

Read the passage & Take notes

↓

Listen to the lecture & Take notes

↓

Respond

Strategies for Task 4

- Quickly understand what the question asks you to do
- Find the two examples of the main idea when you listen to the lecture
- As you read and listen, organize the major ideas in an outline
- Practice expressing key ideas in complete sentences
- Relax and speak clearly and confidently
- Do not hesitate or mumble, even when you make mistakes
- Remember, your time is limited

Q The professor describes the halo effect by providing two examples. Explain how these examples demonstrate how the halo effect works and how it is applied.

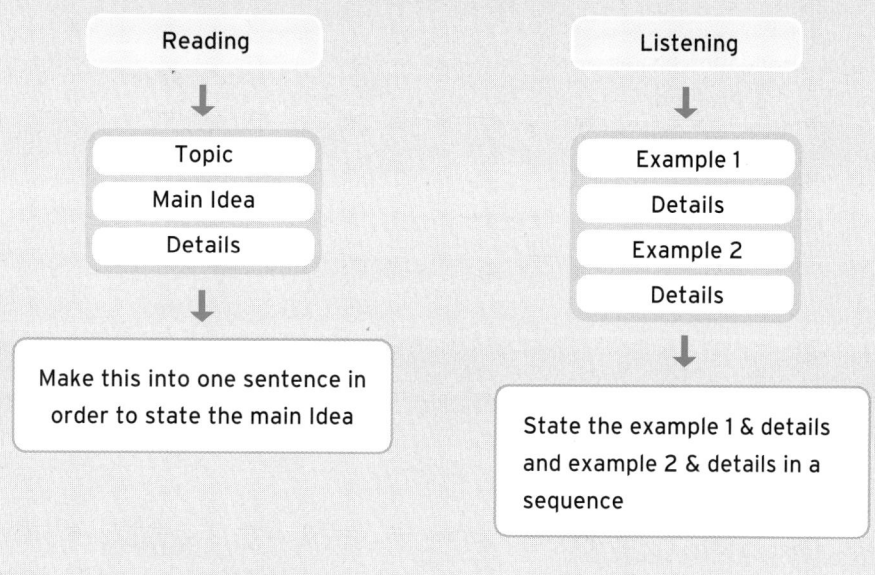

Tip Try to understand the main idea of the reading passage and jot down two examples of the main idea as you listen to the lecture. It is very important to logically connect the main idea of the reading with the given examples in the lecture when responding to the question.

Task 5

What does the question ask?

: It asks you to listen to a conversation between two students. They will discuss an issue related to campus life. After listening to the conversation, the question will ask you to state the main student's problem along with two possible solutions to the problem mentioned in the conversation. Then, you will be asked to choose one of the two solutions and explain why you chose it.

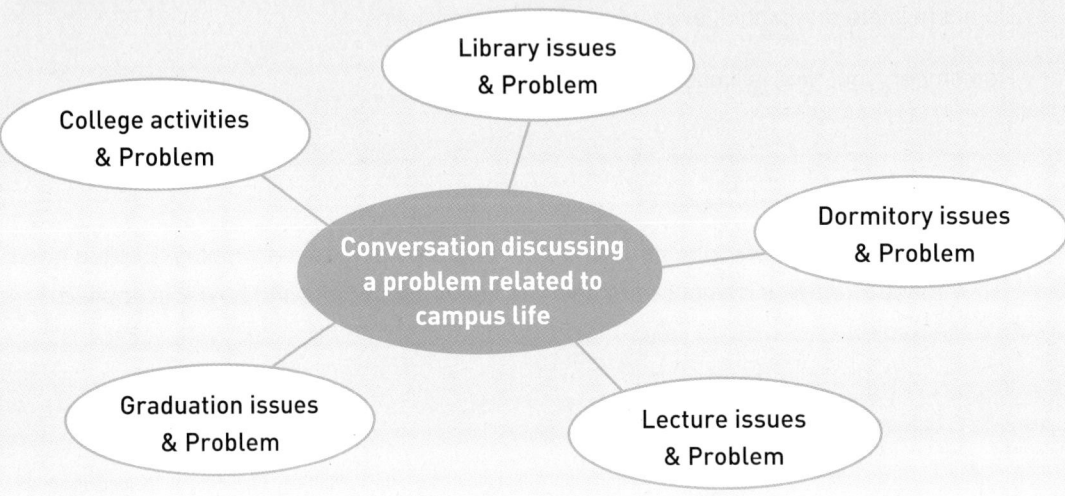

How much time do I have?

: 80 seconds

Question Types for Task 5

- The students discuss two possible solutions to the man's problem. Describe the problem. Then state which of the two solutions you prefer and explain why.

- The two speakers discuss two possible solutions to the woman's problem. Describe the problem. Then state which of the two solutions you prefer and explain why.

Responding Process of Task 5

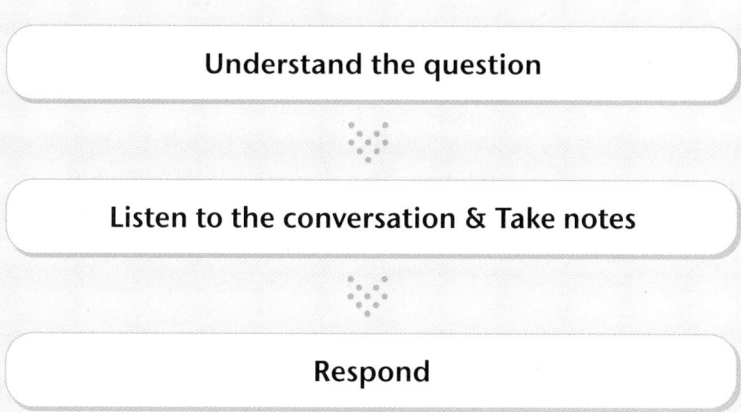

Strategies for Task 5

- Quickly understand what the question asks you to do
- Note the problem and two solutions when you listen to the conversation.
- Quickly choose a solution you prefer and provide reasons for it
- Practice expressing key ideas in complete sentences
- Relax and speak clearly and confidently
- Do not hesitate or mumble, even when you make mistakes
- Remember, your time is limited

Q The students discuss two possible solutions to the woman's problem. Describe the problem. Then state which of the two solutions you prefer and explain why.

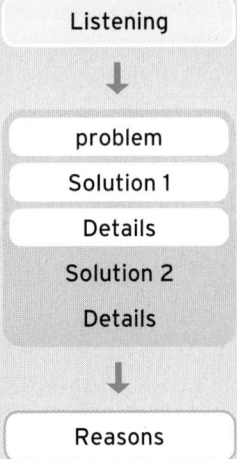

Tip While listening, try to understand the main student's problem and the two possible solutions to the problem as quickly as you can. Then, choose one of the two solutions that you think is better and provide reasons for your choice.

Task 6

What does the question ask?

It asks you to listen to part of a lecture taken from an academic field such as Psychology, Biology, Sociology, Anthropology, Music, Literature, Business, American history, et cetera. When you listen to the lecture, you need to understand the main idea of the lecture and the two following examples of the main point. Your main task is to organize the lecture content and rephrase the lecture points in your own style.

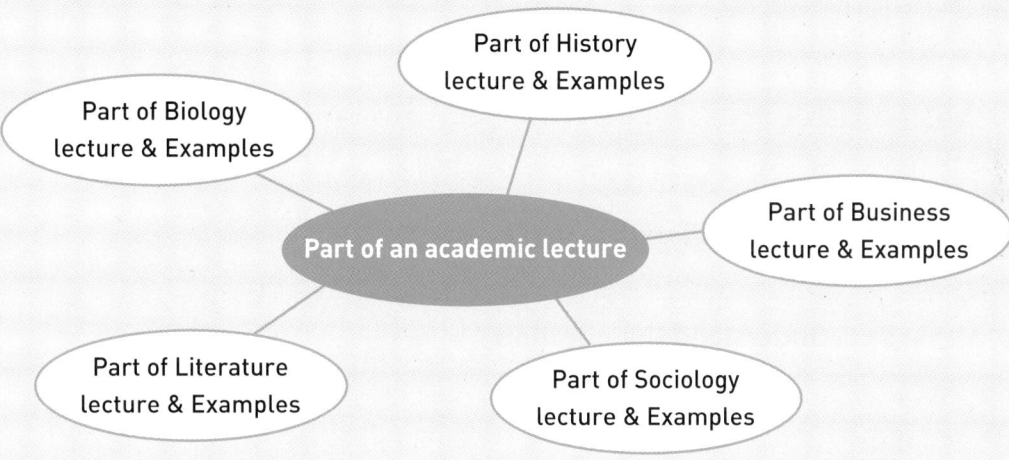

How much time do I have?

80 seconds

Preparation: 20 seconds

Answer: 60 seconds

Question Types for Task 6

- Using points and examples from the talk, explain how the desire for more land and taxation without representation led to the American Revolution.

- Using points and examples from the talk, explain how sublimation and activism have motivated writers to create literature.

- Using points and examples from the talk, explain how the ability to build a resistance to toxins is harmful to humans.

- Using points and examples from the talk, explain how the situations of Presidents Nixon and Bush illustrate the concept of checks and balances.

Responding Process of Task 6

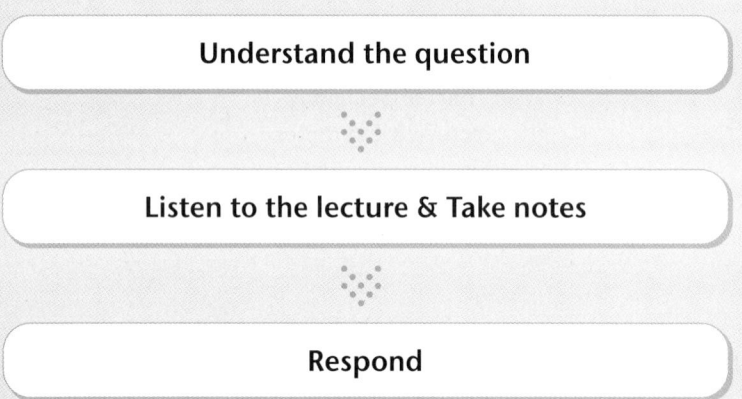

Strategies for Task 6

- Quickly understand what the question asks you to do
- Note the main idea of the lecture and the two following examples with specific details
- As you listen, organize the major ideas of the lecture and make a clear outline
- Practice expressing key ideas in complete sentences
- Relax and speak clearly and confidently
- Do not hesitate or mumble, even when you make mistakes
- Remember, your time is limited

Q Using points and examples from the talk, explain how the electric guitar and the multi-track recorder illustrate the role of technology in music.

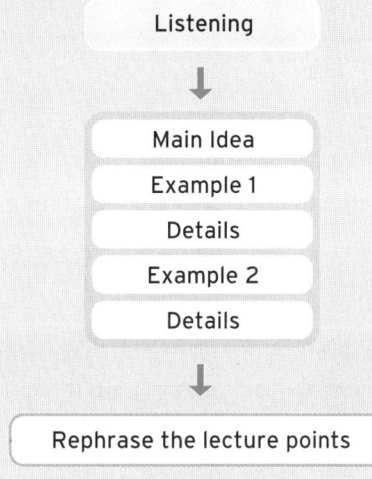

Tip As you listen to the lecture, you need to write down a few things in abbreviated forms. Jot down only key ideas that best describe the lecture. Always listen carefully for the main idea along with its explanation and the two following examples with specific examples or details. Your task is to rephrase the lecture points in an orderly manner.

Fit & Explain

Task 3 consists of a question related to college life. You will read a passage and listen to a conversation between two students discussing the reading. You will need to understand their conversation and state the main student's opinion, reasons, and details accordingly.

Sample Question MP3 4

Reading   The university is planning to renovate the library building. Read the announcement made by the construction office.

Announcement from the Construction Office

Due to the lack of adequate space, the college will restructure the top three floors of its library for renovation. Over the next three months, we will be working on these floors in order to create space for more rows of bookshelves. Because of safety concerns, we will have to close this area off to anyone who isn't on the construction crew. If students need to retrieve materials from these floors, they must submit a request form to the library's main circulation desk. The floors will be closed starting today.

Reason / Policy / Detail

Checkpoints
- Policy
- Reason
- Details

Listening   Now listen to two students as they discuss the announcement.

M: Tammy! Hey, how are you doing?

W: I'm doing okay, but I'm a little annoyed about the library.

M: Oh, you mean that announcement about closing the top three floors?

W: Yeah. I mean, they don't have to close off portions of the library just to make more space for books. They have a lot of room in the library's basement, which is mostly unused storage. If they cleared that out, then they could put all of their older books down there. Instead, they've made parts of the library inaccessible, so now students can't get books from the top floors when they need them.

M: Well, you can get them, but you just have to ask the circulation desk for them.

W: Have you ever requested a book at the circulation desk? It can take a long time for them to find certain books, and sometimes they can't find your book at all. I would much rather have a small number of books I can find than a large number of books that I can't find.

Checkpoints
- Opinion
- Reason 1
- Details
- Reason 2
- Details

3. Fit & Explain

Q The woman expresses her opinion of the announcement made by the Construction Office. State her opinion and explain the reasons she gives for holding that opinion.

| Preparation time : 30 seconds |
| Response time   : 60 seconds |

Responding process of Task 3

Opinion > **Reason 1 & Details** > **Reason 2 & Details**

Reading note

Policy
  Library reno.

Reason
  Lack of space

Details
  - Top 3 fls. to be closed for 3 months.
  - Submit a req. form to get matls.

Listening note

Opinion
  Disagree

Reason 1
  Closing: not necessary

Details
  - Can use space in the basmt.

Reason 2
  Rather have a small number of books she can find

Details
  - Circ. desk: takes a long time / can't find books sometimes.

Sample Response

Disagree
  → The woman is against the university's plan to temporarily close off part of the library.

Closing: not necessary – can use space in the basement
  → She opposes the plan because she thinks that the closing is not really necessary. She says that the university can use the space in the library's basement to keep their older books, instead of closing the top floors.

Rather have a small number of books she can find – circ. desk: takes a long time / can't find books sometimes
  → She also says that she would rather have a small number of books she can find than a large number of books that she can't find. That is because it takes a long time for the people at the circulation desk to find books, and sometimes they can't even find the books at all.

1 Outlining

> Take notes as you read the passage and listen to a conversation.

1

Reading   The university is planning to extend the running time of its campus buses. Read the announcement from the Office of Student Services.

Announcement from the Office of Student Services

Due to the increase in passengers, the university has decided to run its campus buses past 6:00 p.m. Buses will run until 9:00 p.m. in an effort to accommodate passengers who attend late night classes and other various campus activities. This means that there will be more pedestrians walking in the dark. To discourage dangerous driving in these conditions, speed limits will be strictly enforced, and there will be a major increase in fines for traffic violations on campus.

Listening   Now listen to two students discussing the announcement. MP3 5

Reading note

Policy
Buses run til 9

Reason
More riders

Details
- More peds. at night/ Higher spd. fines

Listening note

Opinion
Disagree

Reason 1
Will be late for class

Details
- Can't drive fast w/ buses

Reason 2
No need for buses

Details
- Never sees anyone at night

2

Reading   The university is planning a ban on loud music in the dormitories after 6:00 p.m. Read the letter sent to the school newspaper.

Letter to the Editor

I would just like to say thank you to the school for banning loud music in the dorms after 6:00 p.m. I have had trouble studying, sleeping, and even talking on the phone because of people down the hall who blast their music at all hours—up until the early morning! The noise also drowned out fire alarms when we had fire drills. Now we'll be able to hear them if there's actually a fire in the middle of the night.

A concerned student

Listening   Now listen to two students discussing the announcement.

Reading note

Policy

Opinion

Reasons

Listening note

Opinion

Reason 1

Details

Reason 2

Details

2 Speaking Grammar

■ **Sentence Structure:** Simple, compound, & complex sentences

Simple sentences: S + V	The man **agrees** with the university's policy. The woman **disagrees** with the university's policy.
Compound sentences: S + V, (FANBOYS) S + V	The letter **is opposed** to the university's policy, but the woman **agrees** with the university's policy.
Complex sentences: Independent + Dependent	The man disagrees with the policy because he believes students have rights to express their opinions.

* FANBOYS: For, And, Nor, But, Or, Yet, and So
* Subordinators: (When, After, Because, Although, Since, etc.) can be placed in front or middle.

■ **Templates**

- Templates for Opinion Sentences

The man / woman agrees with...	**The man agrees with** the university's policy to limit the number of audit students in each class.
The man / woman disagrees with ...	**The woman disagrees with** the university's policy to limit the number of audit students in each class.

- Templates for Reason Sentences

First, she points out that...	**First, she points out that** the class quality has been very poor because of an excessive number of audit students.
Second, she mentions that...	**Second, she mentions that** audit students do not concentrate on lectures because they have no need to take exams and write papers.

- Templates for Detail Sentences

What he means is that...	**What he means is that** audit students have no pressure to do well in class. Thus, they discourage students who need to study hard to pass the course.
For instance,	**For instance,** many audit students ask questions that aren't directly related to lectures. So, it bothers students who are taking the class for credits.

3. Fit & Explain

» **Complete and speak your answers.**

1 Notes for Question 1

Reading note

Policy
Buses run til 9

Reason
More riders

Details
- More peds. at night/ Higher spd. fines

Listening note

Opinion
Disagree

Reason 1
Will be late for class

Details
- Can't drive fast w/ buses

Reason 2
No need for buses

Details
- Never saw anyone at night

Policy The university has decided to run busses until 9 p.m. because there are many passengers who attend late night classes and campus activities.

Opinion The man disagrees with the announcement that campus buses will run until nine in the evening.

Reason 1 First, he points out that the buses will prevent him from driving quickly enough to get to class on time.

Details What he means is that speed limits will be enforced more and fines for traffic violations will increase, too. So, he will get into trouble if he drives as fast as he'd like to.

Reason 2 Second, he mentions that the policy change is unnecessary.

Details For instance, he argues that he never saw pedestrians or drivers on campus at night, so he doesn't think the buses will help any extra passengers.

Speaking Grammar

2 Use your Notes for Question 2.

Reading note	Listening note
Policy	Opinion
Reason	Reason 1
	Details
Details	Reason 2
	Details

Policy _____

Opinion The woman disagrees with _____

Reason 1 First, she points out that _____

Details What she means is that _____

Reason 2 Second, she mentions that _____

Details For instance, _____

66 •• i SPEAKING

③ Delivery

3. Fit & Explain

1 Put a slash ("/") where you want to pause (before commas, prepositions, conjunctions, etc.) and respond slowly.

> The university / has decided to run buses until 9 p.m. / because there are many passengers / who attend late night classes / and campus activities. / The man disagrees / with the announcement / that campus buses will run until nine / in the evening. / First, / he points out that the buses will prevent him / from driving quickly enough to get to class on time. / What he means is that speed limits / will be enforced more / and fines for traffic violations will increase, too. / So, he will get in trouble / if he drives as fast as he'd like to. / Second, / he mentions that the policy change is unnecessary. / For instance, / he argues that he never saw pedestrians / or drivers on campus at night, / so he doesn't think / the buses will help any extra passengers.

* As shown above, practice the delivery with your answer for Q2.

Read the evaluation questions and check the level of your delivery. On a scale from 1 to 5 (1=very poor, 2=poor, 3=OK, 4=good, 5=very good), rank your delivery accordingly.

Could you complete your response?	1	2	3	4	5
Is your answer coherent and unified?	1	2	3	4	5
Do you find a sequence in your response?	1	2	3	4	5
How is the use of vocabulary?	1	2	3	4	5
Does your response show grammatical structures?	1	2	3	4	5
How is the use of idiomatic expressions?	1	2	3	4	5
Is your response fluent and smooth?	1	2	3	4	5
Is your pronunciation clear?	1	2	3	4	5
How is the use of stress and intonation?	1	2	3	4	5

* Use the extra evaluation sheet provided at the end of the main textbook (p.227) and evaluate your delivery for Q2.

Practice Questions

1

Announcement from the Athletics Office

Due to the arrival of basketball season, the locker rooms in the university stadium will be off limits to anybody who isn't on the men's or women's basketball teams. This policy is the result of the locker rooms being vandalized recently, and the school wants to keep these facilities clean and orderly not only for our team but for visiting teams, as well. Anyone who tries to enter the locker rooms will be escorted off the premises by security.

The man expresses his opinion of the announcement made by the Athletics Office. State his opinion and explain the reasons he gives for holding that opinion.

Preparation time : 30 seconds
Response time : 60 seconds

2

Book Sale This Friday

This is just a reminder to all students that the campus book store will be holding a special sale for all used textbooks this Friday. None of the items on sale will be required for any classes next year. All used textbooks on sale will be marked down by thirty percent, and all of the proceeds from this special sale will go to local charities. If any students would like to donate any used textbooks, please drop them off at the book store before Wednesday.

The woman expresses her opinion of the school's plan for the book sale. State her opinion and explain the reasons she gives for holding that opinion.

| Preparation time : 30 seconds |
| Response time : 60 seconds |

Practice Questions

3

Announcement from the Academic Office

Due to the large number of new students arriving, the university has decided to offer freshmen three-hour long courses next year. These classes will only meet one day a week for three hours, and they will be offered for every introductory class in all departments. It should be noted that the university is only offering these classes, not requiring them. This only means that freshmen will have more options in arranging their academic schedules.

The man expresses his opinion of the announcement made by the Academic Office. State his opinion and explain the reasons he gives for holding that opinion.

| Preparation time : 30 seconds |
| Response time   : 60 seconds |

3. Fit & Explain

4

Letter to the Editor

I am not happy that the school decided to replace our parking stickers with tags. Why did they feel that this was necessary? Now, I have to hang this new tag on my rear view mirror, and it gets in the way of my view. At least the old stickers were tucked away in a windshield corner where you couldn't see them. Oh, and these tags fall off all the time. At least a parking sticker stays stuck to the car window!

A Sophomore

The man expresses his opinion of the letter published in the school newspaper. State his opinion and explain the reasons he gives for holding that opinion.

| Preparation time : 30 seconds |
| Response time   : 60 seconds |

Vocabulary Study — Campus life

- **maintenance office**   office for staff members
- **off campus**   outside of campus
- **postgraduate**   *n.* graduate student
- **resident assistant**   dormitory staff
- **mid term test**   test taken in the middle of a semester
- **audit student**   a student taking classes for no credits
- **loan**   *n.* borrowed money
- **gymnasium**   *n.* sports hall
- **extracurricular activities**   activities performed by students
- **academic year**   the spring and the winter semesters
- **student council**   student committee
- **add/drop form**   a form for adding or dropping courses
- **academic warning**   notice that a student's scholastic record is unsatisfactory
- **admissions committee**   a group of admission officials
- **circulation desk**   the service point for library uses to check in & check out books
- **inter-library loan**   a system through which one can borrow books or receive photocopies of documents owned by another library
- **writing sample**   writing example
- **tuition**   *n.* education fee
- **transcript**   *n.* record
- **alumni**   *n.* graduates of the school
- **applicant**   *n.* a person who applies for something
- **assistant professor**   beginning level professor
- **final test**   a test taken at the end of a college course
- **handout**   *n.* a copied set of readings or exercises
- **withdrawal**   *n.* giving up taking classes
- **job fair**   an exposition for recruiters and employers to meet with prospective job seekers
- **academic adviser**   someone who guides students to academic success by providing informed advice
- **advance registration**   registering for classes early
- **study abroad program**   studying in a foreign country for a limited time
- **research paper**   a type of paper dealing with investigation of a significant topic
- **prerequisite course**   required course
- **liberal arts**   academics focused on broadening general knowledge and developing intellectual capabilities
- **undergraduate**   *n.* education taken prior to gaining a bachelor's degree
- **international student office**   an office providing services for foreign students and study abroad programs

A Choose the word which is closest in meaning to the vocabulary listed below.

1. Loan
2. Student council
3. Prerequisite course
4. Postgraduate
5. Admissions committee
6. Transcript
7. Withdrawal
8. Tuition
9. Off campus
10. Gymnasium

(a) Required course
(b) Student committee
(c) A group of admission officials
(d) Sports hall
(e) Borrowed money
(f) Graduate student
(g) Education fee
(h) Giving up taking classes
(i) Outside of campus
(j) Record

B Complete the sentences by filling in the blanks.

academic warning	circulation desk	alumni	assistant professor
academic adviser	audit students	job fairs	off campus
research paper	extracurricular activities		

1. I have to visit my college because I am a member of the _____ association.

2. Many people believe that _____ are becoming a more common method of entry level recruiting and initial screening.

3. Freshmen are easily placed on _____ because they are not accustomed to studying hard.

4. You should listen to your _____ because he can assist you in choosing the proper classes to succeed in college.

5. All of my friends live _____, so that I don't have anyone to play soccer with on campus.

TASK 04

General / Specific

In Task 4, you will read an article, a textbook, or a journal. As soon as the reading time expires, you will listen to part of a lecture. Here, you need to integrate information from both the reading and listening passages and answer the question accordingly.

Sample Question MP3 11

Reading   Now read a passage about role conflict.

Role Conflict — Topic

Every person has different roles to play in life. A man may be both a father and a husband. Each of these roles carries its own set of responsibilities that the man must try to fulfill. Role conflict occurs when the responsibilities imposed by one role directly contradict the responsibilities of another role, making it impossible to fulfill the responsibilities of both roles. Role conflicts must be resolved by abandoning the responsibilities of one role.

Checkpoints
☐ Topic
☐ Main Idea
☐ Details

Listening   Now listen to part of a lecture in a sociology class.

Today we are going to talk about situations in which a person's professional duties conflict with his personal ones. If you look at lawyers, for example, there are many times when a lawyer may know his client is guilty of the crime he has been accused of. Now, it is the lawyer's job to make sure his client gets the best possible defense, meaning that the lawyer has to try to make sure his client doesn't go to jail. But obviously, as a responsible citizen, the lawyer doesn't want to help a criminal go free. So what can he do in this situation? In most cases, the lawyer tells himself that his duties as a lawyer are more important and works to free his client. Psychologists face similarly difficult situations. One of the duties of a psychologist is to keep everything a patient tells him a secret. But let's say that patient tells his psychologist that he is planning to hurt himself. Again, the psychologist's professional responsibility is to keep this secret, but obviously, as a caring person, the psychologist is going to want to tell someone to stop the patient from hurting himself. In this case, the psychologist may tell himself that his ultimate responsibility is to protect his patient, even if that means violating the patient's trust.

Checkpoints
☐ Example 1
☐ Details
☐ Example 2
☐ Details

74 •• i SPEAKING

4. General / Specific

Q The professor discusses problems faced by lawyers and psychologists. Explain how these problems relate to the concept of role conflict.

| Preparation time : 30 seconds |
| Response time   : 60 seconds |

| Responding process of Task 4 |

Main Idea > **Reason 1 & Details** > **Reason 2 & Details**

Reading note

Topic
Role conflict

Main Idea
When resp. of 1 role conflict w/ other roles

Details
- Everyone has diff. roles w/ diff. responsibilities.
- Impossible to play both roles in role conflict.
- 1 role must be abandoned

Listening note

Example 1
Lawyer: aware of client's guilt

Details
- Job: protect client & Citz.: put crim. in jail. Chooses job over citz.

Example 2
Psychologist: knows patient's going to hurt self

Details
- Job role: keep pat. secrets & Caring role: tell secrets
- May have to tell pat. secrets to help him

Sample Response

Role conflict — when resp. of 1 role conflict w/ other roles
→ The professor explains the concept of role conflict by talking about situations where a person's professional responsibilities and personal ones are in conflict.

Lawyer: aware of guilt - Job: protect client - Citz.: put crim. in jail - Usu. chooses job over citz.
→ The professor provides two examples. The first one is the situation in which a lawyer knows that his client is guilty. In this situation, the lawyer's job is to protect his client, while his role as a responsible citizen tells him not to do that.

Psychologist: knows patient's going to hurt self - Job role: keep pat. secrets - Caring per. role: stop pat. from hurting self - May have to tell pat. secrets to help him
→ The second example is a situation faced by a psychologist who knows his patient is planning to hurt himself. As a psychologist, he has a duty to keep this fact a secret, but since he is also a caring person, he feels that he should let this fact be known so that he can save his patient. The lawyer or the psychologist must give up one role to resolve role conflict.

1 Outlining

> Take notes as you read the passage and listen to a lecture.

1

Reading   Now read the passage about omnivorous advantage.

Omnivorous Advantage

Omnivorous animals feed on all kinds of organisms, including animals, plants, fungi, and decomposing materials. Being omnivorous provides these animals with a crucial advantage. While the bodies of purely carnivorous animals can only assimilate nutrients from other animals, omnivores have the ability to consume any available organic matter. Thus, they have the flexibility to obtain necessary sustenance should environmental changes cause their food source to become unavailable. Even if an omnivore relies primarily on meat or vegetables, it can resort to an alternative food source if its normal diet is disrupted.

Listening   Now listen to part of a lecture on this topic in a zoology class. MP3 12

Reading note

Topic
 Omnivorous advantage

Main Idea
 - Omnv. animals eat meat & veg.

Details
 - Can get nutr. from any org. source
 - Can eat if env. destroys main food
 - Adv. over anmls. That rely on only meat or veg.

Listening note

Example 1
 Large cats; e.g. lions (non-omnv.)

Details
 - Rely on gazelles
 - Can only dig. meat
 - Die if all gazelles die

Example 2
 Wild dogs (omnv.)

Details
 - W. dogs mainly eat meat
 - Can subsist on nuts, berries
 - Can survive if gazelles die

4. General / Specific

2

Reading Now read the passage about tragic flaw.

Tragic Flaw

A tragic flaw is the characteristic of a literary or dramatic character that leads to his destruction. While the character is in some way remarkable, his tragic flaw is either a moral imperfection in his character or a mistake he makes, and it is always an essential part of this character's personality. Additionally, because the character is remarkable, he is also very powerful. Because he wields so much power, his tragic flaw has disastrous consequences for both him and the story's other characters.

Listening Now listen to part of a lecture on this topic in a literature class. MP3 13

Reading note

Topic

Main Idea

Details

Listening note

Example 1

Details

Example 2

Details

2 Speaking Grammar

■ **Sentence Structure: Subject + Predicate**

Subject: Who, That, Which	He is the man **who** proved the behavior of SUV drivers is related to risk compensation.
Object: Who, Whom, That, Which	The fact **that** the behavior of SUV drivers is related to risk compensation is not logical to the professor.
Possessive: Whose	The result includes people **whose** behaviors are related to risk compensation.

■ **Templates**

- Templates for Definition Sentences

(A) refers to...	Symbiosis **refers to** a close relationship between two organisms living together.
(A) is seen when	Animal deception **is seen when** animals adopt certain characteristics in order to protect themselves from predators.

- Templates for Citation Sentences

According to the reading...	**According to the reading,** creative destruction renders old products obsolete.
The professor says that...	**The professor says that** humans and gut flora get mutual benefits through their relationship.

- Templates for Explanation Sentences

The professor discusses (A) and (B) to illustrate (C).	**The professor discusses** computers and automobiles **to illustrate** creative destruction.
The first example of (A) discussed by the professor is (B).	**The first example of** animal deception **discussed by the professor is** mimicry.

4. General / Specific

» **Complete and speak your answers.**

1 Notes for Question 1

Reading note

Topic
  Omnivorous advantage

Main Idea
  Omnv. animals eat meat & veg.

Details
  - Can get nutr. from any org. source
  - Can eat if env. destroys main food
  - Adv. over anmls. That rely on only meat or veg.

Listening note

Example 1
  Large cats; e.g. lions (non-omnv.)

Details
  - Rely on gazelles
  - Can only dig. meat
  - Die if all gazelles die

Example 2
  Wild dogs (omnv.)

Details
  - W. dogs mainly eat meat
  - Can subsist on nuts, berries
  - Can survive if gazelles die

Definition Omnivorous animals are species that feed on all kinds of organisms including animals, plants, etc.

Citation According to the reading, omnivorous advantage is the advantage in surviving that omnivores have over non-omnivores.

Explanation The professor discusses wild cats and wild dogs to illustrate how omnivores have an advantage over non-omnivores. First, wild cats and other felines are solely carnivorous. This is because their digestive system can only digest meat. The professor says if gazelles, which lions eat, were to die off, the lions would eventually starve to death because they can only absorb nutrients from other animals. Second, the professor says that wild dogs are omnivorous, so they can consume any organic matter, such as fruits, nuts, and grass. Even though wild dogs may hunt gazelle as their main food source, they would have an advantage over lions if the gazelle population died off because dogs can resort to an alternative food source.

Speaking Grammar

2 Use your notes for Question 2.

Reading note	Listening note
Topic	Example 1
	Details
Main Idea	
	Example 2
Details	
	Details

Definition

Citation

Explanation

3 Delivery

| 4. General / Specific |

1 Put a slash ("/") where you want to pause (before commas, prepositions, conjunctions, etc.) and respond slowly.

> Omnivorous animals are species / that feed on all kinds of organisms / including animals, plants, etc. / According to the reading, / omnivorous advantage is the advantage / in surviving that omnivores have over non-omnivores. / The professor discusses wild cats / and wild dogs to illustrate how omnivores have an advantage over non-omnivores. / First, / wild cats and other felines / are solely carnivorous. / This is because their digestive system / can only digest meat. / The professor says if gazelles, / which lions eat, / were to die off, / the lions would eventually starve to death / because they can only absorb nutrients from other animals. / Second, / the professor says that / wild dogs are omnivorous, / so they can consume any organic matter, / such as fruits, nuts, and grass. / Even though wild dogs may hunt gazelle / as their main food source, / they would have an advantage over lions / if the gazelle population died off / because dogs can resort to an alternative food source.

* As shown above, practice the delivery with your answer for Q2.

Read the evaluation questions and check the level of your delivery. On a scale from 1 to 5 (1=very poor, 2=poor, 3=OK, 4=good, 5=very good), rank your delivery accordingly.

Could you complete your response?	1	2	3	4	5
Is your answer coherent and unified?	1	2	3	4	5
Do you find a sequence in your response?	1	2	3	4	5
How is the use of vocabulary?	1	2	3	4	5
Does your response show grammatical structures?	1	2	3	4	5
How is the use of idiomatic expressions?	1	2	3	4	5
Is your response fluent and smooth?	1	2	3	4	5
Is your pronunciation clear?	1	2	3	4	5
How is the use of stress and intonation?	1	2	3	4	5

* Use the extra evaluation sheet provided at the end of the main textbook (p.227) and evaluate your delivery for Q2.

Practice **Questions**

1 MP3 14

Behavior Modification

Behavior modification is a technique that administrators use in psychotherapy to attempt to change or control a person's behavior. An administrator can modify a person's behavior through two different methods: reinforcement and punishment. Reinforcement involves rewarding the person when he behaves in a way the administrator desires. Punishment, on the other hand, involves creating unpleasant conditions for a person when he behaves undesirably. Both kinds of behavior modification are used to help people adapt to all kinds of situations and conditions.

The professor talks about rewarding and punishing students. Explain how this relates to the concept of behavior modification.

| Preparation time : 30 seconds |
| Response time   : 60 seconds |

2

Opportunity Costs

Opportunity costs are the losses someone must undergo when choosing to produce or purchase one product over another product. These losses can be either materials or opportunities. The choice between the two different products must be made because the person lacks the resources needed to get both options. Because the person cannot have both options, he will normally choose the option where either the quality or the quantity of the chosen product's benefits outweighs the loss of the other product.

The professor talks about why entrepreneurs study public demand for certain goods. Explain how this relates to the concept of opportunity costs.

| Preparation time : 30 seconds |
| Response time   : 60 seconds |

Practice Questions

3

Nervous System

The nervous system is a network of nerves that essentially regulates all of the body's voluntary and involuntary organ functions and muscle movements. One of the most important features of this system is that it divides body functions into voluntary and involuntary actions. Body functions that are necessary to maintain life are controlled by the nervous system automatically and humans essentially have no control over them. However, the system also allows a person direct conscious control over certain muscles. This allows the person to perform helpful auxiliary tasks of his own volition.

The professor talks about voluntary and involuntary organic functions in humans. Explain how this demonstrates the functioning of the nervous system.

| Preparation time : 30 seconds |
| Response time   : 60 seconds |

Short Term Memory

Short term memory is the part of a person's memory used to store small bits of information for a short period of time. Information in the short term memory is immediately available for someone, but it can vanish through two different ways: decay and interference. Decay is the gradual disappearance of information in the short term memory that isn't repeatedly applied. Interference is the blocking of short term information with the learning or memorizing of new information.

The professor talks about ways to study for a chemistry exam. Explain how her discussion of this relates to short term memory.

Preparation time : 30 seconds
Response time   : 60 seconds

Vocabulary Study — Lectures

Psychology

- **intuition** *n.* instinctive knowledge
- **amnesia** *n.* memory loss
- **retarded** *adj.* mentally deficient
- **empathy** *n.* the act of having compassion
- **insight** *n.* profound understanding
- **egocentric** *adj.* self-centered
- **illusion** *n.* daydream or fantasy
- **cognition** *n.* conscious mental process
- **insanity** *n.* madness
- **impulse** *n.* a strong desire to do something

Business / Economics

- **acquisition** *n.* gain
- **facilitate** *v.* promote
- **conflict** *n.* disagreement, fight
- **enthusiasm** *n.* zeal
- **socialize** *v.* meet other people socially
- **subsidize** *v.* to pay part of the cost of something
- **tariff** *n.* a charge for goods entering a country
- **welfare** *n.* the state's help given to people below the poverty line
- **monopoly** *n.* complete control over something
- **prosperity** *n.* success or great wealth

Biology

- **replicate** *v.* copy
- **absorb** *v.* to take in something
- **stimulate** *v.* arouse someone to feel excited
- **inhibit** *v.* restrain or slow down
- **bipolar** *adj.* relating two opposing elements
- **deprive** *v.* without or deny something
- **discriminate** *v.* treat unequally
- **cacophony** *n.* a mixture of noise
- **velocity** *n.* speed
- **receptive** *adj.* easily approachable

Art & Literature

- **catharsis** *n.* the release of strong sentiments through a particular experience
- **explicit** *adj.* open, obvious
- **spontaneous** *adj.* suddenly happening without any planning
- **fallacy** *n.* misleading notion or belief
- **inference** *n.* belief that something is true on the basis of information presented
- **extrinsic** *adj.* coming from outside
- **resentment** *n.* anger
- **suppress** *v.* hold back or hide
- **integrity** *n.* honesty
- **manifest** *adj.* apparent

A Choose the word which is closest in meaning to the vocabulary listed below.

1. Enthusiasm
2. Manifest
3. Suppress
4. Conflict
5. Absorb
6. Amnesia
7. Explicit
8. Fallacy
9. Insight
10. Intuition

(a) Disagreement, fight
(b) Profound understanding
(c) Misleading notion or belief
(d) Zeal
(e) Instinctive knowledge
(f) Apparent
(g) Open, obvious
(h) Hold back or hide
(i) Memory loss
(j) To take in something

B Complete the sentences by filling in the blanks.

| discriminate | egocentric | catharsis | stimulate | facilitate |
| replicate | integrity | explicit | spontaneous | manifest |

1. The professor found the fact that most people are not aware that they _____ against others on the basis of their race.

2. It seemed her outburst wasn't planned, but _____.

3. The government official says IT industries will _____ distributing knowledge.

4. There is no one who can _____ Nature's beauty.

5. Abraham Lincoln was a man of _____.

TASK 05

Problem & Solution

Task 5 consists of a conversation between two speakers. One of the two speakers will explain his or her problem related to campus life. Your task is to summarize the problem and state the two possible solutions mentioned in the conversation. Then, choose a solution that you think is better and explain why.

Sample Question MP3 18

Listening   Now listen to a conversation between two students.

M: Hi, Helen! How are you doing today?

W: I'm okay, but I've got a bit of a problem.

M: Oh? And what would that be?

W: Well, I have this English paper due Friday, and I have to find a certain book to use for quotations. The trouble is that the library doesn't have this book, so I really don't know what to do. *— Problem*

M: Well, I have a suggestion. You could buy the book from a nearby bookstore. We have a lot of bookstores on and around campus that may very well have what you're looking for. You can even make notes on the pages once you buy it. *— Solution 1 / Detail*

W: Yeah, but I don't know if I want to spend money on a new book.

M: Another option you have is to go on the Internet and see if you can find selected passages from the book. There are many academic websites that have pages and sometimes entire chapters from different books. They might have the information you need for your paper. Plus, it doesn't cost anything. *— Solution 2 / Detail*

W: I'm not really sure what to do right now.

Checkpoints
- Problem
- Solution 1
- Details
- Solution 2
- Details

5. Problem & Solution

Q The students discuss two possible solutions to the woman's problem. Describe the problem. Then state which of the two solutions you prefer and explain why.

| Preparation time : 20 seconds |
| Response time   : 60 seconds |

Responding process of Task 5

Problem → Solutions → Reasons

Listening note

Problem
Book missing from lib — need quotes for Eng. paper

Solution 1
Buy book
- Can leave notes on pgs.
- Have entire book, cost $

Solution 2
Find pass. On I-net
- Find pgs. & chs. w/ quotes
- No cost, not entire book

Reasons
1) May not find info. online. It's wasting time.
2) Buy book: Use it again in the future wherever she needs it.

Sample Response

Book missing from lib. — need quotes for Eng. paper
→ The woman's problem is that a book she needs to write her English paper is missing from the library.

Buy book vs. Find pass. on I-net
→ The man suggests that she either buy the book at a bookstore or find the passages she needs on the Internet.

(1) Safer — may not find info on I-net → waste of time (2) can use it again
I prefer buying the book over finding the passages on the Internet. That's because she may not be able to find the exact information she wants on the Internet. If that is the case, she'll only be wasting her time. Also, if she buys the book, she can use it again in the future whenever she needs it.

1 Outlining

≫ Take notes as you listen to a conversation.

1

Listening   Now listen to a conversation between two students. MP3 19

Listening note

Problem
Interview w/ a professor
- Intv. History prof. for project – Hist. prof. is on a field trip

Solution 1
Interview him later
- More time to prepare questions
- Work on rest of proj. til ten

Solution 2
Interview diff. prof. now
- Have to change questions
- More time to work on proj.

Reasons
1) Already have questions for the prof. – Int. will not be difficult
2) The prof. will come back soon – Finding ano. prof. and preparing intv. might take longer

| 5. Problem & Solution

2

Listening   Now listen to a conversation between two students. MP3 20

Listening note

Problem

Solution 1   Solution 2

Reasons

Part B. Integrated Tasks

2. Speaking Grammar

■ **Sentence Structure:** Adverb Clauses

Time: Before, after, when, etc	The professor had left **before** the student arrived.
Cause & Effect: Because, since, as, etc	He works a lot of overtime **because** he is expecting to be promoted this year.
Opposition: Although, whereas, as, etc	**Although** his math class was extremely difficult, he managed to pass the course with a good grade.

■ **Templates**

- Templates for Problem Sentences

The man's problem is that...	**The man's problem is that** he doesn't get along with his girlfriend because she has serious attitude problems.
The woman is having problems ~ing...	The woman is **having problems finding** an apartment to live in next semester.

- Templates for Solution Sentences

The man suggests that she either... or...	**The man suggests that she either** get some sleep at home **or** go see a doctor.
The woman advises that he should... or...	**The woman advises that he should** get a job or join the Peace Corps.

- Templates for Reason Sentences

I think the first solution is better because...	**I think the first solution is better because** he won't have to worry about other people disturbing him.
I think (A) is better than (B). That is because...	**I think** getting another roommate **is better than** living alone. **That is because** he would never get lonely if he has someone to talk to.

5. Problem & Solution

» **Complete and speak your answers.**

1 Notes for Question 1

Listening note

Problem
Interview w/ a professor
- Intv. History prof. for project - Hist. prof. is on a field trip

Solution 1
Interview him later
- More time to prepare question.
- Work on rest of proj. til then

Solution 2
Interview diff. prof. now
- Have to change questions
- More time to work on proj.

Reasons
1) Already have questions for the prof. — Int. will not be comparatively easy
2) The prof. will come back soon — Finding ano. prof. and preparing int. might take longer

Problem — The man's problem is that he has to interview his history professor for a project due in one week, but the professor is on a field trip.

Solution — The woman suggests that he either interview him later while working on the project or change his questions and interview a different professor now.

Reason — I think the first solution is better because he already has prepared questions for the professor. He can work on strengthening his questions until his professor comes back. Then the interview will be comparatively easy, since he is well-prepared to interview the history professor. Also, the professor may return soon, so he could be back in less time than the student would have to find another professor and change his questions.

Speaking Grammar

2 Use your notes for Question 2.

Listening note

Problem

Solution 1   Solution 2

Reasons

Problem

_____

_____

_____

Solution

_____

_____

_____

Reason

_____

_____

_____

_____

_____

3 Delivery

| 5. Problem & Solution |

1 Put a slash ("/") where you want to pause (before commas, prepositions, conjunctions, etc.) and respond slowly.

> The man's problem is that / he has to interview his history professor / for a project due in one week, / but the professor is on a field trip. / The woman suggests that / he either interview him later / while working on the project / or change his questions / and interview a different professor now. / I think the first solution is better / because he already has prepared questions / for the professor. / He can work on strengthening his questions / until his professor comes back. / Then the interview will be comparatively easy, / since he is well-prepared / to interview the history professor. / Also, / the professor may return soon, / so he could be back in less time / than the student would have to find another professor / and change his questions.

＊ As shown above, practice the delivery with your answer for Q2.

Read the evaluation questions and check the level of your delivery. On a scale from 1 to 5 (1=very poor, 2=poor, 3=OK, 4=good, 5=very good), rank your delivery accordingly.

Could you complete your response?	1	2	3	4	5
Is your answer coherent and unified?	1	2	3	4	5
Do you find a sequence in your response?	1	2	3	4	5
How is the use of vocabulary?	1	2	3	4	5
Does your response show grammatical structures?	1	2	3	4	5
How is the use of idiomatic expressions?	1	2	3	4	5
Is your response fluent and smooth?	1	2	3	4	5
Is your pronunciation clear?	1	2	3	4	5
How is the use of stress and intonation?	1	2	3	4	5

＊ Use the extra evaluation sheet provided at the end of the main textbook (p.227) and evaluate your delivery for Q2.

Practice Questions

1 MP3 21

The students discuss two possible solutions to the woman's problem. Describe the problem. Then state which of the two solutions you prefer and explain why.

Preparation time : 20 seconds
Response time   : 60 seconds

5. Problem & Solution

2 MP3 22

The students discuss two possible solutions to the man's problem. Describe the problem. Then state which of the two solutions you prefer and explain why.

| Preparation time : 20 seconds |
| Response time   : 60 seconds |

Practice Questions

3 MP3 23

The students discuss two possible solutions to the woman's problem. Describe the problem. Then state which of the two solutions you prefer and explain why.

| Preparation time : 20 seconds |
| Response time   : 60 seconds |

5. Problem & Solution

4

The students discuss two possible solutions to the man's problem. Describe the problem. Then state which of the two solutions you prefer and explain why.

| Preparation time : 20 seconds |
| Response time   : 60 seconds |

Vocabulary Study — Campus life

- **syllabus** *n.* a course outline
- **snack bar** a small restaurant
- **override** *v.* permission to take the class
- **assignment** *n.* homework
- **credit hours** the number of credit units

- **curriculum** *n.* the course of study
- **lab** *n.* short for laboratory
- **dean** *n.* a leader in charge of a college, faculty, or division
- **probation** *n.* a trial period to improve grades before disciplinary action
- **course withdrawal** a policy that removes a student from official registration

- **matriculation** *n.* acceptance in a degree-granting program
- **college catalog** catalog for perspective students
- **study lounge** a quiet area of a dormitory where students can study
- **tenure** *n.* an academic rank that guarantees permanent status
- **distance learning** receiving instruction through a computer

- **advisor** *n.* a faculty member or counselor assigned to help students for academic success, career planning, etc.

- **coed** *adj.* having men and women study together
- **minor** *n.* a secondary area of study
- **tuition hike** an increase in fees for instruction
- **term paper** an assigned paper in each class
- **GPA** Grade Point Average

- **sorority** *n.* an organization for female students
- **pop quiz** a quiz given without notice
- **intercollegiate sports** sports teams that compete with other colleges' sports teams
- **pass/fail grade** a grading policy that allows students to earn either a pass grade or a fail grade
- **placement service** a campus office that assists students in finding jobs

- **practicum** *n.* an evaluation in which students must perform specific required tasks
- **professor/academic rank** a system of evaluating faculty members
- **semester** *n.* the length of time during which a class is offered
- **shuttle service** free transportation offered by a school.
- **plagiarism** *n.* using someone else's work without giving the person credit

- **work-study** *n.* a program that lets students work on campus when they have no classes.

A Choose the word which is closest in meaning to the vocabulary listed below.

1. Override
2. Study lounge
3. Lab
4. Tuition hike
5. Snack bar
6. Syllabus
7. GPA
8. Curriculum
9. Credit hours
10. Assignment

(a) A small restaurant
(b) Grade Point Average
(c) The course of study
(d) A quiet area where students can study
(e) Homework
(f) Permission to take the class
(g) An increase in fees for instruction
(h) Short for laboratory
(i) The number of credit units
(j) A course outline

B Complete the sentences by filling in the blanks.

| dean | work-study | sorority | coed | intercollegiate sports |
| term paper | probation | matriculation | override | placement service |

1. Some people believe _____ schools are better than single-sex schools.

2. A(n) _____ is a social organization of women students at a college or university.

3. He is worried because he must submit his _____ by this Thursday.

4. The advisor explained that a(n) _____ allows students to enroll in a class.

5. Many student job seekers do not know how the _____ can help them.

Task 06

Summary

Task 6 contains a lecture on an academic subject. After listening to the lecture, you need to summarize the content of the lecture and state the topic, examples, and supporting details.

Sample Question MP3 25

Listening Now listen to part of a lecture in a music history class.

When we think of classical music, we tend to think of a large and complex orchestra. Now, how many of you have ever wondered *how the orchestra grew to such a large size* [Main Idea]? Well, what we know is that the modern orchestra expanded gradually over the past four hundred years. However, two developments helped the modern orchestra expand in its early days. *One was the introduction of the opera; the other was the invention of valves* [Main Idea]. *Opera became a popular form of musical theater in the early seventeenth century* [Example 1]. *Before opera, many rich European families hired groups of musicians for personal performances, but these were fairly small groups* [Detail]. *When opera came along, composers began to write music for a theatrical audience, and this required not only more musical instruments, but also specific written parts for those instruments* [Detail]. *The Italian composer Claudio Monteverdi was one of the first to assemble considerably larger orchestras and give them specific parts* [Detail]. This set a standard for later composers, who further increased the orchestra's size for operas they wrote. *New inventions like the valve also led to the expansion of the modern orchestra* [Example 2]. *In the early eighteenth century, the valve was added to brass instruments* [Detail]. *This made it easier to change the pitch, which provided players with a new range of pitches* [Detail]. *Valves eventually led to the use of several improved brass instruments, such as the trumpet, cornet, and tuba* [Detail]. All of these new instruments would be added to the modern orchestra, providing it with not only more instruments, but also a greater variety of sounds.

Checkpoints
☐ Main idea
☐ Example 1
☐ Details
☐ Example 2
☐ Details

102 ●● i SPEAKING

6. Summary

Q (1) Using points and examples from the talk, (2) explain how the invention of the opera and valves helped create the modern orchestra.

| Preparation time : 20 seconds |
| Response time   : 60 seconds |

Responding process of Task 6

Main Idea → Example 1 & Details → Example 2 & Details

Listening note

Main Idea
How orchestra became large & complex
- 2 inventions: opera & valves

Example 1
Opera (early 17th century)

Details
- Eur. families paid small mus. groups
- Opera req. more players, spec, parts
- Monteverdi exp. size of orch. early on

Example 2
Valves (early 18th century)

Details
- New invention on brass inst.
- Easier to change pitch, wider range
- Improved inst: tuba, cornet, & trumpet
- More inst. & var. of sounds

Sample Response

How orchestra became large & complex - 2 inventions: opera & valves
→ In her lecture, the professor discusses two factors that brought about an increase in the size and complexity of the orchestra. Those two factors were the invention of the opera and valves.

Opera (early 17th C) - Eur. families paid small mus. groups - Opera req. more players, spec, parts
- Monteverdi exp. size of orch. early on
→ According to the lecture, the opera became popular in the early seventeenth century in Europe. Since the opera required a greater number of players and specific parts for each instrument, the orchestra became larger and more complex.

Valves (early 18th C) - New invention on brass inst. - Easier to change pitch, wider range - Improved inst: tuba, cornet, & trumpet - more inst. & var. of sounds
→ Another factor was the invention of the valve that occurred in the early eighteenth century. The professor says that the valve eased the way for brass instruments to change the pitch, creating a new range of pitches. As a result, newly improved instruments, such as the trumpet, cornet, and tuba, were added to the orchestra, providing it with a variety of sounds.

1 Outlining

>> Take notes as you listen to a lecture.

1

Listening   Now listen to part of a lecture on water circulation.   MP3 26

Listening note

Main Idea
Water circulation
- Lots of water const. circ.
- Endless cycle refr. water sources

Example 1
Solar radiation

Example 2
Geothermal activity

Details
- Heats up oceans, makes vapor
- Vapor rises, becomes precip.
- Scatters on land as rain & snow

Details
- Magma heats up sea floor
- Hot water rises, cold water sinks
- Creates currents, like in North Atl.

| 6. Summary |

2

Listening Now listen to part of a lecture in a botany class. **MP3 27**

Listening note

Main Idea

Example 1   Example 2

Details   Details

2 Speaking Grammar

■ **Sentence Structure: Participle phrases**

Present Participle: Ends with "~ing"	We didn't know that our mother was a **working** woman.
Past Participle: Ends with "~ed"	Because of the car accident, he has an **injured** arm.
Perfect Participle: Ends with "having + ~ed"	**Having improved** her English pronunciation, she could communicate with native English speakers much more smoothly.

■ **Templates**

- Templates for Topic Sentences

The lecture is mainly about…	**The lecture is mainly about** the use of perspective in Renaissance paintings.
The professor discusses…	**The professor discusses** the effects of the Industrial Revolution.

- Templates for Example Sentences

He gives two examples of… One is… The other is…	**He gives two examples of** artistic imitation. **One is** exaggerated drawings in newspapers. **The other is** impersonation, wherein good imitators try to look and to act like their subjects.
(A) is another example of…	Reducing humidity **is another example of** preventing food deterioration.

- Templates for Detail Sentences

(A) enabled (B).	The development of technology **enabled** distance learning and teaching.
(A) is the most important factor in…	According to the professor, an experience one has early in life **is the most important factor in** determining one's personality.

6. Summary

>> Complete and speak your answers.

1 Notes for Question 1

Listening note

Main Idea
Water circulation
- Lots of water const. circ.
- Endless cycle refr. water sources

Example 1	Example 2
Solar radiation	Geothermal activity

Details
- Heats up oceans, makes vapor
- Vapor rises, becomes precip.
- Scatters on land as rain & snow

Details
- Magma heats up sea floor
- Hot water rises, cold water sinks
- Creates currents, like in North Atl.

Main Idea The professor discusses two power sources that help water circulation around the planet.

Example 1 He gives two examples of water circulation. One is solar radiation and the other is geothermal activity. According to the professor, heat from solar radiation will evaporate water and cause it to rise into the atmosphere, where it loses heat to cooler air. This transforms the water into precipitation that is scattered over the earth, such as rain or snow.

Example 2 Geothermal activity is another example of water circulation. This activity heats up deep ocean water, usually with the heat from magma flowing beneath the earth's crust. As the warm water rises, cooler waters in the ocean begin to sink, and these actions form ocean currents. Currents like the ones in the North Atlantic Ocean then enable water distribution throughout the planet's oceans.

Speaking Grammar

2 Use your notes for Question 2.

Listening note

Main Idea

Example 1   Example 2

Details   Details

Main Idea

_____
_____
_____

Example 1

_____
_____
_____
_____
_____

Example 2

_____
_____
_____
_____
_____

③ Delivery

6. Summary

1 Put a slash ("/") where you want to pause (before commas, prepositions, conjunctions, etc.) and respond slowly.

> The professor discusses two power sources / that help water circulation / around the planet. / He gives two examples / of water circulation. / One is solar radiation / and the other is geothermal activity. / According to the professor, / heat from solar radiation will evaporate water / and cause it to rise into the atmosphere, / where it loses heat to cooler air. / This transforms the water into precipitation / that is scattered / over the earth, / such as rain or snow. / Geothermal activity / is another example of water circulation. / This activity heats up deep ocean water, / usually with the heat from magma flowing beneath the earth's crust. / As the warm water rises, / cooler waters in the ocean begin to sink, / and these actions form ocean currents. / Currents like the ones / in the North Atlantic Ocean / then enable water distribution / throughout the planet's oceans.

* As shown above, practice the delivery with your answer for Q2.

Read the evaluation questions and check the level of your delivery. On a scale from 1 to 5 (1=very poor, 2=poor, 3=OK, 4=good, 5=very good), rank your delivery accordingly.

Could you complete your response?	1	2	3	4	5
Is your answer coherent and unified?	1	2	3	4	5
Do you find a sequence in your response?	1	2	3	4	5
How is the use of vocabulary?	1	2	3	4	5
Does your response show grammatical structures?	1	2	3	4	5
How is the use of idiomatic expressions?	1	2	3	4	5
Is your response fluent and smooth?	1	2	3	4	5
Is your pronunciation clear?	1	2	3	4	5
How is the use of stress and intonation?	1	2	3	4	5

* Use the extra evaluation sheet provided at the end of the main textbook (p.227) and evaluate your delivery for Q2.

Practice Questions

1 MP3 28

Using points and examples from the talk, explain how reliability and external appearance help determine the products a consumer buys.

| Preparation time : 20 seconds |
| Response time   : 60 seconds |

2

Using points and examples from the talk, explain how sublimation and activism have motivated writers to create literature.

| Preparation time : 20 seconds |
| Response time   : 60 seconds |

Practice Questions

3 MP3 30

Using points and examples from the talk, explain how direct advertisements and indirect advertisements contribute to the success of a small company.

| Preparation time : 20 seconds |
| Response time   : 60 seconds |

4 MP3 31

Using points and examples from the talk, explain how the desire for more land, and taxation without representation, led to the American Revolution.

| Preparation time : 20 seconds |
| Response time   : 60 seconds |

Vocabulary Study — Lectures

Psychology

- **assertive** *adj.* self-confident
- **cynical** *adj.* believe that people are only interested in themselves and are not sincere.
- **panic** *n.* terror
- **phobia** *n.* irrational fear
- **subconscious** *n.* the part of your mind that remembers information that you're not aware of
- **agnosia** *n.* inability to recognize objects due to brain damage
- **delusion** *n.* belief in something that is not true
- **extroverted** *adj.* outgoing or sociable
- **perception** *n.* the process or act of understanding
- **stimulus** *n.* something that rouses action

Business / Economics

- **transaction** *n.* the process of buying or selling something
- **accumulation** *n.* collection over time
- **patent** *n.* a legal right to make and sell a newly created item
- **privilege** *n.* a special right or opportunity that only a selected individual or group(s) can enjoy
- **portable** *adj.* small enough to carry around
- **device** *n.* a method, machine, or invention
- **equivalent** *adj.* having the same amount, quality, or value
- **continuity** *n.* uninterrupted succession
- **substitution** *n.* replacement
- **monopoly** *n.* complete control over something

Biology

- **adaptation** *n.* The process of adjusting to a new environment
- **ferment** *v.* to cause a chemical change through the action of living substances such as yeast.
- **optical** *adj.* having to do with sight
- **plasticity** *n.* ability to be changed into a new shape
- **sequence** *n.* a process
- **gravity** *n.* the force that makes things fall to the ground
- **particle** *n.* a small piece of matter
- **reinforce** *v.* to make something stronger
- **enlargement** *n.* extention in height or width
- **capture** *v.* seize or to take captive

Art & Literature

- **aesthetic** *adj.* beauty in an artistic sense
- **absurd** *adj.* unreasonable
- **applied art** the application of design to objects of function and everyday use
- **evoke** *v.* to cause someone to remember something
- **paradox** *n.* contradiction
- **probability** *n.* likelihood
- **literate** *adj.* able to read and write
- **tangible** *adj.* able to be seen or touched
- **allegory** *n.* a story that uses heavy symbolism
- **calligraphy** *n.* the art of fine handwriting

A. Choose the word which is closest in meaning to the vocabulary listed bleow.

1. Paradox
2. Literate
3. Portable
4. Substitution
5. Particle
6. Phobia
7. Extroverted
8. Calligraphy
9. Assertive
10. Capture

(a) The art of fine handwriting
(b) A small piece of matter
(c) Self-confident
(d) Able to read and write
(e) Small enough to carry around
(f) Irrational fear
(g) Replacement
(h) Contradiction
(i) Seize or take captive
(j) Outgoing or sociable

B. Complete the sentences by filling in the blanks.

| monopoly | equivalent | reinforce | cynical | aesthetic |
| adaptation | transaction | portable | patent | plasticity |

1. I noticed that she was _____ about everything except friendship.

2. In biology, _____ is the process through which an organism becomes better adjusted to its habitat.

3. A(n) _____ exists when an individual or a company has complete control over a particular product.

4. The Japanese Defense Ministry wants to _____ its army with more aircraft.

5. I found out that there was an unauthorized _____ made by the bank two weeks ago.

Part B. Integrated Tasks

PART C

Actual Test

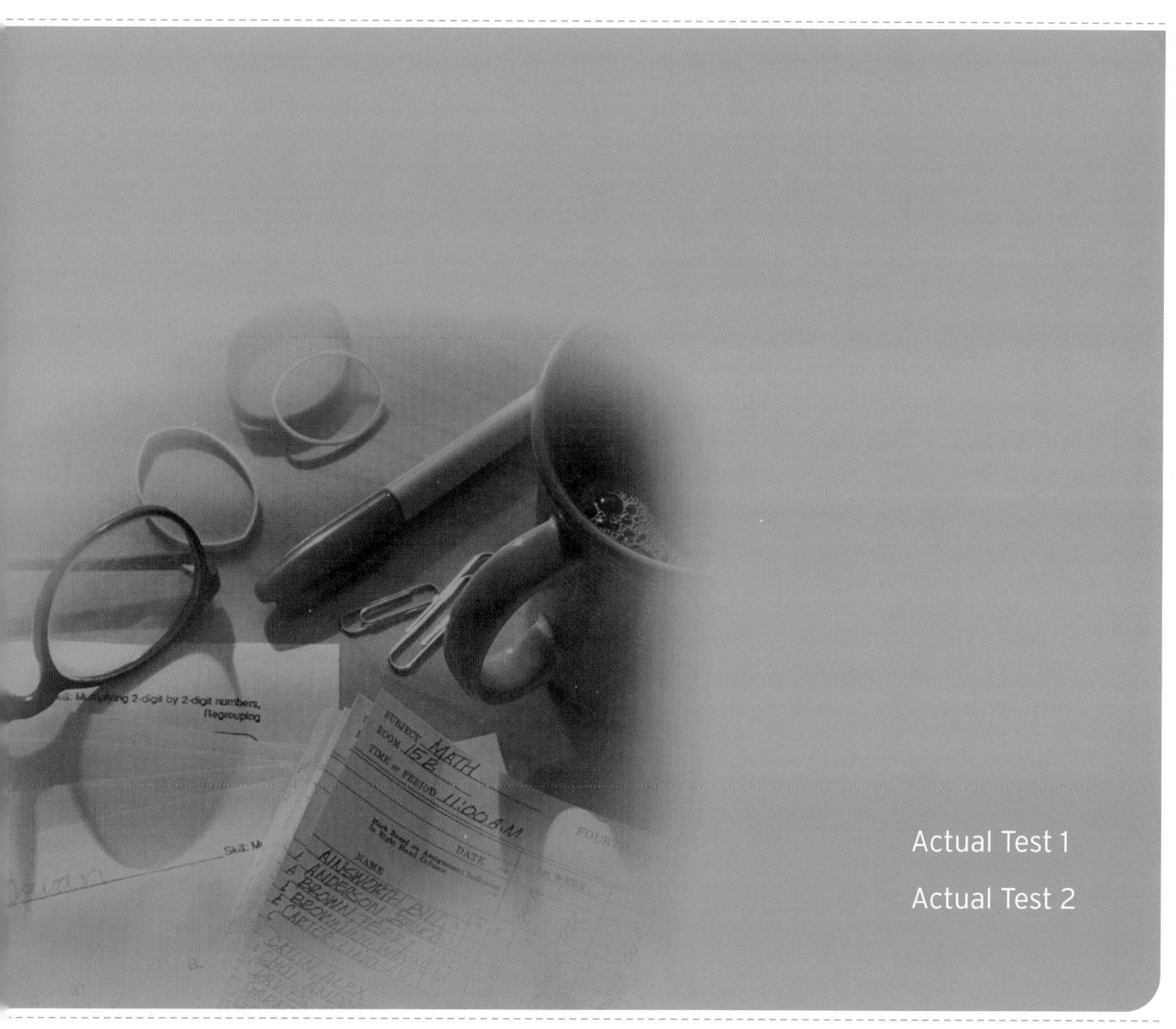

Actual Test 1

Actual Test 2

Actual Test 1

TOEFL SPEAKING

Speaking Section Directions

In this section of the test, you will be asked to demonstrate your ability to speak about a variety of topics. You will answer six questions by speaking into the microphone. Answer each of the questions as completely as possible.

In questions 1 and 2, you will speak about familiar topics. Your response will be scored on your ability to speak clearly and coherently about the topics.

In questions 3 and 4, you will first read a short text. The text will go away and you will then listen to a talk on the same topic. You will then be asked a question about what you have read and heard. You will need to combine appropriate information from the text and the talk to provide a complete answer to the question. Your response will be scored on your ability to speak clearly and coherently and on your ability to accurately convey information about what you have read and heard.

In questions 5 and 6, you will listen to part of a conversation or a lecture. You will then be asked a question about what you have heard. Your response will be scored on your ability to speak clearly and coherently and on your ability to accurately convey information about what you heard.

You may take notes while you read and while you listen to the conversations and lectures. You may use your notes to help prepare your response. Listen carefully to the directions for each question. The directions will not be written on the screen.

For each question, you will be given a short time to prepare your response. A clock will show how much preparation time is remaining. When the preparation time is up, you will be told to begin your response. A clock will show how much response time is remaining. A message will appear on the screen when the response time has ended.

Click on **Continue** to go on.

Actual Test 1

TOEFL SPEAKING Question 1 of 6

Describe your favorite item of clothing and why it is your favorite. Please include specific details and examples in your response.

| Preparation time : 15 seconds |
| Response time   : 45 seconds |

Some people think that a company should only promote people who work hard, while other people believe that a company should promote people who have worked there a long time. Which opinion do you agree with and why?

Preparation time : 15 seconds
Response time : 45 seconds

Actual Test 1

Reading Time: 45 seconds

Announcement from the Residence Office

Due to increasing safety concerns, the college will no longer allow students to keep personal microwaves in dorm rooms, starting next semester. This policy is being issued because of the possibility that microwaves could ignite any flammable items and start a fire in one of the dorm rooms. Any microwaves that are found in dorm rooms next semester will be confiscated by the director of the dormitory, and the owner will be fined one hundred dollars.

The woman expresses her opinion of the announcement. State her opinion and explain the reasons she gives for holding that opinion.

Preparation time : 30 seconds
Response time   : 60 seconds

Reading Time : 45 seconds

Vision Disorders

Among various vision problems, the most common conditions are related to refractive disorders. Refractive disorders occur when the shape of the eye is not a perfect sphere and cannot bend light correctly. The retina of the eyeball is the membrane that processes signals we receive to form images. When light rays hit the middle of the eye and don't reach the retina, a person will only be able to see close objects. If light does pass the retina, only distant objects will be clearly seen. Although such disorders can be attributed to genetic inheritance, they can be treated with corrective procedures.

The professor describes vision problems in humans. Explain how the two problems discussed by the professor relate to the way in which light strikes the retina.

| Preparation time : 30 seconds |
| Response time   : 60 seconds |

The students discuss two possible solutions to the woman's problem. Describe the problem. Then state which of the two solutions you prefer and explain why.

Preparation time : 20 seconds
Response time   : 60 seconds

TOEFL SPEAKING — Question 6 of 6

Using points and examples from the talk, explain how growing opposition to slavery and cultural differences between Northern and Southern states led to the American Civil War.

Preparation time : 20 seconds
Response time   : 60 seconds

Actual Test 2

TOEFL SPEAKING

Speaking Section Directions

In this section of the test, you will be asked to demonstrate your ability to speak about a variety of topics. You will answer six questions by speaking into the microphone. Answer each of the questions as completely as possible.

In questions 1 and 2, you will speak about familiar topics. Your response will be scored on your ability to speak clearly and coherently about the topics.

In questions 3 and 4, you will first read a short text. The text will go away and you will then listen to a talk on the same topic. You will then be asked a question about what you have read and heard. You will need to combine appropriate information from the text and the talk to provide a complete answer to the question. Your response will be scored on your ability to speak clearly and coherently and on your ability to accurately convey information about what you have read and heard.

In questions 5 and 6, you will listen to part of a conversation or a lecture. You will then be asked a question about what you have heard. Your response will be scored on your ability to speak clearly and coherently and on your ability to accurately convey information about what you heard.

You may take notes while you read and while you listen to the conversations and lectures. You may use your notes to help prepare your response.

Listen carefully to the directions for each question. The directions will not be written on the screen.

For each question, you will be given a short time to prepare your response. A clock will show how much preparation time is remaining. When the preparation time is up, you will be told to begin your response. A clock will show how much response time is remaining. A message will appear on the screen when the response time has ended.

Click on **Continue** to go on.

Actual Test 2

TOEFL SPEAKING — Question 1 of 6

Describe one thing you regret not doing in your life and explain why you regret not doing it. Please include specific details and examples in your response.

Preparation time : 15 seconds
Response time   : 45 seconds

Question 2 of 6

Some people believe that students should be allowed to graduate from high school early, while other people believe that students should all graduate at the same time. Which opinion do you agree with and why?

Preparation time : 15 seconds
Response time   : 45 seconds

Letter to the Editor

I am just writing to say how angry I am that the school will no longer allow students to walk their dogs on campus after 6:00 p.m. The only nearby park where I can take my dog out for a walk is the university campus, and I don't get out of class until after 6:00. Why doesn't the university just change the policy so that people are required to have their dogs on leashes? It would make the campus safer and also allow people to walk their dogs here.

A concerned student

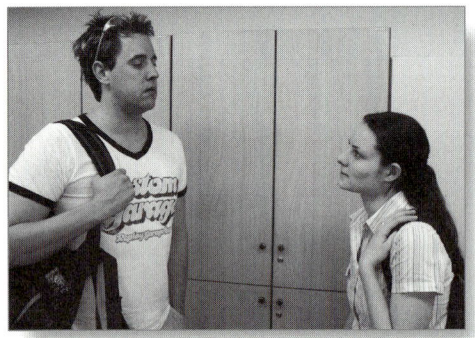

The man expresses his opinion of the letter published in the school newspaper. State his opinion and explain the reasons he gives for holding that opinion.

Preparation time : 30 seconds
Response time   : 60 seconds

Learned Helplessness

Learned helplessness is a psychological condition in which a person has been repeatedly exposed to unpleasant experiences and, as a result of these past experiences, believes that he is helpless in all unpleasant situations. The person's initial experience would have been one in which he truly had no control, and the constant exposure to such unpleasant conditions has caused him to become passive and resigned to his fate. As a result of this, his defensive behavior will vanish so that he instinctively becomes helpless in future situations that he could actually control.

The professor discusses why many women who were abused as children also get abused as adults. Explain how this relates to the concept of learned helplessness.

Preparation time : 30 seconds
Response time   : 60 seconds

Actual Test 2

Question 5 of 6

The students discuss two possible solutions to the man's problem. Describe the problem. Then state which of the two solutions you prefer and explain why.

Preparation time : 20 seconds
Response time : 60 seconds

Using points and examples from the talk, explain how setting up physical barriers and preserving vegetation can prevent soil erosion.

Preparation time : 20 seconds
Response time : 60 seconds

Workbook

1. Independent Task Skills
2. Integrated Task Skills
3. Pronunciation
4. Grammar

Workbook

01

Independent Task Skills

Exercise 1.   뜻이 비슷한 단어
Exercise 2.   모양·발음이 비슷한 단어
Exercise 3.   능동 vs. 수동
Exercise 4.   함께 쓰는 단어
Exercise 5.   숙어(Phrasal Verbs)
Exercise 6.   콩글리쉬(Broken English)
Exercise 7   풀어말하기
Exercise 8.   동사의 패턴
Exercise 9.   부사절이 포함된 문장
Exercise 10. 명사절이 포함된 문장
Exercise 11. 형용사절이 포함된 문장
Exercise 12. 둘 이상의 종속절이 포함된 문장

i-Speaking

Exercise 1 뜻이 비슷한 단어

비슷한 뜻의 어휘를 모아서 정리해 놓은 "thesaurus" 사전을 본 적이 있을 것이다. 그러나 같은 그룹에 속하더라도 그 단어들을 아무렇게나 바꾸어 쓸 수 있는 것이 아니다. 뜻이 비슷하더라도 쓰임새가 저마다 다르기 때문이다. 어휘력을 향상시키기 위해서는 머리 속에 각자의 thesaurus를 만들어 가야 한다. 비슷한 뜻을 갖는 단어들을 한 그룹으로 모아 생각하되, 각각 어떤 경우에 쓰이는지 구별할 수 있어야 한다.

A 다음 문장의 빈칸에 가장 적합한 말을 괄호 안에서 골라 써 보자.

1. It's hard to understand Cheryl because of her British ___accent___.
   (accent / intonation / pronunciation)

2. We are not able to communicate well, and it has become a big _____.
   (matter / problem / question / affair)

3. I think the professors should hold a calm, reasonable _____.
   (quarrel / argument / fight / debate)

4. What he said was _____, but how he said it was very rude.
   (real / genuine / true)

5. My father doesn't _____ why I want to go to university in a different city.
   (realize / understand)

6. It seems rather _____ that you got sick before your test.
   (comfortable / convenient)

7. There was a _____ misunderstanding about why Mr. Deane was not at the meeting.
   (total / whole)

8. In her first book, the author took us on an emotional _____ that ended in betrayal.
   (travel / trip / journey)

9. Due to problems with her health, Susan is _____ to participate in sports.
   (unable / impossible)

10. Give me one good _____ why I should finish school.
    (cause / reason)

1. Independent Task Skills

B 영어 문장의 빈칸을 채워 우리말과 같은 뜻이 되도록 말해 보자.

1. 우체국에서 그의 편지를 받았니?
   → Did you ____receive____ his letter from the post office?

2. 그 컴퓨터는 비쌀 거야.
   → That computer will _____ a lot of money.

3. 그 사고 이후, 그의 외상은 빠르게 나았으나, 정신적으로는 여전히 회복되고 있는 상태였다.
   → After the accident, his physical wounds _____ quickly, but emotionally he was still recovering.

4. 인생에서 어떤 길을 가야 할지 결정하는 일은 대개 쉽지 않다.
   → It is often not easy to _____ upon which path to take in life.

5. 프랑스에서 산 것은 나의 프랑스어 듣기와 말하기 실력을 향상시키는 데 매우 효과적인 방법이었다.
   → Living in France was a very _____ way to improve my French listening and speaking skills.

6. 나의 아버지는 내가 의학과 법학 중에 선택하길 바라시지만, 나는 공학을 공부하고 싶다.
   → My father wants me to choose _____ medicine and law, but I want to study engineering.

7. 군대에 가기로 결정하는 것은 쉬웠으나, 힘들었던 부분은 기초 훈련이었다.
   → The _____ to join the military was easy; the hard part was basic training.

8. 나는 그 기업이 환경 파괴에 대해 시민들에게 보상할 것이라는 것을 믿어 의심치 않았다.
   → I had no _____ that the company would compensate the citizens for the environmental damage.

9. 그 식당은 위생 기준을 개선해야 해. 안 그러면 문을 닫게 될 거야.
   → The restaurant must _____ its health standards, or it will be closed.

10. Emily는 예절 수업을 들어서 매우 예절이 바르다.
    → Emily took lessons in etiquette, so she has very _____ manners.

Exercise 2 모양·발음이 비슷한 단어

모양이나 발음이 비슷해서 혼동되는 단어들은 따로 정리하여 두고, 쓸 때마다 주의를 기울일 필요가 있다. 아래에 제시된 혼동하기 쉬운 주요 단어를 익혀 두도록 하자.

• affection	애정		• *gold	금으로 만든
• affectation	가식		• *golden	아주 좋은
• alone	혼자 있는		• human	인간의, 인류의
• lone	고독한		• humane	자비로운, 인도적인
• *base	(건물의) 기초		• loose	느슨한
• *basis	(세상의) 기초, 근거		• lose	잃다
• beside	~의 옆에		• noble	귀족
• besides	게다가		• novel	소설
• casual	태평한, 격이 없는		• precede	~ 보다 먼저 일어나다
• causal	인과관계의, 원인이 되는		• proceed	앞으로 나아가다
• *classic	전형적인		• persecute	박해하다
• *classical	클래식 풍의		• prosecute	집행하다
• conscious	의식이 있는		• quiet	조용한
• conscientious	양심적인		• quite	아주, 꽤
• *continual	반복적으로 지속되는		• resource	자원
• *continuous	(선 등이) 끊김 없는		• source	근원
• corpse	시체		• respectable	훌륭한, 존경받는
• course	강의, 시간의 흐름		• respective	각각의
• decent	우아한, 훌륭한		• rise	오르다, 올라가다
• descent	하강, 자손		• raise	올리다
• decreased	감소된, 줄어든		• sensible	이성적인, 자각 있는
• deceased	죽은, 고인이 된		• sensitive	예민한
• delusion	망상		• shade	그늘
• illusion	환상		• *shadow	그림자
• desert	버리다, 사막		• *sociable	사교적인
• dessert	디저트, 후식		• *social	사회의
• eminent	저명한		• terrible	끔찍한
• imminent	긴급한, 임박한		• terrific	굉장히 좋은
• extend	연장하다, 확장하다		• transfer	옮기다, 옮겨 가다
• expand	늘어나다, 팽창하다		• transform	변형시키다

* 표시가 있는 단어들은 경우에 따라 같은 뜻으로 사용되기도 한다. 본 리스트에서는 편의상 다른 뜻으로 쓰이는 경우의 뜻을 표시하였다.

1. Independent Task Skills

 A 다음 문장의 빈칸에 적합한 말을 괄호 안에서 골라 써 보자.

1. Gas will _____expand_____ when it gets hot.
   (extend / expand)

2. After my travels through China, I'd like to finish my journey with a _____ trip.
   (desert / dessert)

3. What, _____ first-rate skiing, does the city have to offer tourists?
   (beside / besides)

4. I think the fact that he was driving a sports car was a _____ factor in why the police stopped him.
   (casual / causal)

5. Samuel thought it best for the meeting to _____ the luncheon, so that people could leave when they were finished eating.
   (precede / proceed)

6. The students were disappointed because their principal decided to _____ school into the summer.
   (expand / extend)

7. The government will _____ the old fish market into a tourist attraction.
   (transform / transfer)

8. The theme of the detective novel was a _____ case of mistaken identity.
   (classical / classic)

9. I don't think there is anything _____ about preventing refugees from leaving the camps
   (human / humane)

10. Over the last 10 years, the population in the rural farming areas has _____ significantly.
    (decreased / deceased)

11. My biggest _____ of inspiration came from my grandfather; he was a musician, too.
    (resource / source)

12. Due to the irreversible effects of global warming, a change to alternative sources of energy is _____.
    (eminent / imminent)

13. The doctors in the refugee camp tried to provide adequate medical care, but recurring shortages in clean water was a _____ problem.
    (continual / continuous)

14. If James continues to _____ Ralph, I know it will end in violence.
    (prosecute / persecute)

15. It was _____ how Mary Anne was able to gain the trust of the clients so quickly.
    (terrible / terrific)

Exercise 3 능동 vs. 수동

동사에서 파생된 형용사 중에는 능동의 의미를 갖는 것과 수동의 의미를 갖는 것이 있다. 형용사가 현재 분사의 형태이면 능동의 의미이고, 과거분사의 형태이면 수동의 의미이다. 예를 들어, "disappointing"은 "실망스러운"(=실망하게 하는)이란 뜻이 되고, "disappointed"는 "실망한"이란 뜻이다.

예외 delightful (NOT delighting), impressive (NOT impressing)

A 다음 문장에서 밑줄 친 단어가 올바르게 사용되었으면 빈칸에 OK로 표시하고, 잘못된 경우에는 바르게 고쳐 써 보자.

1. The audience was amazing by the enthusiastic performance of the band.
   → _____amazed_____

2. Larry was annoying everyone with his rude, inappropriate behavior.
   → _____

3. The instructor felt the students were bored with the material, so he assigned a special group project. → _____

4. Vivian felt that the exam questions were confused, and so she thinks she may have failed.
   → _____

5. Kevin thought it was depressed to see how much of the forest had been cleared for housing.
   → _____

6. Alexander had been hesitant to attend; but it turned out to be a delightful party.
   → _____

7. My parents must have felt embarrassed when they saw me scolded by my teacher.
   → _____

8. The spectators at the soccer game became more and more exciting as the game went into the second half. → _____

9. Darren feels that by impressing the boss with his knowledge of the competition, he can get promoted quickly. → _____

10. How could I ever forget such an inspired song? → _____

1. Independent Task Skills

B 우리말과 같은 뜻이 되도록 영어 문장의 빈칸에 알맞은 말을 넣어 문장을 완성해 보자.

1. Jacob은 밖에서 들리는 소음 때문에 짜증이 나서 공부에 집중할 수 없었다.
   → Jacob couldn't concentrate on his studies because he was ___annoyed___ ___by___ the noise from outside.

2. 나는 그에게 그 일자리에 관심이 있다고 말했다.
   → I told him that I was _____ _____ the job offer.

3. 그 어린이 자선단체는 금전적인 지원과 더불어 더 많은 자원봉사자를 요청하는 매우 감동적인 탄원을 했다.
   → The children's charity made a very _____ plea for more volunteers as well as monetary assistance.

4. 사장님이 당신의 발표를 흡족해 하시는 것 같다.
   → It seems the boss is _____ _____ your presentation.

5. 뒤뜰에 있는 테라스에서 쉬면서, 나는 내가 직접 이것을 만들었다는 것을 만족스럽게 생각했다.
   → While I was relaxing on the patio in the backyard, I found it _____ that I had built it with my own two hands.

6. 그 사이클 선수가 기록 단축을 위해 약물을 복용한 것이 사실로 드러났다고 들었지만 그다지 충격적이지 않았다.
   → It was not all that _____ to hear that the cyclist was found guilty of using performance enhancing drugs.

7. 나는 공항에서 호텔까지 가는 데 실제로 걸린 시간에 대해 놀랐다.
   → I was _____ by the time it had taken to actually travel from the airport to the hotel.

8. Jade는 어릴 때 무서운 경험을 해서 그네를 타지 않는다.
   → Jade doesn't go on swings because she had a _____ experience when she was little.

9. 나는 연습에 참가하지 않음으로써 코치 선생님을 실망시켰다.
   → I made my coach _____ by not participating in the training session.

10. 그 영화는 너무도 강렬해서 영화가 끝나고 났을 때 나는 정신적으로 아주 기진맥진해 졌다.
    → The movie was so powerful that by the time it was over, I was emotionally _____.

Exercise 4 함께 쓰는 단어

"Win a lottery (복권이 당첨되다)", "shake hands (악수하다)" 처럼 함께 쓰이는 동사와 명사가 있다. 이들을 '연어 (collocation)'라고 한다. 어떤 단어들이 함께 쓰이는지를 기억해 놓으면 자동적으로 구(phrase)를 말할 수 있게 되므로 영어의 유창함(fluency)이 크게 향상된다.

   주어진 명사와 함께 쓰일 수 있는 동사들을 보기에서 골라 구(phrase)를 3개씩 만들어 보자.

보기				
make	break	lose	shut out	can't stand
get	pick up	look for	cause	become
suffer	relieve	suffer from	prevent	keep
cope with	from	have	tell	meet

1. habit → break a habit   pick up a habit   become a habit
2. stress → _____   _____   _____
3. job → _____   _____   _____
4. noise → _____   _____   _____
5. damage → _____   _____   _____
6. secret → _____   _____   _____
7. disease → _____   _____   _____
8. appointment → _____   _____   _____
9. friend → _____   _____   _____
10. heart → _____   _____   _____

1. Independent Task Skills

B 앞에서 만든 구(phrase) 중에서 다음 빈칸에 알맞은 것을 골라 써 보자. (필요한 경우에는 동사의 시제를 변형시켜야 한다.)

1. I've _made an appointment_ with the dentist for 10:30 tomorrow morning.

2. Listening to music helps me _____ caused by my job.

3. I began to _____ so I could pay my rent.

4. When you study, you must _____ so you can concentrate.

5. Termites can _____ to your house.

6. You have to be careful of what you say when you _____.

7. If I ever _____, I hope that someone can take care of me.

8. She was so beautiful that I _____ to her when we met.

C 다음 문장의 빈칸에 알맞은 동사를 써 보자.

1. My wife and I both _share_ an interest in animals, so we have many pets.

2. The teacher always makes us laugh when she _____ a joke.

3. I'm tired from work, so I'd like to _____ a holiday.

4. I damaged my friend's car, so I had to _____ an apology to her.

5. It took a long time, but we finally _____ progress on our research project.

6. If you want to learn Spanish, you must _____ an effort to study it.

7. Once we _____ the end of our long drive, we decided to have a picnic.

8. If someone is sad, you can _____ the situation by being nice to him or her.

Exercise 5 숙어 (Phrasal Verbs)

Phrasal verbs란 동사에 전치사나 부사가 합쳐져서 마치 하나의 동사처럼 쓰이는 것을 말한다. Phrasal verbs를 사용하면 적은 수의 기본 동사를 활용하여 다양한 표현을 할 수 있으며, 관용적인 영어 (idiomatic English)를 구사하는 능력을 보여 줄 수 있어 시험에서 가산 점수를 받을 수 있는 요소가 된다. Phrasal Verbs를 사용할 때는 뜻뿐 아니라 자동사인지 타동사인지, 분리되어 사용할 수 있는지 없는지 등을 정확히 알고 사용하도록 하자.

1) 동사 + 부사: Phrasal Verbs가 목적어를 취하지 않고 자동사처럼 쓰이는 경우.

- **blow up** 폭발하다
- **close down** 문을 닫다, 폐점하다
- **eat out** 외식하다
- **get away** 도망치다
- **go off** 폭발하다, 상하다.
- **break down** 고장나다
- **give in** 굴복하다
- **go on** 계속되다, (어떤 일이) 일어나다
- **slow down** 느려지다, 속도를 줄이다
- **show off** 자랑하다

2) 동사 + 목적어 + 전치사/부사: 목적어가 명사일 때는 위치가 자유롭다. (목적어가 대명사일 때는 항상 가운데에 들어감)

- **bring O ↔ up** (어떤 문제를) 꺼내다, ~을 키우다
- **give O ↔ up** ~을 포기하다, (담배 등을) 끊다
- **let O ↔ down** ~을 실망시키다
- **look O ↔ up** ~을 (컴퓨터, 사전 등에서) 찾아보다
- **make O ↔ up** ~을 지어내다, 꾸며내다
- **pick O ↔ up** ~을 집어 들다, 배우다, 습득하다
- **put O ↔ off** ~을 연기하다, 미루다
- **take O ↔ up** (취미를) 시작하다
- **think O ↔ over** ~에 대해 곰곰이 생각해 보다
- **turn O ↔ down** (열, 소리를) 줄이다, (제안을) 거절하다
- **wear O ↔ out** ~을 닳을 때까지 쓰다
- **write O ↔ down** ~을 적다, 메모하다

3) 동사 + 전치사/부사 + 목적어: Phrasal Verbs가 하나의 타동사처럼 쓰이면서 분리될 수 없는 경우.

- **account for O** (비중을) 차지하다, ~의 이유를 설명하다, 출석을 확인하다
- **come across O** ~을 우연히 만나다, 발견하다
- **count on O** ~에 의지하다
- **deal with O** ~을 다루다, 처리하다
- **do without O** ~없이 지내다
- **get over O** ~을 극복하다
- **go through O** ~을 겪다
- **look after O** ~을 돌보다
- **look into O** ~을 조사하다
- **run into O** ~와 우연히 마주치다
- **take after O** ~을 닮다

4) 동사 + 전치사/부사 + 전치사/부사 + 목적어: Phrasal Verbs가 하나의 타동사처럼 쓰이면서 분리될 수 없는 경우.

- **carry on with O** ~을 계속하다
- **catch up with O** ~을 따라잡다
- **cut down on O** ~의 양을 줄이다
- **come up with O** ~을 떠올리다, 생각해 내다
- **find out about O** ~에 대해 알아내다
- **get away with O** ~에 대한 처벌을 모면하다
- **make up for O** ~을 보상하다
- **put up with O** ~을 참고 견디다
- **run out of O** ~이 떨어지다
- **speak up for O** ~을 위해 목소리를 내다

1. Independent Task Skills

A 다음 문장의 밑줄 친 부분과 바꾸어 쓸 수 있는 표현을 보기에서 골라 보자.

보기
breaks down   carry on with   get over   run out of
let down   blows up   put up with   speak up for

1. When I graduated from the university, I decided not to <u>disappoint</u> my parents again.
 → (*let down*)

2. My teacher let me <u>continue</u> my drawing because I wasn't distracting anyone.
 → ( )

3. If that microwave <u>explodes</u>, it could cause a fire.
 → ( )

4. We <u>used up</u> the milk, so I'm going to buy some more at the store.
 → ( )

5. If we don't <u>speak in support of</u> neglected animals, then who will help them?
 → ( )

6. When a car <u>stops working</u>, it can cost a lot to repair it.
 → ( )

7. You must <u>soothe</u> your anger over losing the game and just try harder next time!
 → ( )

8. I've <u>lived with</u> that noise for a month, but I am finally tired of it.
 → ( )

B 어떤 phrasal verbs는 둘 이상의 뜻이 있다. 다음 문장에서 밑줄 친 phrasal verbs의 뜻을 괄호 안에서 골라 보자.

1. (A) When you do roll call, make sure you can <u>account for</u> all the students. (설명하다 /⃝출석을 확인하다⃝)
 (B) Can you <u>account for</u> the missing money? (⃝설명하다⃝/ 출석을 확인하다)

2. (A) I want to <u>bring up</u> my son the same way my parents raised me. (키우다 / (문제를) 꺼내다)
 (B) Please don't <u>bring up</u> politics around Amy, or she'll argue. (키우다 / (문제를) 꺼내다)

3. (A) He needs to <u>give up</u> his job as a waiter and go back to college. (포기하다 / 끊다)
 (B) I've heard that it's difficult to <u>give up</u> smoking, but people can quit. (포기하다 / 끊다)

4. (A) Please <u>turn down</u> the air conditioner, because it is too cold in here. (거절하다 / (소리, 열 등을) 줄이다)
 (B) I hate to <u>turn down</u> your invitation, but I have other plans. (거절하다 / (소리, 열 등을) 줄이다)

5. (A) We need to <u>check out</u> of the hotel before we can pay the bill. (확인하다 / 체크아웃 하다)
 (B) Let's <u>check out</u> the newspaper to see who won the game. (확인하다 / 체크아웃 하다)

Exercise 6 콩글리쉬 (Broken English)

한국인이 콩글리쉬를 쓰게 되는 것은 한국어와 같은 패턴으로 영어를 사용하기 때문이다. 콩글리쉬를 쓰지 않기 위해서는 영어식 사고 방식에 익숙해져야 하며, 이를 위해서는 영어환경에 스스로를 많이 노출시켜야 한다. 하지만 무작정 읽고 듣기만 한다고 되는 것이 아니다. 콩글리쉬를 빨리 뿌리뽑으려면 영어로 말할 때 자신의 말에 귀를 기울여야 한다. 말이든 글이든, 항상 자신이 사용한 표현 중에 어떤 것이 콩글리쉬인지 확인하고 그것을 자연스러운 영어 표현으로 고치는 연습을 해야 한다. 그러다 보면 어떤 표현이 머리 속에 떠오를 때 '아, 이건 콩글리쉬야' 하고 감이 올 것이다.

  다음 우리말 문장을 영어로 표현한 두 문장 중 더 자연스러운 표현을 골라 보자.

1. Alice의 눈은 아름답고 파란 색이며, 머리는 곱슬거리고 갈색이다.

    (A) Alice's eyes are beautiful and blue, and her hair is curly and brown.

    (B) Alice has beautiful blue eyes and curly brown hair.

2. 엠파이어 스테이트 빌딩의 꼭대기에서 아래를 내려다 보았을 때, 나는 현기증을 느꼈다.

    (A) I felt dizzy when I looked down from the top of the Empire State Building.

    (B) I felt dizziness when I looked below the top of the Empire State Building.

3. 매우 부자인 Kane씨는 세계에서 두 번째로 비싼 자동차를 소유하고 있다.

    (A) Mr. Kane, a very rich man, owns the second most expensive car in the world.

    (B) Mr. Kane, a very rich man, is owning the secondly most expensive car in the world.

4. 교통량이 많지 않으면 내가 학교까지 가는 데는 대략 한 시간이 걸린다.

    (A) I spend about an hour to go to school if there are not many cars on the road.

    (B) It takes me about an hour to get to school if there's not much traffic.

5. 벨기에 작가인 Amélie Notomb는 일본에서 태어나 5살까지 살았기 때문에 일본을 고국으로 생각한다.

    (A) The Belgian writer Amélie Nothomb thinks Japan as her real country, because she was born in Japan and lived 5 years.

    (B) The Belgian writer Amélie Nothomb considers Japan her mother country, because she was born there and stayed until she was 5 years old.

1. Independent Task Skills

B 다음 문장의 밑줄 친 부분은 어색한 표현이다. 자연스러운 표현이 되도록 고쳐 말해 보자.

1. Only high people are allowed in this club. (상류층 사람들만 이 클럽에 입장할 수 있다.)
   → upper class people

2. We need to reference other countries' policies. (우리는 다른 나라의 정책을 참고해야 한다.)
   → _____

3. I don't spray perfume because I am too sensitive to scents.
   (나는 향기에 너무 민감해서 향수를 뿌리지 않는다.)
   → _____

4. This one is a service. (이번 잔은 서비스입니다.)
   → _____

5. Children usually spend their time under the sight of their parents.
   (아이들은 부모가 지켜보는 가운데 많은 시간을 보낸다.)
   → _____

C 다음 문장은 어색한 표현이 사용되었다. 자연스러운 문장이 되도록 고쳐 말해 보자.

1. Parents can afford to give valuable lessons to their children.
   (부모는 아이들에게 귀중한 교훈을 가르쳐 줄 수 있다.)
   → Parents can teach valuable lessons to their children.

2. This way, I could know studying ways of friends.
   (이렇게 해서 나는 친구들로부터 공부 방법을 배우게 되었다.)
   → _____

3. A telescope shows the universe to us more closely.
   (사람들은 망원경을 통해 우주를 더 자세히 관찰할 수 있다.)
   → _____

4. Riding a bicycle gives much benefit than driving a car.
   (자전거를 타면 차를 운전하는 것보다 많은 이점이 있다.)
   → _____

5. It is important for adults to express positive words toward their spouses in front of children.
   (성인들이 아이들 앞에서 배우자에 대해 긍정적인 말을 하는 것이 중요하다.)
   → _____

Exercise 7 풀어 말하기

어떤 단어가 영어로 무엇인지 모르거나, 알더라도 금방 생각나지 않을 때에는 다른 말로 그 단어를 설명할 수 있어야 한다. 예를 들어 "목격자 (witness)"단어가 생각나지 않을 경우, "someone who has seen a crime or an accident"라고 풀어 설명할 수 있다. 이렇게, 정확한 단어를 알지 못하더라도 풀어 말할 수 있는 것은 자신의 의사를 전달하는 데 있어 꼭 필요한 능력이다.

 다음 단어를 영어로 풀어 설명해 보자.

1. tuition
   → *the money you pay for attending school*

2. majority
   → _____

3. vandalize
   → _____

4. aggravate
   → _____

5. premises
   → _____

6. pedestrian
   → _____

7. scholarship
   → _____

8. inaccessible
   → _____

9. donate
   → _____

10. deforestation
    → _____

| 1. Independent Task Skills |

B 다음 우리말 단어에 해당하는 영어 단어를 아는 경우에는 (A)에 그 단어를 쓰고 (B)에 그 뜻을 영어로 풀어 써 보자. 해당 영어 단어를 모르는 경우에는 (A)를 빈 칸으로 남겨 두고 (B)에서 다른 말로 풀어 영어로 설명해 보자.

1. 수족관 (A) _aquarium_
           (B) _a building where people go to look at water animals_

2. 지출   (A) _____
           (B) _____

3. 고고학 (A) _____
           (B) _____

4. 표절   (A) _____
           (B) _____

5. 보상하다 (A) _____
           (B) _____

6. 잠재력 (A) _____
           (B) _____

7. 상호작용 (A) _____
           (B) _____

8. 습도   (A) _____
           (B) _____

9. 만성적인 (A) _____
           (B) _____

10. 혁신   (A) _____
           (B) _____

Exercise 8 동사의 패턴

많은 학생들이 동사의 뜻만 암기하고 그 동사를 안다고 생각한다. 예를 들면 'remind'는 '~을 떠올리게 하다'라고 외우고 마는 것이다. 그러나 막상 '그 축제는 내게 2009년 인천 세계 도시 축전을 떠올리게 했다.'라는 문장을 영어로 정확히 말할 수 있는 학생은 많지 않다. 이것은 'remind'가 'remind A of B' 패턴으로 사용되는 것을 잘 모르기 때문이다. 이처럼, 동사는 뜻과 함께 그 패턴을 반드시 기억해야 한다.

A 괄호 안의 두 동사 중에서 알맞은 것을 골라 보자.

1. I (suggested / (advised)) my sister to visit Paris because it is a nice city.

2. I (think / regard) Jim as a good friend because he helped me out when I was in trouble.

3. He could not (explain / tell) the model well enough for me to understand how to apply it to my research.

4. In order to (discuss / talk) issues about effective economies, we first need to have a basic understanding of economics.

5. The ice on the road (made / caused) me to lose control of the car.

B 괄호 안에 주어진 동사를 빈칸에 알맞은 형태로 써 보자.

1. I asked the waiter _____to bring_____ some more water, but he hasn't yet.   (bring)

2. Donald considered _____ in a consultant so that we could finish the project before the deadline.   (call)

3. I suggested that we _____ a long lunch break because we had worked so much.   (take)

4. My daughter was spending too much time on the computer, so I tried to encourage her _____.   (read)

5. If you commit yourself to _____ the piano, you will be a talented pianist.   (play)

152 •• i SPEAKING

1. Independent Task Skills

C 빈칸에 알맞은 전치사를 써넣어 보자.

1. You must communicate ___with___ your colleagues in order to do a good job.
2. Mom tried to prevent Dad _____ buying a new car.
3. Did you contribute any money _____ charity last year?
4. I can relate _____ Billy because we both have vision problems.
5. I really prefer watching TV _____ taking out the garbage.

D 우리말과 같은 뜻이 되도록 영어 문장의 빈칸을 채워 말해 보자.

1. Chang 교수님은 우리에게 소그룹으로 협력하여 공부하라고 조언하셨다.
   Professor Chang ___advised___ us ___to___ ___study___ collaboratively in small groups.

2. 이 연구 논문 쓰는 것을 피할 수 있었으면 좋겠어.
   I wish I could _____ _____ this research paper.

3. 우리는 우리 치약이 최고라는 것을 고객들에게 확신시켜야 한다.
   We have to _____ customers _____ our toothpaste is the best.

4. 전에 Darrel 은 내가 대학에 조기 입학 지원을 하는 게 좋겠다고 말했지만, 언제 지원할지는 말해주지 않았다.
   Darrel mentioned one day that I should apply for early admission to the university, but he didn't _____ me _____ _____ apply.

5. 나의 교수님은 한 연구 프로젝트를 진행 중이신데, 내가 조사를 하나 맡아 주었으면 좋겠다고 말했다.
   My professor is involved in a research project, and she mentioned that she would _____ me _____ _____ a survey.

6. 법에 따라 모든 운전자는 운전면허증을 소지해야 한다.
   The law _____ all drivers _____ _____ a drivers license.

7. 나는 어떤 하키 선수가 최고인지에 대해 내 친구들과 늘 언쟁을 한다.
   I always _____ with my friends _____ which hockey player is the best.

8. 정확히 어쩌다 그 일이 일어났는지 이해가 잘 안 된다. Vanessa에게 그 사고에 대해 더 물어봐야겠다.
   I'm not sure exactly how it happened, so I need to _____ Vanessa more _____ the accident.

Workbook • • 153

Exercise 9 부사절이 포함된 문장

부사절은 문장에서 부사와 같은 역할을 하며, if, when, because, although와 같은 종속접속사로 시작된다. 때로는 as soon as와 같이 둘 이상의 단어가 모여 종속접속사의 역할을 하기도 한다. 다음은 부사절을 이끄는 대표적인 종속접속사와 그 의미이다.

• when	~할 때	• while	~하는 동안, ~한 반면
• as	~하므로, ~하면서, ~하듯이	• before	~하기 전에
• after	~한 후에	• since	~한 이래로
• until	~할 때까지	• if	~한다면
• unless	~하지 않는다면	• so that/in order that	~하도록
• because	~하기 때문에	• since	~하기에, ~한 이래로
• though/although	비록 ~하지만, ~함에도 불구하고	• even if/though	~하더라도
• where	~하는 곳에서	• the way	~하는 방식으로

A 빈칸에 알맞은 종속접속사를 괄호 안에서 골라 보자.

1. _____After_____ they saw the suspect, the police officers tried to catch him.
   (After / If)

2. The police were busy controlling the crowd, _____ the firefighters fought the blaze.
   (though / while)

3. We need to educate the public on matters of public health and safety, _____ we can reduce incidences of illness and injury.
   (because / so that)

4. _____ criminals show regret or not, they need to serve the full term of their sentence. (Because / Whether)

5. Fossil fuel deposits will be depleted _____ we begin to seriously develop alternative fuel supplies.
   (unless / if)

6. The fire damage to the house was so severe _____ it had to be torn down and re-built.
   (that / when)

7. I will continue my physical therapy _____ my leg has healed completely and I can walk without crutches.
   (until / unless)

8. The inmate was denied parole _____ he had served his minimum sentence and was a model prisoner.
   (the way / even though)

| 1. Independent Task Skills |

B 다음 두 문장 중 하나를 부사절로 만들어 두 문장을 한 문장으로 합쳐 보자.

1. We went sailing yesterday. + We got caught in a rainstorm.

    → We went sailing yesterday though we got caught in a rainstorm.

2. Polar bears come from there. + Climate is ideal for walruses and seals.

    → _____

3. Price of land near the lake has fallen. + They discovered deposits of toxic chemicals in the area.

    → _____

4. The oranges will freeze and the crop will be destroyed. + There is an early frost.

    → _____

5. There was a 10-car pile up. + The snow storm caused zero visibility.

    → _____

C 주어진 문장에 적절한 내용의 부사절을 첨가하여 좀 더 구체적인 내용이 되도록 말해 보자.

1. I believe most people are honest.

    → Although some people take advantage of others, I believe most people are honest.

2. This place seems familiar.

    → _____

3. I took the bus instead of driving yesterday.

    → _____

4. My sister and I have a lot of things in common.

    → _____

5. I'd rather live in my own country than live abroad.

    → _____

Exercise 10 명사절이 포함된 문장

명사절은 문장 내에서 명사의 역할, 즉 주어, 목적어, 보어, 전치사의 목적어 역할을 한다. 가장 흔히 사용되는 명사절을 정리해 보면 다음과 같다.

1) 타동사의 목적어 역할을 하는 that절 (that은 생략 가능)
   Ex I can't believe (that) you guys haven't met before.

2) Be동사의 보어 역할을 하는 that절 (that은 생략 가능)
   Ex The fact is (that) nobody wants to waste time and money.

3) 동격으로 사용된 that절 (that은 생략 불가능)
   Ex I agree with the idea that high school students should be allowed to vote.

4) 형용사 (sure, afraid, aware, sorry, etc) 뒤에 나오는 that절 (that은 생략 가능)
   Ex I'm not sure (that) this is the shortest way.

5) 의문사절 - Can you tell me what you think of this poem?

6) If 또는 whether로 시작하는 명사절 - I don't know if I did the right thing.

 다음 문장의 빈칸에 가장 적합한 말을 괄호 안에서 골라 보자.

1. I think ____that____ you should've left a phone number.
   (that / if)

2. I can't wait to see _____ my grandmother lived as a child.
   (why / where)

3. The problem is _____ our car hit a very expensive car.
   (that / what)

4. Do you know _____ I can borrow that book?
   (where / what)

5. I expressed the idea _____ every child has the right to education.
   (which / that)

6. Max was disappointed _____ not many people showed up at the party.
   (that / why)

7. My fondest memory is of _____ we ate at that little Italian restaurant.
   (how / when)

8. I'm not quite sure _____ day it is to do the laundry, mine or yours.
   (who / whose)

9. I will support your decision _____ you decide to go to school.
   (whatever / wherever)

1. Independent Task Skills

B 괄호 안에 있는 명사절을 밑줄 친 대명사 대신 삽입하여 문장을 다시 써 보자.

1. is a tough choice. (whether I should drive or walk)
   → Whether I should drive or walk is a tough choice.

2. won't be revealed until tomorrow. (where the actress is to be married)
   → _____

3. I can't believe! (that the woman has not stopped talking)
   → _____

4. will not be made public. (what is talked about in the meeting)
   → _____

5. They now know. (why the world's climate is warming)
   → _____

C 괄호 안의 단어들을 적절히 배열하여 다음 문장의 빈칸에 들어갈 내용을 써 보자.

1. Today we learned how __pretzels are made__.
   (are, pretzels, made)

2. The professor expressed the hope that _____.
   (students, the program, join, more, would)

3. Do you know _____?
   (he, made, him, what, that, sick, ate)

4. Scientists say _____.
   (can, in front of, cancer, that, microwave, cause, a working, standing)

5. The disagreement began over _____, the husband's or the wife's.
   (priorities, were, important, whose, more)

6. The police found _____.
   (stolen, hid, the criminal, where, the bank, from, the money)

Exercise 11 형용사절이 포함된 문장

형용사절은 관계절(relative clause)이라고도 하며, 관계대명사나 관계부사가 이끄는 절을 말한다. 형용사는 명사를 앞에서 수식하지만, 형용사절은 명사를 뒤에서 수식한다. 형용사절을 사용하면 문장을 쉽게 확장할 수 있다. 한국어는 형용사절이 흔히 사용되는 구조가 아니어서 한국인들은 부사절이나 명사절에 비해 형용사절을 잘 활용하지 못하는 경향이 있고, 그래서 더 많은 연습이 필요하다.

A 다음 문장에서 밑줄 친 형용사절이 꾸며 주는 선행사를 찾아 동그라미 쳐 보자.

1. I want to invest in an apartment that I can rent out to a nice family.
2. The area where the typhoon caused such damage has been declared a disaster area.
3. The car that was used in the robbery was stolen from a parking lot.
4. I was trying to find the book that my grandfather had given me as a child.
5. I am concerned about the environment, so I want to buy a car that also uses electrical power.
6. I can't remember exactly the year when my whole family had a reunion.
7. A child that had been lost for a week in the mountains was finally found.
8. An artist whose art is too abstract might have a difficult time being accepted by the general public.

B 다음 문장에서 밑줄 친 선행사를 꾸며 주는 형용사절을 찾아 동그라미 쳐 보자.

1. For many young lovers, love is the only thing that matters.
2. In the case of many car accidents, it's not the volume of traffic that is at fault, but how people drive that really causes the problem.
3. In many cultures around the world, it is the eldest son who must bear the responsibility of maintaining family unity.
4. It was not the acting, but the subject matter of the movie that really offended me.
5. As a nature photographer, I wanted to take pictures of eagles, so I had to hike up into the mountains where they made their nests.
6. Many parents look forward to the day when their children marry and move away from home, so that they can enjoy traveling.

1. Independent Task Skills

C 다음 문장을 읽고 괄호 안에서 알맞은 관계사를 골라 보자.

1. My biology professor is the woman (whom / **(who)**) received a grant to study cancer cells.

2. I'm not sure yet if the new governor is a man in (whom / that) people can put their trust.

3. I'd like to live in a city (where / which) I can afford to buy a home as well as have easy access to cultural facilities.

4. I remember, with great pride, the time (which / when) my husband sold his first painting.

5. It was the summer of 2002 (when / where) Korea co-hosted World Cup soccer with Japan.

6. I can't remember the name of the dish (that / what) we had at the Indian restaurant, but it was delicious.

7. Yellow dust, (which / when) comes from the Gobi Desert in the spring, is the source of tremendous air pollution all over Asia.

8. The picture in the newspaper was of the woman (whose / who) identity was stolen.

D 괄호 안의 단어들을 적절히 배열하여 다음 문장의 빈칸에 들어갈 내용을 써 보자.

1. 서울은 도시의 이점을 충분히 누릴 수 있는 도시이다.
   → Seoul is a city _____*where you can fully enjoy the advantages of city life*_____.

2. 파리는 박물관, 연극, 오페라와 같은 무한한 문화적 활동을 제공하는 도시이다.
   → Paris is a city _____.

3. 박지성은 영국 프리미어 리그(Premier League)에서 활동하는 유명한 한국 축구 선수이다.
   → Park Ji Sung is a famous Korean soccer player _____.

4. Margaret Atwood는 캐나다 작가로, 종종 페미니스트 작가로 일컬어진다.
   → Margaret Atwood is a Canadian writer _____.

5. 새벽에 일어나 일출을 보는 것은 내가 올해 하고 싶은 일 중 하나이다.
   → Waking up at dawn to see a sunrise is one of the things _____.

Exercise 12 둘 이상의 종속절이 포함된 문장

둘 이상의 종속절이 포함된 문장을 틀리지 않고 구사할 수 있다면 상당한 영어 실력을 가졌다고 자부해도 좋다. Speaking 시험에서도 이런 문장들이 자주 사용된 응답은 높은 점수를 받는다. 앞에서 학습한 부사절과 명사절, 그리고 형용사절을 자유롭게 섞어 쓸 수 있도록 꾸준히 연습하자.

A 다음 문장에서 종속절을 모두 찾아 밑줄을 쳐 보자.

1. I love the times <u>when I hang out with my old friends</u>, <u>because we share a lot of common interests</u>.

2. Which career you choose will determine the classes that you decide to take.

3. When Dad's favorite football team wins, he brags to his friends who don't like that team.

4. Let's see the movie you told me about after we eat dinner.

5. This building, which was constructed a hundred years ago, will endure whatever conditions weather can create.

B 괄호 안에 주어진 내용을 종속절로 만들어 제시된 문장을 좀 더 구체적으로 만들어 말해 보자.

1. The couch that you bought will look nice. (우리가 그 소파를 놓을 장소를 찾는다면)
   → The couch that you bought will look nice when we find a place for it.

2. Whoever wants a ticket must wait. (판매원이 올 때까지)
   → _____

3. Even though it will rain today, students want to go on a picnic.
   (소풍이 재미있을 거라고 생각하기 때문에)
   → _____

4. Students who had low grades need extra lessons. (그 보충 수업은 도움이 될 것이다)
   → _____

5. The factory is where most people in town work. (그 공장에서는 자동차를 만든다)
   → _____

C 다음 문장은 하나의 종속절을 포함하고 있다. 여기에 하나 이상의 종속절을 더 삽입하여 문장을 다시 말해 보자.

1. In Korea, you are not allowed to drive until you are eighteen.
   → In Korea, you are not allowed to drive until you are eighteen, which is one or two years older than in the US.

2. Mary learned how fractions work.
   →

3. What his uncle said was very clever.
   →

4. I am scared of driving because of a car wreck.
   →

5. You'll have to travel with whomever you can find.
   →

6. The road is where these two streets separate.
   →

7. While the children are asleep, let's set out the presents.
   →

8. Whatever you want to discuss is fine.
   →

9. Whether the professor approves of your project or doesn't, you can be proud of the great effort.
   →

10. Some scientists are convinced that global warming is due to human activity.
    →

02

Integrated Task Skills

Exercise 1. 비슷한 말(Synonym)로 바꾸어 말하기
Exercise 2. 문장 구조를 바꾸어 말하기
Exercise 3. 내용을 단순화시키기
Exercise 4. 다양한 Paraphrase
Exercise 5. 기호·약어 사용하기
Exercise 6. 중요한 내용 찾기
Exercise 7 대화 듣고 Note-taking 하기
Exercise 8. 강의 듣고 Note-taking 하기
Exercise 9. 주제(Main Idea) 찾기
Exercise 10. 뒷받침 내용(Supporting Points) 찾기
Exercise 11. 노트 보고 요약하기 (독해)
Exercise 12. 노트 보고 요약하기 (청취)

Exercise 1 비슷한 말 (Synonym)로 바꾸어 말하기

문장의 일부를 비슷한 말로 바꾸어 표현하는 것은 가장 쉽고 기본적인 **paraphrasing** 방법이다. 일반적으로 **paraphrasing**은 어떤 문장을 머리 속에서 이해하여 표현하는 것이므로, 원래 문장보다 쉽고 간단한 표현으로 이루어진다.

> **Ex** They installed the new computer network at last.
> → They finally set up the new computer network.

A 다음 문장의 밑줄 친 표현을 비슷한 말로 바꾸어 문장을 다시 써 보자.

1. Plant life generates oxygen in abundant quantities.
   → Plant life produces lots of oxygen.

2. The escalating tension between Russia and America jeopardized peace.
   → _____

3. Now, who knows what the miscellaneous causes of the bubonic epidemic were?
   → _____

4. I've exhausted all of my money on tuition for classes.
   → _____

5. All organisms must utilize water to survive.
   → _____

6. Can you locate my residence hall on that campus map?
   → _____

7. I checked out a good deal of resources from the library.
   → _____

8. If you perspire too much during gym, take a sip of water.
   → _____

B 다음 문장의 일부를 비슷한 말로 바꾸어 표현해 보자.

1. The Berlin Wall was a partition that didn't prevent people from leaving East Berlin.
   → The Berlin Wall was a barrier that didn't stop people from leaving East Berlin.

2. I had a quarrel with my roommate, and now she is snubbing me.
   → _____

3. Freud speculated that our dreams manifest our deepest yearnings.
   → _____

4. You have a lot of liberty in a democracy, but you must be cautious when using it.
   → _____

5. The accumulation of dust in the atmosphere creates clouds.
   → _____

C 들려주는 문장을 듣고 비슷한 표현을 써서 paraphrasing을 해 보자. MP3 44

1. 🎧
   → Space travel may be limited, but it can give us important information.

2. 🎧
   → _____

3. 🎧
   → _____

4. 🎧
   → _____

5. 🎧
   → _____

Exercise 2 문장 구조를 바꾸어 말하기

문장의 구조를 바꾸어 말함으로써 paraphrasing을 할 수 있다. 이것은 비슷한 말을 사용하는 것보다 좀 더 어려운 방법이다. 문장의 구조를 바꾼다는 것은 능동태를 수동태로 표현한다거나 구(phrase)를 절(clause)로 풀어 쓴다거나 하는 것을 말한다.

Ex Careful planning for the future can ensure that technology will improve the quality of life.
→ Technology can improve the quality of life if we plan carefully for the future.

A 주어진 문장의 첫머리에 맞추어 다음 문장을 변형해 보자.

1. Abuse of power by the czar incited the Russian Revolution.
   → The Russian Revolution was incited _by the czar's abuse of power_.

2. Stinging tentacles are mechanisms that jellyfish use to defend themselves.
   → Jellyfish use _____.

3. The assignment that we received yesterday is difficult.
   → We received _____.

4. The place where President Lincoln was assassinated was Ford's Theater.
   → President Lincoln _____.

5. Clouds of cosmic dust will eventually compress in order to form stars.
   → Stars form _____.

6. It is required that new students attend the orientation that takes place next week.
   → New students must _____.

7. The graduation test must be taken by seniors who are graduating.
   → Seniors are _____.

8. Back in medieval Europe, the belief that the sun orbited the Earth was very popular.
   → A popular belief in medieval Europe _____.

| 2. Integrated Task Skills |

B 다음 문장의 구조를 바꾸어 paraphrasing을 해 보자.

1. If there are any problems, they can be reported to your Resident Assistant.
   → You can report any problems to your Resident Assistant.

2. There are a variety of meal plans that are available for you to choose from.
   → _____

3. In order to override a presidential veto, a two-thirds majority is required of Congress.
   → _____

4. Something that may have made the dinosaurs go extinct, or so many scientists believe, is a meteorite.
   → _____

5. Next Tuesday would be a good time for you to move into the dorm.
   → _____

C 들려주는 문장을 듣고 문장 구조를 바꾸어 paraphrasing을 해 보자. MP3 45

1. 🎧
   → The student council will meet once a week.

2. 🎧
   → _____

3. 🎧
   → _____

4. 🎧
   → _____

5. 🎧
   → _____

Exercise 3 내용을 단순화시키기

길고 복잡해 보이는 문장이지만 다 읽고 보면 단순한 아이디어를 담고 있는 경우가 많다. 어려운 표현으로 된 문장의 내용을 단순화시켜 가능한 한 짧고 간결한 표현으로 말하는 연습을 해 보자. 이것은 paraphrasing뿐 아니라 note-taking과 summarizing에도 도움이 된다.

Ex The average global temperature is increasing.
→ It's getting hotter all around the world.

  주어진 문장의 첫머리에 맞추어 다음 문장을 단순화시켜 보자.

1. The hours of service for the computer lab have ended for today.
   → The computer lab is _now closed_____.

2. Only one vote can be attributed to each individual who votes in the United States.
   → Each American voter _____.

3. It takes me too long to walk to English class.
   → My English class _____.

4. My calculus professor has a real strict policy about whispering in class.
   → We can't _____.

5. A massive super continent once consisted of all the land masses on earth.
   → All of the earth's land was _____.

6. One result of emotional trauma is the persistent recurrence of nightmares.
   → Emotional trauma can _____.

7. Rocket technology made great advancements during World War II.
   → Improved rockets were _____.

8. Taking pop quizzes is an effective method of getting prepared for tests.
   → Pop quizzes are _____.

| 2. Integrated Task Skills

B 다음 문장의 내용을 단순화시켜 **paraphrasing**을 해 보자.

1. The shower stalls in that dorm could benefit from a good scrubbing.
   → The dorm's showers are overly dirty.

2. Turtles possess shells that function as a buffer against different kinds of dangers.
   →

3. Metaphors are used to illustrate similarities between two different objects or ideas.
   →

4. Jonathan Swift often made humans' irrational behavior the target of his ridicule.
   →

5. Not only does this essay cover complex material, but it also has to be at least ten pages!
   →

C 들려주는 문장을 듣고 문장 구조를 바꾸어 **paraphrasing**을 해 보자. **MP3 46**

1. 🎧
   → The Treaty of Versailles ended World War I.

2. 🎧
   →

3. 🎧
   →

4. 🎧
   →

5. 🎧
   →

Exercise 4 다양한 Paraphrase

하나의 문장에 대한 paraphrase는 하나뿐이 아니다. 또한 앞에서 배운 세 가지 방법 중 어느 하나만을 사용해야 하는 것도 아니다. 세 방법을 적절히 혼합하여 다양한 paraphrase를 만드는 연습을 하면 어떤 문장에 대해서도 쉽게 paraphrasing을 할 수 있게 될 것이다.

> **Ex** The global average temperature is increasing due to global warming.
> → It's getting hotter all around the world because of global warming.
> → Global warming makes the earth hotter.
> → Global warming causes the world's temperature to rise.
> → The world's temperature is getting higher as global warming takes hold.

 빈칸을 채워 주어진 문장에 대한 다양한 paraphrase를 만들어 보자.

1. Corporations rely on private investors for financing.
   → Private investors _finance corporations_____.
   → Businesses rely on private investors for _funding_____.
   → When they need financial assets, corporations _turn to private investors_____.

2. Few people are on campus on Friday afternoons, so lunch isn't served then.
   → _____ since no one's on campus.
   → The campus is _____ on Friday afternoons, so lunch is _____.

3. While sailing for India, Columbus found North America.
   → Columbus _____ North America while _____ for India.
   → _____, Columbus stumbled upon North America.

4. Citric acid has numerous applications, including cleaning surfaces and healing cells.
   → Citric acid can _____ and _____.
   → _____ can be done with citric acid.
   → Citric acid has many uses, like _____.

5. When a person joins the fraternity, he or she has to promise to keep its secrets.
   → Fraternity members _____.
   → When _____ is _____ into the fraternity, he or she has to _____ to keep its secrets.
   → Anyone _____ has to promise to keep its secrets.

2. Integrated Task Skills

B 다음 문장에 대해 둘 이상의 paraphrasing을 해 보자.

1. Several nations in Europe adopted the euro as their primary currency.
   → Many European nations mainly use the euro.
   → The euro was adopted by a number of European nations as their main currency.

2. Class presidents have a lot of power.
   → _____
   → _____

3. College radio DJs must work around their classes.
   → _____
   → _____

4. The Cherokee tribe developed its own alphabet and published a newspaper.
   → _____
   → _____

5. Due to an oncoming thunderstorm, softball practice has been called off.
   → _____
   → _____

C 들려주는 문장을 듣고 문장 구조를 바꾸어 paraphrasing을 해 보자. **MP3 47**

1. 🎧
   → The bookstore sells chemistry lab notebooks.
   → Chemistry lab manuals can be purchased at the bookstore.

2. 🎧
   → _____
   → _____

3. 🎧
   → _____
   → _____

Workbook •• 171

Exercise 5 기호·약어 사용하기

Note-taking의 기본은 짧은 시간 내에 많은 내용을 적는 것이다. 이를 위해서는 긴 단어나 문장을 그대로 받아 적지 않고 기호와 약어를 사용하여 간단히 표시하는 것이 필요하다. 다음은 흔히 사용되는 기호와 약어들이다. 이 외에 자신만 알아볼 수 있는 기호와 약어를 사용할 수도 있다. 중요한 것은 꾸준한 note-taking 연습을 통해 이러한 약어와 기호의 사용에 익숙해지는 것이다.

기호	의미	약어	의미
→	leads to, results in (결과)	w/	with
←	is a result of (원인)	w/o	without
↑	increases (증가)	b/c	because
↓	decreases (감소)	e.g.	for example
+ 또는 &	and, plus, in addition (첨가)	esp.	especially
=	equals, is the same as (같음)	dept.	department
≠	is not the same as (같지 않음)	b/w	between
↔	is the opposite of (반대)	wt.	weight
〉	is more than (이상)	ht.	height
〈	is less than (이하)	sth.	something
/	per (~당)	sb.	somebody
#	number (숫자)	ASAP	as soon as possible

 기호와 약어를 적절히 사용하여 다음 문장에 대한 노트를 작성해 보자.

1. The Department of Justice is managed by the United States Attorney General.
   → <u>US Atty. Gen. Runs Dept. of Just.</u>

2. Not only do plants provide nutrients, but they also produce oxygen.
   → _____.

3. The distance from Earth to Jupiter is farther than a shuttle can travel.
   → _____.

4. I can't make the college basketball team because I'm less than six feet tall.
   → _____.

5. If you finish your research paper by Friday afternoon, you'll pass the class.
   → _____.

2. Integrated Task Skills

6. Because of drought, farms can't produce any crops; therefore, they usually close down.

→ _____.

7. Public works might benefit if they were purchased by corporations.

→ _____.

8. I lost my backpack, so I'll have to attend class without my textbook.

→ _____.

9. Your risk of getting heart disease increases if you eat fatty foods, especially red meat.

→ _____.

10. The art department is showing some student art on Wednesday to raise money for the art center.

→ _____.

B 들려주는 문장을 듣고 기호와 약어를 적절히 사용하여 노트를 작성해 보자. MP3 48

1. 🎧
  → *bikes to class b/c wants wt. ↓*

2. 🎧
  → _____

3. 🎧
  → _____

4. 🎧
  → _____

5. 🎧
  → _____

Workbook •• 173

Exercise 6 중요한 내용 찾기

Note-taking을 할 때 읽거나 듣는 내용을 모두 적으려고 하는 경우가 있는데, 모든 내용을 다 적을 시간도 없을 뿐더러, 그래야 할 필요도 없다. 지문을 읽거나 들으면서 핵심적인 내용이 무엇인지 파악하여 적는 것이 효과적인 note-taking이다. 적어야 할 내용은 다음과 같다.

1) **토픽 (Topic):** 글의 소재 또는 무엇에 대한 내용인지를 간단히 적는다.
2) **주제 (Main idea):** 글의 전체 내용 및 방향을 요약해서 완전한 문장이 아닌 주요 어구 위주로 간단히 적는다.
3) **뒷받침 내용 (Supporting points):** 주제를 뒷받침하거나 주제와 밀접한 관련 내용을 간단히 적는다.

Ex Humans have a skeletal system inside their bodies. In contrast to this, an ant has an exoskeleton, or a thick shell on the outside of its body. This exoskeleton essentially maintains the shape of the ant's body and holds it together, but it also serves as a kind of armor, protecting the body from harm. When ants must grow, they will shed these exoskeletons and grow new ones. The system of an exoskeleton can also be found in most insects, spiders, and many other animals like lobsters and turtles.

Sample Note

Topic	exoskeleton of ants . shell surrounding ant's body
Main idea	maintains body shape + protects body from harm
Supporting Ideas	ants grow → shed & grow new ones

A 다음 지문을 읽고 아래 노트를 완성해 보자.

1. The development of the Sputnik satellite was one of the most important events after World War II. First, it was a big turning point in the race for technological superiority between Russia and America. Not only that, but the Sputnik satellite also made history as being the first object launched into orbit around the Earth. This new occurrence helped inspire the desire to explore space further.

Topic

Main idea

Supporting Ideas

| 2. Integrated Task Skills |

2. Medieval Europeans launched the Crusades in an attempt to take the city of Jerusalem back from the Muslims who controlled it. Many attempts were made over the centuries, but none was very successful. However, the knights who returned from the Crusades brought back new ideas in science and philosophy from the Middle East. These new ideas would lead to the Renaissance, where arts and science would advance.

Topic

Main idea

Supporting Ideas

3. A form that most sixteenth century British writers used in their plays was blank verse. Blank verse is poetry in which each line has ten syllables, and there is no rhyme scheme. British writers predominantly used blank verse because it fit into the natural rhythm of spoken English, and because the lack of rhymes made it sound more like normal speech. Thus, it was both poetic and believable.

Topic

Main idea

Supporting Ideas

Exercise 7 대화 듣고 Note-taking 하기

일반적으로 두 사람의 대화를 듣고 note-taking을 할 때에는, 어떤 사람이 어떤 말을 했는지 구분하여 표시해 두는 것이 좋다. 이를 위해 두 가지 note-taking 방법을 사용할 수 있다. 대화가 이루어지는 순서를 그대로 따라서 남녀 화자의 말을 번갈아 기록하는 방법이 있고, 처음부터 남자와 여자 화자를 구분한 후 각 화자가 말한 내용을 해당 공간에 적는 방법이 있다. 본인에게 맞는 방법을 택하도록 한다.

❏ 순서대로 적는 방법

> W: A term paper due end of vac.; visit home during vac.; need books to write pap.
> M: Borrow books from lib.; no limits on days
> W: What if books must be returned? Fine $2/day
> M: Mail books to lib.
> W: Shipping = expensive
> M: But less than fine; vacation is long

❏ 화자를 나누어 적는 방법

Woman	Man
A term paper due end of vac.; visit home during vac.; need books to write pap.	Borrow books from lib.; no limit on days
What if books must be returned? Fine $2/day	Mail books to lib.
Shipping = expensive	But less than fine; vacation is long

A 들려주는 대화를 듣고 노트를 작성해 보자.

1. MP3 49

2. 🎧 MP3 50

3. 🎧 MP3 51

Exercise 8 강의 듣고 Note-taking 하기

학술적인 내용의 강의는 대부분 같은 순서로 구성된다. 도입부에서 토픽과 주제를 제시한 후, 본론에서 주제를 뒷받침하는 내용을 전개한다. 결론은 제시되기도 하고 제시되지 않을 수도 있다. 내용이 전환되는 것을 알리는 표현들을 signal words라고 한다. 일반적으로 signal words 뒤에 나오는 내용은 중요한 내용이다. 그러므로 signal words를 알아 두고 주의를 기울이면 note-taking해야 할 내용이 무엇인지 보다 쉽게 판단할 수 있다. 다음은 강의에서 흔히 사용되는 signal words이다.

1) 토픽을 소개할 때 사용하는 표현

- This is called …
- Okay, now let's talk about …
- Today we are going to discuss …
- Today we are going to talk about …
- That brings us to …
- This is what we call …
- I'd like to tell you about …
- One of the … is …

2) 내용을 전환할 때 사용하는 표현

- However …
- But …
- On the other hand …
- On the contrary …
- Then …
- Next, I want to mention …
- Now let's consider …
- Another point is …

3) 예를 들 때 사용하는 표현

- For example …
- Let's look at an example.
- Take … for example.
- For instance …
- Let's talk about the case of …
- Take another example …
- My other example is …
- Let's consider the case of …
- Let's say that …

4) 강조할 때 사용하는 표현

- Most importantly …
- Especially …
- Significantly …
- One important factor/ cause/point/problem is …
- Amazingly …
- Please note that …
- Be sure to note that …
- Pay special attention to …

2. Integrated Task Skills

A 들려주는 강의를 듣고 노트를 작성해 보자.

1. 🎧 MP3 52

2. 🎧 MP3 53

3. 🎧 MP3 54

Exercise 9 주제 (Main Idea) 찾기

요약의 기본은 내용의 주제(main idea)를 찾는 것이다. 글의 주제는 대부분 주제문(topic sentence)을 변형·확장한 것이다. 주제문은 맨 처음에 제시되는 경우가 가장 일반적이나, 중간이나 끝에 제시되는 경우도 있다. "However" 같은 signal word가 나오면서 내용이 전환될 경우에는 그 다음에 나오는 내용이 주제문일 경우가 많다. 하지만 반드시 그런 것은 아니므로 기계적으로 찾기보다는 글 전체의 내용을 이해하여 주제문을 찾도록 하자. 간혹 주제문이 제시되지 않는 경우도 있는데, 이런 경우에는 글 전체의 내용을 종합하여 요약하도록 한다.

A 다음 짧은 글을 읽고, 글의 내용을 한 문장으로 요약해 보자.

1. According to the weather forecast, there's a very good chance that it will rain on campus this Saturday. Hopefully it won't rain, because we have our graduation ceremony outside on Saturday. If it does, we'll have to move the ceremony from the football field to the gymnasium. Unfortunately, that will mean that we have less room for seating, and the light will be dimmer in there.

   → _____
   _____

2. Like hair, nails on the fingers and toes are constantly growing, and they must be trimmed. However, if these nails are not trimmed properly, then they can become ingrown, or curved so that they grow into the flesh surrounding a finger or toe. An ingrown nail may cut into the surrounding flesh, making the area susceptible to germs and possibly causing an infection.

   → _____
   _____

3. When we think of dreams, we may think of strange images that don't make sense. Sigmund Freud, however, argued that dreams do make sense. He believed that a person's dreams are really symbols that represent wishes that are so secret that the person may not realize he or she has them. Freud argued that dreams must then be interpreted symbolically in order to understand what a person's secret wishes are.

   → _____
   _____

B 들려주는 내용을 듣고, 그 내용을 한 문장으로 요약해 보자.

1. MP3 55
   → _____
   → _____

2. MP3 56
   → _____
   → _____

3. MP3 57
   → _____
   → _____

Exercise 10 뒷받침 내용 (Supporting Points) 찾기

> 짧은 글을 요약할 때는 주제(main idea) 한 문장만 쓰면 되지만, 긴 글을 요약할 때에는 여러 문장으로 이루어진 summary가 필요하다. 이 때 summary에 포함되는 것은 주제(main idea)와 뒷받침 내용(supporting points)이다. 뒷받침 내용은 주제를 직접 뒷받침하거나 주제와 밀접하게 관련된 내용이다. 주제와 직접적인 관련이 없는 내용은 summary를 할 필요가 없다. 좋은 summary란 주제와 중요한 내용을 포함하는 것이며, 잘못된 summary는 내용이 원글과 다르거나 중요하지 않은 내용을 포함한 것이다.

A 다음 글을 읽고, 글의 내용을 요약한 두 summary 중 올바른 것을 골라 보자.

1. You are probably wondering why there are so many school buses in the front parking lot. That's because there's a class visiting campus. Some students from the local middle school wanted to take a tour of this school so they could see what an average university was like. It's interesting to see the kids, but it does create a problem in trying to park around here. I mean, I had to walk all the way over from the other side of campus because the school buses are taking up all of the nearby lots.

   | Summary A | The speaker at first wonders where all the school buses came from. The speaker then becomes annoyed after realizing that children are visiting the university.

   | Summary B | Students from the local middle school went on a field trip to the university to see an average college. The speaker is annoyed because their school buses have taken all of the nearby parking spaces.

2. If you are going to graduate next semester and you aren't sure of what job you'd like to get after college, then you should go to the career fair being held this weekend. The career fair will have people representing different companies and fields. These representatives will speak with you about jobs that are related to the field you are studying. However, you must make sure that you fill out an application by Wednesday with all your student information on it, particularly your major and any careers you're interested in.

   | Summary A | The career fair this weekend will help graduating students decide which jobs they'd like. There, representatives from different fields will help students find careers related to their studies. Interested students must apply by Wednesday, listing majors and career interests.

   | Summary B | A career fair is being held on Wednesday, and students who attend will get information on jobs they would like after college. Students can meet representatives who took the same college courses, and the jobs they are offering have high salaries. Students need to fill out the application and turn it in at the career fair.

2. Integrated Task Skills

B 들려주는 내용을 듣고, 내용을 요약한 두 summary 중 올바른 것을 골라 보자.

1. 🎧 MP3 58

| Summary A | Marsupials like kangaroos are animals that carry and protect their offspring in pouches on their bodies. A marsupial needs this pouch because it gives birth to its offspring quickly, and the baby must nurse from the mother for a long time.

| Summary B | Kangaroos are famous for having pouches on the front of their bodies, and they use these to carry their offspring. Kangaroos give birth to these offspring quickly, which distinguishes this creature from other marsupials. In an attempt to protect its newborn, a kangaroo can enfold its offspring in its pouch.

2. 🎧 MP3 59

| Summary A | Because bison were so numerous and grazed all over North America, the Plains Indians hunted them for food. However, the Plains Indians began to commercially hunt the bison, so this animal became completely extinct. Even though the government tried to stop this and help the Plains Indians, they lost their main source of food and eventually had to leave their land.

| Summary B | American hunters commercially hunted the large North American bison population to the brink of extinction. The United States government decided not to protect the bison because it wanted to take land from the Plains Indians, who relied on bison for food, clothing, and other basic needs.

Exercise 11 노트 보고 요약하기 (독해)

긴 글을 요약할 때에는 중요한 내용을 모두 기억할 수 없으므로, 중요 내용을 note-taking 한 후 그것을 기초로 하여 summary를 작성하는 것이 효율적이다. 또한 노트를 작성하면 글의 구조를 더욱 확실히 이해하게 되므로 내용 요약에 도움이 된다.

 다음 글에 대한 노트를 바탕으로 요약문을 작성해 보자.

1. In the late nineteenth century, there was some debate in the United States over what to do with the vast amount of western land. Many Americans wanted to settle this land and use it for agriculture, but there were already many different native tribes living in the West. Thus, Americans came up with the idea of Manifest Destiny. Manifest Destiny was the American belief that their society was destined to cover all of North America, so conquering the West was both inevitable and morally right. Manifest Destiny eventually became an excuse to drive Indian tribes off their homelands.

> Manifest Destiny: Amer. dest. to conq. N. Amer. + conq. of west was right
> - 19th c US deb. what to do w/ west ? tribes alr. there
> - Man. Des. was exc. to take land from tribes

→ _____
_____
_____

2. The earth's crust is composed of a number of tectonic plates, and these plates drift on a layer of magma just below the crust. Now, the boundaries of these plates are constantly grinding against each other, and sometimes they will strain while grinding and suddenly slip, releasing energy waves that rattle the earth's surface. This is an earthquake. Earthquakes can be very intense and cause a lot of damage. As a result, some cities located near grinding plate boundaries, such as San Francisco, have been destroyed almost completely by earthquakes.

> Earthquake
> - tect. plates drif. on mag.; plate bou. grind each other; can strain & slip
>   → ener. waves shakes sur.
> - e.quakes are int. & dam. + destroy cities

→ _____
_____
_____

B 다음 글에 대한 노트를 작성한 후, 그것을 바탕으로 요약문을 작성해 보자.

1. In the business world, a corporation can be made and destroyed by people who might invest money in its stock. Now, an executive in this company can influence an investor by giving him private company information that affects the price of stock. This is called insider trading. Most forms of insider trading are illegal because executives can abuse their power. For instance, the executive might tell his friends to invest in another company's stock because he plans on selling his business to this second company. These traders would profit while the employees of the company would lose their jobs.

Exercise 12 노트 보고 요약하기 (청취)

청취 내용을 요약하는 경우에는 note-taking의 중요성이 더욱 크다. Signal words에 주의를 기울이고 강의의 흐름을 잘 따라가면서 주제와 뒷받침 내용을 찾아 note-taking한다. 이 때 주의할 점은, 강의의 주제를 직접 뒷받침하는 중요한 예는 summary에 포함시켜야 하며, 주제와 직접 관련없는 예는 포함시키지 않아야 한다는 것이다. 항상 주제를 중심으로 생각하면 어떤 것이 중요한 내용인지 판단할 수 있다.

A 들려주는 강의에 대한 노트를 바탕으로 요약문을 작성해 보자.

1. MP3 60

> Possible impact of asteroid collision
> - impact may or may not kill all life dep. on size
> - any imp. kicks up lots of dust _ dust block out sun _ new ice age

→ _____
_____
_____

2. MP3 61

> UN Security Council
> - creation of UN: after WW2 - to avoid war + resolve conflict
> - 5 fund. nat = Am., Russ., Brit., China, France = perm. mem. of U.N. Sec. Coun.
> - can veto enf. plans

→ _____
_____
_____

2. Integrated Task Skills

B 들려주는 강의에 대한 노트를 작성한 후, 그것을 바탕으로 요약문을 작성해 보자.

1. 🎧 MP3 62

   → _____
   _____
   _____

2. 🎧 MP3 63

   → _____
   _____
   _____

3. 🎧 MP3 64

   → _____
   _____
   _____

03

Pronunciation

Exercise 1. 자음 & 모음
Exercise 2. 묵음 & 강조
Exercise 3. 문장 강조

Exercise 1 자음 & 모음

A 들려주는 두 단어의 발음이 똑같은 경우에는 O로, 다른 경우에는 X로 표시해 보자. **MP3 65**

1. __X__   2. _____   3. _____   4. _____   5. _____
6. _____   7. _____   8. _____   9. _____   10. _____

B 들려주는 단어가 다음 중 어느 것인지 골라 보자. **MP3 66**

1. leaf, (leave)
2. word, world
3. lay, ray
4. bear, bell
5. really, lily
6. size, thighs
7. think, sink
8. that, dad
9. some, thumb
10. sued, soothe

C 박스 안에 있는 단어의 밑줄 친 s와 같이 발음되는 단어의 번호를 빈칸에 써 보자. **MP3 67**

① co**s**metic	② tran**s**parent	③ plea**s**ure

silent ___②___	standing _____	televi**s**ion _____	va**s**t _____
scared _____	con**s**ervative _____	neighbor**s** _____	inva**s**ion _____
enormou**s** _____	confu**s**ing _____	unu**s**ual _____	exa**s**perate _____
an**s**wer _____	clo**s**ed _____	clo**s**ely _____	pha**s**e _____

(오디오 파일을 듣고 자신의 분류가 정확한지 확인하여 보자.)

D 다음 문장을 듣고 밑줄 친 자음 중 잘못 발음된 것을 가려내 보자. **MP3 68**

1. We ha<u>d</u> a <u>r</u>eally (<u>g</u>)rea<u>t</u> <u>t</u>ime.
2. Mere<u>d</u>ith is going to <u>l</u>eave <u>f</u>or Switzerland <u>t</u>omorrow.
3. <u>Th</u>is song is <u>wr</u>itten by the <u>l</u>ead <u>v</u>ocalist of the <u>b</u>and.
4. John, <u>pl</u>ease <u>s</u>top talking nonsense. I've had enough.
5. He's <u>f</u>orgotten a<u>b</u>out getting to the <u>v</u>illage.
6. The on<u>l</u>y <u>th</u>ing we can do i<u>s</u> keep <u>tr</u>ying.

3. Pronunciation

E 다음을 듣고 밑줄 친 모음의 발음이 나머지 세 단어와 다른 것 하나를 골라 보자. MP3 69

1. (add), addition, adjust, adopt
2. caught, lost, fall, dawn
3. driven, slip, prison, life
4. most, cope, sport, pole
5. drag, wake, sanity, class
6. civilized, running, credit, practically
7. behave, have, locate, great
8. younger, but, future, discuss
9. please, teacher, pleasant, feature
10. thirsty, mistake, until, wish

F 박스 안에 있는 단어의 밑줄 친 a와 같이 발음되는 단어의 번호를 빈칸에 써 보자. MP3 70

① advertise	② parents	③ amend

Asian ②	anthropology ___	ancient ___	calligraphy ___
Saturday ___	satellite ___	sacred ___	age ___
compatible ___	lateral ___	gravity ___	human ___
label ___	literature ___	narrative ___	narrator ___

오디오 파일을 듣고 자신의 분류가 정확한지 확인하여 보자.

G 다음 문장을 듣고 밑줄 친 모음 중 잘못 발음된 것을 가려내 보자. MP3 71

1. The author has written four novels and two plays.
2. The old man poured hot liquid iron into the mold.
3. The owl is a nocturnal bird that hunts at night.
4. Valves eventually led to the use of several improved brass instruments.
5. Magma leaks out of holes in the ocean floor.

Exercise 2 묵음 & 강조

A 다음 단어 중 묵음인 부분에 밑줄을 쳐 보자. MP3 72

1. num<u>b</u>
2. knight
3. fasten
4. chalk
5. doubt
6. debt
7. receipt
8. pneumonia
9. psychiatrist
10. climbing

B 다음 단어의 강세를 표시해 보자. MP3 73

1. techníque
2. advertising
3. eventually
4. adjust
5. photographer
6. indirect
7. garage
8. display
9. allies
10. detail

C 괄호 안에 주어진 품사에 따라 강세를 표시해 보자.

1. objéct (verb)
2. record (noun)
3. present (verb)
4. address (verb)
5. discharge (noun)
6. export (verb)

D 괄호 안에 주어진 품사에 따라 강세를 표시해 보자. MP3 74

1. applý, application
2. occur, occurrence
3. contribute, contribution
4. arrive, arrival
5. pursue, pursuit
6. hostile, hostility
7. desire, desirable
8. emit, emission
9. ècology, ecological
10. resolve, resolution

3. Pronunciation

E 다음 문장에서 밑줄 친 단어들의 강세를 표시해 보자. MP3 75

1. The Civil War was the bloodiest cónflict ever fought in America.

2. Today we will discúss something that's always been a serious threat to agriculture.

3. Physical barriers set up on farmland absórb or defléct natural ágents of erósion.

4. This is why many agricúltural commúnities reforest areas by planting new trees.

5. Even before slávery was óutlawed, there were several ways people could defý slavery.

6. The runaway sláves took long, indiréct routes through désolate areas.

7. Snakes can bite animals and injéct them with vénom.

8. It's the school's responsibílity to repláce them with louder alárms.

9. There are situátions in which a person's proféssional duties conflíct with his personal ones.

Exercise 3 문장 강조

A 들려주는 문장을 듣고 크고 높은 소리로 들리는 단어들만 받아 적어 보자. MP3 76

1. What, up, lately
2. _____
3. _____
4. _____
5. _____
6. _____
7. _____
8. _____
9. _____
10. _____

B 들려주는 문장을 듣고 강세가 오는 단어에 밑줄을 쳐 보자. MP3 77

1. Did <u>you</u> <u>hear</u> about those <u>new</u> <u>three-hour</u> <u>courses</u> being <u>offered</u> to <u>freshmen</u>?

2. With the tag, at least a campus cop knows to check for it on your rear view mirror.

3. Sometimes animals will go extinct because they can't adapt to subtle habitat changes.

4. This would have dramatic effects on the animals that prey on these gazelles.

5. Without any animals to feed on, they too would become extinct.

6. Othello becomes enraged when he mistakenly believes that she is unfaithful to him.

7. Before an entrepreneur can make his fortune, he must decide on what kind of business he'd like to start.

8. If they decide to build cars, then they probably won't be able to build houses as well.

9. He will usually see which industry has the most customers at a certain place or time.

10. Humans, like most other animals, have a series of different organs, all used for different tasks.

3. Pronunciation

 다음 응답을 듣고 강세가 오는 단어에 밑줄을 쳐 보자.

1. MP3 78

I prefer to do activities on a holiday rather than just stay home and relax. One reason I prefer doing activities is that I have something to discuss with friends when I do an activity on a holiday. For example, I can tell stories about the time I went to the countryside for a picnic or rode my bicycle down a new trail. Moreover, I believe it is a waste of time to sit around and do nothing, because a holiday is such a good time to do things I want to do. I feel like I wasted a whole day when I just sit around and watch TV. In other words, it can be a more meaningful way of spending time if you do something worth doing.

2. MP3 79

I personally think that a person that has a great influence on people's lives today is Bill Gates. To start, he sells a lot of computer programs, more than anyone else. This means that people rely on him for their computers to work, and computers are needed for almost everything that we do. Next, Bill Gates donates lots of money to charity. He has given billions of dollars to help people in Africa. By using his money and power like this, he can influence others to give too, and this can help everyone. In conclusion, Bill Gates is someone who has a great influence on people's lives today.

04

Grammar

Exercise 1.   주어 동사 일치
Exercise 2.   자동사와 타동사
Exercise 3.   사역동사
Exercise 4.   감각을 표현하는 동사
Exercise 5.   동사의 시제
Exercise 6.   간접 의문문
Exercise 7.   To부정사와 -ing를 취하는 동사
Exercise 8.   울타리 표현(Hedging)
Exercise 9.   비교급과 최상급
Exercise 10. 형용사의 쓰임

Exercise 1 주어 동사 일치

1) **And로 연결된 주어**: 복수 취급한다.
   - Your enthusiasm and participation have been much appreciated.

2) **Or로 연결된 주어**: 동사와 가까운 주어에 일치시킨다.
   - Either you or your boss has to attend the meeting.

3) **주어에 수식어구가 따라 나오는 경우**: 혼동하지 않도록 주의한다.
   - Engaging in team sports builds character and self-esteem.

4) **관계절의 동사**: 선행사에 일치시킨다.
   - Rupert is one of those people who are late for everything.

5) **기간이나 수량을 나타내는 말**: 한꺼번에 말할 때는 단수 취급, 하나 하나를 강조할 때는 복수 취급
   - Three hours is plenty of time.

6) - **Either, neither, everything, everybody, anything, anybody, each, every**: 항상 단수 취급
   - **All, more, most, some, any**: 복수 명사와 함께 쓰이면 복수 취급, 단수 명사와 함께 쓰이면 단수 취급
   - Neither of them wants to go. / Some children don't like to dance.

7) **Staff, family, couple, police와 같은 집합 명사**: 집단 전체로 말할 때는 단수로, 개개인을 강조할 때는 복수로 취급한다.
   - The couple get along very well together. / The couple has adopted an orphan.

8) **특이한 형태의 명사**: s로 끝나도 단수인 명사가 있는가 하면, s로 끝나지 않아도 복수인 명사가 있음에 주의
   Ex phenomena, criteria, graffiti, customs, mathematics, data
   - The media influence us as individuals and as a society.

A 괄호 안에서 알맞은 동사를 골라 보자.

1. The moon and the north star (was, **were**) shining brightly last night.
2. Food and water (is, are) necessary for survival.
3. The singer and the band (was, were) waiting backstage.
4. The soccer team and their coach (is, are) standing over there.
5. Either the bus or the subway (is, are) the best way to get downtown.
6. Either the doctors or the nurses (is, are) going to take care of the patients.
7. The complicated directions Francine gave me (was, were) impossible to understand.
8. The fall of ancient Rome and other powerful empires (was, were) not due to a single reason.

9. A dozen eggs (is, are) probably too many.

10. Everybody (asks, ask) me that question.

11. Most of my friends (lives, live) close by.

12. Ethiopia is one of several African countries that (has, have) been hit by drought.

13. I bought one of the two items that (was, were) recommended by the sales clerk.

14. New data (shows, show) a steady increase in childhood obesity.

15. The police (is, are) investigating reports of an abandoned car found nearby.

B 다음 문장 중 주어와 동사가 일치되지 않는 것을 찾아 바르게 고쳐 보자. 올바른 문장은 OK로 표시하자.

1. I believe that teachers ~~has~~ more educational knowledge and experience than parents do.
   have

2. One reason why I prefer doing outdoor activities are that I can breathe fresh air.

3. I think that parents are the best teachers for their children.

4. I have seen a lot of television programs that shows the suffering of children who have disabilities.

5. Most of the causes of these problems have been identified.

6. The newly elected president has certain characteristics that is seen among great leaders.

7. One of the best ways to improve your writing skills are to write in a journal every day.

8. I think mathematics is the most challenging subject for many students.

9. Some people say five years are not long enough to master a foreign language, but I think it depends on how much effort you put in.

10. Both the reading passage and the lecture discusses the causes of the Iraq War.

Exercise 2 자동사와 타동사

1) **자동사로만 사용되는 동사:** 목적어를 취하지 않으며, 뒤에 명사가 나올 때는 전치사와 함께 쓰인다.
   Ex sleep, rise, coincide, consent, wait, come, remain
   - Stress is a big reason people can't sleep at night.

2) **타동사로만 사용되는 동사:** 항상 동사 바로 뒤에 목적어를 취한다.
   Ex access, accompany, affect, analyze, attribute, discuss, devote, request, contact
   - Let's discuss your problem this afternoon. (O)
   - Let's discuss about your problems this afternoon. (X)

3) **자동사로도 사용되고 타동사로도 사용되는 동사:** 많은 영어 동사는 경우에 따라 자동사로 사용되기도 하고 타동사로 사용되기도 한다.
   Ex compensate, adapt, adjust, approach, assist, comment, communicate, focus, marry
   - Anna is very good at writing. (O)
   - Do you know who wrote *Moby Dick*? (O)
   - Andre wrote about his family in one of his essays. (O)

A. 다음 빈칸에 알맞은 전치사를 넣어 보자. 전치사가 필요 없는 경우에는 X표를 하여 보자.

1. I couldn't access ___X___ my banking information online because I couldn't remember my password.

2. The insurance company will compensate _____ you for any goods lost in the fire.

3. Sheila asked her boyfriend to accompany _____ her to the concert.

4. Given enough time, a person can adapt _____ most changes in his life.

5. It took my eyes a while to adjust _____ wearing glasses.

6. Global problems such as climate change affect _____ everyone in the world.

7. The study analyzed _____ the spending habits of teenagers across the country.

8. It's a good idea to approach _____ strange dogs with caution.

9. I offered to assist _____ my professor with her research so that I could get some lab experience.

10. My doctor attributed _____ my weight gain to lack of exercise and poor diet.

11. My visit to China in two years will coincide _____ the summer Olympics in Beijing.

12. I don't like it when people comment _____ my appearance.

13. The ability to communicate _____ your coworkers well is a necessary skill in the professional world.

14. Karen did not consent _____ having her house searched by the police.

15. I tried to talk to Paul about our argument, but he didn't want to discuss _____ it.

16. Many scholars devote _____ themselves to one area of study for their entire lives.

17. It can be difficult to focus _____ a task if there are many distractions around.

18. I called the airline to request _____ a special meal during my flight to Europe.

19. I will contact _____ you later in the week to set up a meeting.

20. Maria has no desire to marry _____ anyone.

B 다음 문장에서 동사의 사용이 잘못된 부분을 찾아 바르게 고쳐 보자. 올바른 문장은 OK로 표시하자.

1. Marco Polo's book, *Il Milione*, is valuable because he vividly described (about) the Orient.

2. Since Ben has never traveled Asia, he is planning to visit an Asian country this summer.

3. The professor mentions two important factors in conflict resolution.

4. I didn't note at any difference between the two pictures.

5. Marco Polo didn't really socialize with Chinese people.

6. I strongly oppose to the idea that she is a feminist writer.

7. My mom, who was very angry about my behavior, shouted at me and started to talk how rude I was.

8. It contradicts with the fact that there were other European visitors at that time.

9. The professor does not discuss about Chinese traditions such as tea drinking and foot binding.

10. Ken was accused of writing his essay by simply copying from books.

Exercise 3 사역동사

1) **Let + O + do something**: 목적어(O)가 무엇을 하도록 허락하는 것을 말한다.
   - I let Jana do all the work herself.

2) **Have + O + do something**: 목적어가 무엇을 하도록 만들거나 시키는 것으로, make와 비슷하지만 어감이 약하다.
   - I usually have the maid do my laundry.

3) **Make + O + do something**: 목적어가 무엇을 하도록 만들거나 시키는 것으로 강제적인 의미를 내포한다.
   - I can't make you do something you don't want to do.

4) **Get + O + to do something / get + O + doing something**: 목적어 뒤에 동사 원형이 아닌 to부정사나 ~ing를 취한다. 의미는 have와 구분 없이 쓰이기도 하지만, 대체적으로 have보다 좀 더 적극적인 사역의 의미를 담고 있다.
   - I'll get one of my co-workers to do this. (O)
   - I'll get one of my co-workers doing this. (O)
   - I'll get one of my co-workers do this. (X)

5) **Help + (O) + (to) do something**: 목적어가 무엇을 하는 것을 돕는 것으로 동사 원형과 to 부정사 중 어느 것이든 올 수 있으며, 목적어가 생략되기도 한다.
   - My sister helped me clean the house. (O)
   - My sister helped me to clean the house. (O)
   - My sister helped clean the house. (O)
   - My sister helped to clean the house. (O)

6) **Get / have + O + p.p.**: 제3자가 어떤 일을 하는 것을 나타낼 때, 또는 시간과 노력을 들여서 어떤 일을 하는 것을 나타낼 때 사용된다.
   - I had my computer fixed by a local store. (제3자의 행위임을 나타낼 때)
   - I need time to get things settled. (시간과 노력을 들여서 어떤 일을 할 때)

 괄호 안에 주어진 동사를 빈칸에 알맞도록 변형해 보자. 변형할 필요가 없는 경우에는 원형 그대로 쓰도록 한다.

1. Cora has a hairdresser ___do___ her hair once a week. (do)
2. Desmond let his wife _____ the planning for their party. (do)
3. Gerri had some books _____ to her by the librarian. (recommend)
4. I had my messages _____ to my cell phone. (forward)
5. John might get someone _____ his report for him. (do)
6. Melanie wants to get her hair _____ for the party. (style)

4. Grammar

7. The university had tours _____ for prospective students. (arrange)

8. Peter has his secretary _____ all the boring tasks. (do)

9. Ramon had to get his work _____ before going home. (do)

10. We tried to get another copy of the form _____ to us. (send)

B 다음 문장 중 [사역동사 + 목적어 + 동사] 부분이 올바르지 않은 것을 찾아 바르게 고쳐 보자. 올바른 문장은 OK 로 표시하자.

1. She finally made my younger brother (to) take part in a math contest.

2. A good sense of humor can help a leader being more effective in building harmony among group members.

3. Lowering taxes can create more jobs and make people live better lives.

4. Indifference to elections can make the country to collapse.

5. Because I can't spare a moment right now, I'll have one of my co-workers to work on it.

6. Have you ever succeeded in getting someone to stop smoking?

7. Mrs. Smith got the children to clean their room after they finished playing.

8. Josh works so fast that he gets done everything and still has time left.

9. You may make a request to have the book return.

10. We hope to have this project finishing by this Thursday.

Exercise 4 감각을 표현하는 동사

감각	수동적 의미	능동적 의미	Linking Verb
시각	see	look (at), watch	look
청각	hear	listen (to)	sound
촉각	feel	touch, feel	feel
후각	smell	smell	smell
미각	taste	taste	taste

1) **See:** 어떤 것이 눈에 보이는 것, 혹은 볼 수 있는 능력을 나타낼 때 쓰인다.
   - Can you see dust floating in the air?

   Look (at), watch: 어떤 것을 의식적으로 보는 행위를 가리킨다.
   - I looked at the map to find the directions. / I watched the children playing outside.

   Look [linking verb]: '~하게 보인다' '~해 보인다' 는 의미
   - You look great in that suit.

2) **Hear:** 어떤 소리가 귀에 들리는 것, 혹은 들을 수 있는 능력을 나타낸다.
   - I can hear birds singing in the trees outside.

   Listen (to): 어떤 소리를 의식적으로 듣는 행위를 가리킨다.
   - Please stop talking and listen to me.

   Sound [linking verb]: '~하게 들린다' 는 의미
   - Visiting a museum sounds boring to me.

3) **Feel:** ① 어떤 것이 느껴지는 수동적 의미 - I feel pain in my eyes.
   ② 어떤 것을 만져서 느끼는 능동적 의미 - Feel this sand. It's so soft!
   ③ '~하게 느껴진다' 는 의미(linking verb) - Your forehead feels warm.

   Touch: 어떤 것을 만져서 느끼는 능동적 의미 - Don't touch the wall. It's just been painted.

4) **Smell:** ① 어떤 냄새를 느끼는 수동적 의미 - I smell gas inside this house.
   ② 일부러 냄새를 맡는 능동적 의미 - Tania is smelling her new perfume.
   ③ '~한 냄새가 난다' 는 의미(linking verb) - What are you cooking? It smells like heaven.

5) **Taste:** ① 어떤 맛이 나는 것을 느끼는 수동적 의미 - Can you taste salt in it?
   ② 일부러 맛을 보는 능동적 의미 - Jennifer keeps tasting the food while she's cooking.
   ③ '~하게 느껴진다' 는 의미(linking verb) - The food tasted very good.

▶ 감각을 표현하는 동사가 수동적 의미로 쓰이거나 linking verb로 쓰일 때는 진행형을 취하지 않는다.
  - I'm smelling gas inside this house. (X)
  - The food is tasting very good. (X)

▶ See나 hear가 감각을 표현하는 것이 아닌 다른 의미로 쓰일 때는 진행형으로 쓰일 수 있다. (see의 경우 '만나다', hear의 경우 '소식을 듣다')
  - I'm seeing the doctor tomorrow morning. (O)
  - I've been hearing a lot about you. (O)

4. Grammar

A 괄호 안에서 알맞은 동사를 골라 보자.

1. Sharon (felt, touched) a cool wind blowing outside.
2. I can (hear, listen to) thunder coming from the west.
3. I (see, have been seeing) this guy for 6 months, and I like him a lot.
4. My cat likes to (see, look at) birds for hours.
5. Emily and Luke (see, watch) several hours of television each day.
6. William says he (feels, touches) pain around his ears.
7. I like to touch silk because it (feels, is feeling) so nice.
8. Martine can't (hear, listen) well with her right ear.
9. Students cannot (hear, listen to) MP3 players while in class.
10. I (could smell, was smelling) the roses before I could see them.

B 다음 문장 중 감각을 표현하는 동사가 잘못 사용된 것을 찾아 바르게 고쳐 보자. 올바른 문장은 OK로 표시하자.

1. The first time I tasted honey, I didn't like it. → OK
2. The anthropologist used some of the stories she listened from the local people.
3. The theory isn't sounding persuasive anymore because it has been opposed by many scholars.
4. These days, it's not unusual to look at a man wearing pink.
5. A national leader must hear public opinions and share his ideas with people.
6. The wound is not looking serious, but you'd better show it to a doctor.
7. Ellen didn't know what the assignment was because she wasn't hearing what the teacher was saying.
8. I haven't heard from Alice for a while, so I'm a little worried.
9. This soup is tasting weird. Is it safe to eat?
10. I wasn't really listening to the song clearly because of the noise from outside.

Exercise 5 동사의 시제

> 1) **단순 현재 vs. 현재 진행형**
>   ① 단순 현재: 습관이나 일과를 나타낼 때 (usually, every day, sometimes, often 등의 빈도 부사와 종종 함께 쓰임)
>   - I *usually* get up around 7 in the morning.
>   ② 현재 진행형: 현재 진행 중인 동작을 나타낼 때, 또는 가까운 미래를 나타낼 때
>   - I can't talk to you right now, because I'm watching a movie.
>   - Henry is driving me to the airport *tomorrow morning*.
>
> 2) **단순 과거 vs. 현재 완료**
>   ① 단순 과거: 현재와 관련 없는 과거의 일에 대해 말할 때 (구체적인 시간을 나타내는 표현과 함께 쓰임)
>   - I went to visit a friend in Busan *last week*.
>   ② 현재 완료: 현재까지 지속되고 있는 일에 대해 말하거나, '지금까지 살면서'라는 의미로 말할 때 (before, ever, since, for와 같은 말과 함께 쓰임)
>   - It's been raining *since* yesterday. / Have you *ever* been to New Zealand?
>
> 3) **시간을 나타내는 부사절에서 현재가 미래를 대신하는 경우**: 주절이 미래 시제일 때, 시간을 나타내는 부사절에서는 시제가 미래를 대신한다. (시간을 나타내는 부사절은 when, if, after, as soon as, before, once, the moment, the minute, unless, until, by the time 등의 접속사로 시작함)
>   - I'm going to start looking for a job when I become a senior. (O)
>   - I'm going to start looking for a job when I will become a senior. (X)

 괄호 안에서 알맞은 동사를 골라 보자.

1. Patrick (**works**, is working) at the supermarket in the evening.

2. My brother (gives, is giving) good advice to people.

3. I (usually take, am usually taking) the subway home after work.

4. I (take, am taking) the entrance exam for the third time.

5. I (go, am going) to the movie theater now.

6. Jen (walked, has walked) home after the party because she had no money with her.

7. Those two (hated, have hated) each other since they broke up.

8. I (lost, have lost) my wallet this morning.

9. He (was, has been) angry at me for weeks now.

10. I'm going to take a cab if the bus (doesn't come, won't come) soon.

11. They will go to the beach when the weather (warms up, will warm up).

12. Ingrid will travel to Europe unless she (can't afford, won't be able to afford) a plane ticket.

B 다음 문장 중 동사의 시제가 잘못된 것을 바르게 고쳐 보자. 올바른 문장은 OK로 표시하자.

1. I am eating fruit for breakfast if I don't have time to cook.
　　　 eat

2. She has lived there for as long as I can remember.

3. The horse has run away when he got scared.

4. We ate well ever since we hired a cook.

5. Alison has given me this scarf for my birthday.

6. Beautiful flowers have blossomed here before.

7. I won't go home before I will go out for the evening.

8. Tamara is going to call me while she will be on vacation.

9. The workers won't finish today if they waste time talking.

10. Rob's going to work out before he will go to class.

Exercise 6 간접 의문문

1) **Wh - question** → **의문사 + 주어 + 동사**
   - Where is Patrick? → She asked me where Patrick was. (O)
   → She asked me where was Patrick. (X)

2) **Yes / no question** → **whether / if + 주어 + 동사**
   - Do you know her name? → He asked me if I knew her name.

3) **의문사 + to부정사**
   [의문사 + 주어 + can / should / have to / need to / ought to + 동사]로 이루어진 간접의문문을 [의문사 + to부정사]의 형태로 바꿔 쓸 수 있다.
   - Could you tell me where I can buy that CD? → Could you tell me where to buy that CD?

4) **If와 whether의 차이**
   ① 간접의문문을 이끌 때에는 if와 whether 중 어떤 것을 사용해도 좋다.
      - Did she say if she was going to be late? (O)
      - Did she say whether she was going to be late? (O)

   ② "Or not"을 첨가하여 말할 때에는 주로 whether를 사용하며, if를 사용해도 틀리지는 않지만 자주 사용되지 않는다. 또한 if 뒤에는 "or not"이 바로 올 수 없다.
      - I wasn't sure whether I should wake him up or not. (O)
      - I wasn't sure if I should wake him up or not. (△)
      - I wasn't sure whether or not I should wake him up. (O)
      - I wasn't sure if or not I should wake him up. (X)

   ③ Whether 뒤에는 to 부정사가 올 수 있지만 if 뒤에는 올 수 없다.
      - I don't know whether to accept the offer or not. (O)
      - I don't know if to accept the offer or not. (X)

   ④ 전치사 뒤에는 whether를 쓴다.
      - Hamlet was indecisive about whether to take revenge on his uncle Claudius for his father's death.

   ⑤ 특정 동사들은 if보다 whether와 함께 더 자주 사용된다.
      Ex inspect, discuss, ponder, argue, inquire
      - They discussed whether spanking is child abuse or not.

  괄호 안에 주어진 직접 의문문을 간접 의문문으로 바꾸어 빈칸에 써 보자.

1. Toby asked Maria ___*if she was free for dinner*___. ("Are you free for dinner?")

2. She demanded to know _____. ("Where have you been?")

3. He wanted to know _____. ("What is your favorite color?")

4. Could someone tell me _____? ("Where is the elevator?")

4. Grammar

5. Why don't you tell me _____? ("What do you think of this poem?")

6. Jack asked me if _____. ("Can you drive me home?")

7. Do you know _____? ("How old is Danielle?")

8. Sam asked the bus driver _____. ("How can I get downtown?")

9. Elise inquired _____. ("Can I renew my passport?")

10. Please tell me _____. ("Do you need anything?")

B 다음 문장의 밑줄 친 부분을 [의문사 + to부정사]의 형태로 바꾸어 써 보자.

1. I didn't know what I should do first because there were so many things to be done.
 → what to do

2. Bella forgot how she could work her camera because she rarely used it.
 → _____

3. Gina told us what we should bring to the picnic on Saturday.
 → _____

4. Callie wasn't sure where she should go first when she arrived in London.
 → _____

5. Peter didn't know when he should call the doctor about his back pain.
 → _____

6. I can't remember how I can bake cookies because I haven't done it in years.
 → _____

7. The airport is very confusing, and many passengers don't know where they have to go.
 → _____

8. My cat knows how he can find his way home because he is very clever.
 → _____

9. Liam can tell you what you can expect when you travel overseas.
 → _____

10. I have no idea whom I need to see regarding this form I received.
 → _____

Workbook •• 209

Exercise 7 To 부정사와 -ing 를 취하는 동사

1) **동사 + to 부정사:** 동사 뒤에 목적어가 나오지 않고 바로 to 부정사가 나오는 경우
   Ex aim, attempt, afford, decide, deserve, hope, intend, learn, long, manage, plan, prepare, pretend, refuse, seem, tend, wish
   - Anne refused to listen to her father.

2) **동사 + (목적어) + to 부정사:** 동사와 to부정사 사이에 목적어가 나오기도 하고 나오지 않기도 하는 경우
   Ex ask, choose, expect, help, need, pay, prefer, want, would like
   - Dan asked me to dance with him. / Karen asked to go home.

3) **동사 + 목적어 + to 부정사:** 동사 뒤에 목적어가 나오고 그 뒤에 to부정사가 나오는 경우
   Ex allow, choose, convince, enable, encourage, force, order, remind, teach, train, urge
   - My parents allowed me to drink the day I graduated from high school.

4) **동사 + -ing:** 동사 뒤에 -ing 형태를 취하는 경우
   Ex avoid, stand, consider, detest, dislike, mind, enjoy, fancy, finish, give up, imagine, keep, miss, risk
   - Can you imagine traveling to other planets in the future?

4) **동사 + to 부정사 / -ing:** to 부정사와 -ing를 모두 취할 수 있는 동사
   Ex begin, start, like, love, hate, continue, try, stop, remember, forget

   ▶ try, stop, remember, forget은 to 부정사와 –ing를 취할 때 각각 의미가 다르다.
   ① try + to 부정사: ~하려고 노력하다   - Brandon tries to gain some weight.
      try + -ing: 시험삼아 ~해 보다   - Why don't you try living alone for a while?
   ② stop + to 부정사: ~하기 위해 멈추다   - Rob stopped to help me.
      stop + -ing: ~하는 것을 멈추다   - Could you please stop making that noise?
   ③ remember / forget + to부정사: ~해야 할 것을 기억하다 / 잊다   - I keep forgetting to send this letter.
      remember / forget + –ing: ~했던 것을 기억하다 / 잊다
      - I remember having lunch with you guys every day when I used to work there.

 괄호 안에서 알맞은 동사 형태를 골라 보자.

1. I am learning (to play, playing) the cello.

2. We asked (to see, seeing) the dress in another color.

3. Many people enjoy (to swim, swimming) for exercise.

4. Several years ago, my father quit (to smoke, smoking).

5. She suggested (to meditate, meditating) as a good way to relax.

6. I miss (to eat, eating) my grandmother's home-cooked meals.

7. The coach encouraged (the players to try, the players trying) their best.

8. A lot of people forget (to count, counting) their blessings.

9. Don't forget (to give, giving) your phone number to her next time you see her.

10. Lila always remembers (to tidy up, tidying up) before she leaves.

B 다음 문장 중 동사의 패턴이 잘못된 것을 찾아 바르게 고쳐 보자. 올바른 문장은 OK로 표시하자.

1. Ben's dog likes to play catch. → OK

2. Holly stopped to run after she injured her knee.

3. Ian hesitated a lot when he told the story, and this led the police to doubt his word.

4. Emma's essay is coherent and well-written, but she fails reaching a logical conclusion.

5. I started making dinner fifteen minutes ago.

6. I miss to stay up late and hang out with my friends like I did when I was in school.

7. It is easy to forget to praise and reward your dog.

8. I wished having an excellent birthday, but I was not able to do so because an exam fell on that day.

9. No one could convince the old man to leave his house.

10. Citizens want improving the quality of their lives in a more active way.

Exercise 8 울타리 표현 (Hedging)

1) **울타리 표현 (hedging):** 어떤 사실에 대해서 너무 단정적이지 않게 들리도록 표현하는 것을 hedging이라 한다. 즉, hedging은 말하고자 하는 사실에 약간의 거리를 두는 것이라 할 수 있다.

2) **특정 동사를 이용한 hedging:** seem, appear
   ① - It seems that / It appears that
      - It seems that the war is going to be over soon.
      - It appears that the news report is true.
   ② 주어 + seem(s)/appear(s) + to 부정사
      - The machine appears to have flaws.
      - The weather seems to be changing.

3) **수동태를 이용한 hedging:** 수동태로 말하면 능동태로 말하는 것보다 객관적인 느낌을 줄 수 있다. 가령 "I believe that"보다 "It is believed that"말하는 것이다. 이 때 generally, widely와 같은 부사도 종종 함께 사용된다.
   - It is generally believed that diamonds cannot be broken.
   - It is widely recognized that dwarf galaxies are the most common galaxies in the universe.
   - It is not known how Stonehenge was built.

4) **기타:** 다음과 같은 문장 구조를 사용하여 완곡하게 표현할 수 있다.
   ① There is little/some/no doubt that
      - There is little doubt that Sam wrote the letter.
      - There is some doubt that this solution could be effective.
   ② There is little/some evidence of/that
      - There is little evidence that personality is simply genetic.

 빈칸에 알맞은 단어를 아래 보기에서 골라 보자. 답이 두 개 이상인 경우도 있을 수 있다.

보기				
believed	appears	proof	seems	known
recognized	doubt	seem	appear	little

1. It _____appears / seems_____ that no one told Ethan about today's meeting.
2. The computers _____ to stop working at least once a week.
3. It is _____ that most people don't get enough exercise.
4. It _____ that a mistake was found in your paperwork.
5. It is _____ that stress is a major health threat.
6. It is _____ that global temperatures are on the rise.

| 4. Grammar

7. There is no _____ that life can sometimes be difficult.

8. There is no _____ that the man stole your bag.

9. Most people _____ to support the mayor's initiatives.

10. There is _____ evidence of life on Mars.

B 괄호 안에 주어진 표현을 첫머리로 하여 주어진 문장을 다시 써 보자.

1. You were misinformed about the cost of our services. (It seems that)
    → It seems that you were misinformed about the cost of our services.

2. The airline lost your luggage. (The airline appears to)
    → _____

3. This work will have to be redone by someone else. (It appears that)
    → _____

4. My sister is losing weight. (My sister appears to)
    → _____

5. Greta thinks nothing is ever her fault. (Greta seems to)
    → _____

6. Human activity is responsible for global warming. (It is recognized that)
    → _____

7. Many experts believe that the economy will gradually improve. (It is believed that)
    → _____

8. Everyone knows that eating a lot of fast food contributes to obesity. (It is known that)
    → _____

9. Some people doubt that Michael is the most qualified person for the job. (There is some doubt that)
    → _____

10. Most people think that scientists will eventually discover a cure for cancer. (There is little doubt that)
    → _____

Workbook •• 213

Exercise 9 비교급과 최상급

1) 틀리기 쉬운 형용사의 비교급과 최상급

① 2음절 형용사 중 일부는 more를 붙이지 않고, 형용사에 -er/-est을 붙인다.
- prettier, prettiest, scarcer, scarcest, ruder, rudest, fairer, fairest

② 불규칙 비교급, 최상급

good / well	- better	- best
bad / badly / ill	- worse	- worst
many / much	- more	- most
little	- less	- least

far	farther / further	- farthest / - furthest	(거리) / (정도)
late	later / latter	- latest / - last	(시간) / (정도)

③ 어떤 형용사에는 비교급이나 최상급 표현을 쓸 수 없다. **Ex** perfect, unique
- I think Helen's work is more unique than mine. (X)
- My mother is the most perfect woman in the world! (X)

2) 원급 비교

① as … as
- The energy issue is as important as the food issue.

② as … as possible
- Please drive as quickly as possible, because we are running out of time.

③ 배수 as … as
- Jane earns nearly twice as much as her husband does.

3) 최상급과 함께 흔히 사용되는 표현: of the two, of all of us, of the year, in the world, in the country, you've ever made, one of
- China is the most populated country in the world.
- What was the happiest moment in your life?

4) Rather

① would rather … than …
- I'd rather sleep all day than go to an amusement park.

② rather than
- The food was a scrambled egg rather than an omelet.

4. Grammar

A 괄호 안에서 알맞은 표현을 골라 보자.

1. Stephanie is (**taller**, the tallest) than all of her friends.
2. My grandfather is (older, the oldest) person in my family.
3. This book is (less, as) interesting than the last one I read.
4. The world's (biggest, the biggest) lake is in Russia.
5. They say that this summer is going to be almost (hotter than, as hot as) last summer.
6. These are (more delicious, the most delicious) grapes I've ever eaten.
7. The Tokyo subway system is (the busiest, the most busy) in the world.
8. My apartment has a better view than (you, yours).
9. I (would rather, had better) go out tomorrow than tonight.
10. (Rather than, More than) take a cab, Sophie walked home.

B 다음 문장 중 비교급이나 최상급 표현이 잘못된 것을 찾아 바르게 고쳐 보자. 올바른 문장은 OK로 표시하자.

1. Ostriches can run <u>more faster</u> than lions.
   faster
2. Last winter was the coldest in fifty years.
3. Today is the worst day of my life! It is even more bad than when I got lost in Japan last year.
4. My university science classes are more hard than I expected.
5. Many people consider that actress most beautiful woman alive.
6. I will do it myself, than ask someone else.
7. Electric guitars are much louder as acoustic ones.
8. A study shows that military veterans are twice as likely to commit suicide than ordinary people.
9. That was funny movie I have ever seen.
10. Jeanette would rather eat pizza than any other food.

Exercise 10 형용사의 쓰임

1) **형용사 + to부정사**
   ① It's + 형용사 + to부정사
      - It's difficult to master a foreign language.
   ② 주어 + be + 형용사 + to부정사
      - This car is not likely to last not long because it's used.

2) **형용사 + for + 목적어 + to부정사:** for 뒤의 목적어가 to부정사의 의미상 주어가 된다.
   - It's easier for me to study at night because I can concentrate better.

3) **형용사 + 전치사:** 흔히 함께 사용되는 형용사와 전치사를 외워 두는 것이 좋다.

   ① certain about: ~을 확신하는
      optimistic about: ~에 대해 낙관적인
      serious about: ~에 대해 진지한
   ② good at: ~을 잘하는
      bad/poor at: ~을 못하는
      horrible/terrible at: ~을 아주 못하는
      hopeless at: ~에 가망이 없는
      useless at: ~에 쓸모가 없는
   ③ famous for: ~으로 유명한
      late for: ~에 늦은
      ready for: ~에 대한 준비가 된
   ④ interested in: ~에 관심이 있는
      lacking in: ~이 없는
   ⑤ afraid of: ~을 두려워 하는
      fond of: ~을 좋아하는, ~에 호감이 있는
      proud of: ~을 자랑스러워 하는
   ⑥ dependent on: ~에 의존하는
      keen on: ~을 좋아하는
      reliant on: ~에 의지하는
   ⑦ accustomed to: ~에 익숙한
      allergic to: ~에 알레르기가 있는
      sensitive to: ~에 예민한
      essential to/for: ~에 반드시 필요한
   ⑧ angry with: ~에 화가 난 (사람에 대해)
      fed up with: ~에 질린

A 빈칸 앞에 있는 형용사에 유의하여 빈칸에 알맞은 전치사를 넣어 보자.

1. I'm not certain _____about_____ the exact location of the art gallery.
2. I finally got serious _____ my studies when I started university.
3. Kirk's never been good _____ public speaking.
4. My roommate is hopeless _____ using computers.
5. Marta was fed up _____ George's chronic lateness.
6. Kelly was interested _____ learning more about politics.
7. Cafeteria food is generally lacking _____ flavor and creativity.
8. Although I didn't like Simon at first, I've become quite fond _____ him.

9. Bradley was angry _____ Joanne because she broke his MP3 player.

10. Many people are allergic _____ dust and pollen.

B 괄호 안에 주어진 말을 첫머리로 하여 문장을 다시 써 보자.

1. Small children can't stay up late. (It's hard)
→ It's hard for small children to stay up late.

2. Everyone needs to have an occasional break. (It's necessary)
→ _____

3. She doesn't like to clean up after the kids each day. (It's annoying)
→ _____

4. I don't like to do the same thing every day. (It's boring)
→ _____

5. Jim felt unpleasant to remember that time in his life. (It was unpleasant)
→ _____

6. You had better have a good role model. (It's beneficial)
→ _____

7. The sun doesn't usually shine so late into the day. (It's unusual)
→ _____

8. I enjoyed reading the book. (The book was)
→ _____

9. People who love traveling get excited about visiting new countries. (It is exciting)
→ _____

10. Julie is stressed out by working such long hours every day. (It's stressful)
→ _____

Orientation

I. TOEFL iBT/ Next Generation TOEFL
II. 점수 환산 기준

I. TOEFL *i*BT / Next Generation TOEFL

2005년 9월을 기점으로 1998년 미국에서부터 시행된 TOEFL CBT은 인터넷을 기반으로 하는 TOEFL *i*BT 체제로 바뀌었다. 일부에서는 새롭게 시행되는 토플에 한국인들이 특히 강한 문법이 없어지고 한국인들이 상대적으로 약한 Speaking이 추가되어 이제 토플로 고득점을 획득하기는 어려울 것이라 생각하는 경우가 있는 것 같다. 하지만 새로운 토플을 면밀히 분석하여 그에 맞는 공부 방법으로 철저히 대비한다면 *i*BT에서도 고득점을 얻는 것이 충분히 가능하다.

1. TOEFL이란?

TOEFL(Test of English as a Foreign Language)은 영어가 모국어가 아닌 사람(EFL학습자 또는 non-native speakers of English)이 미국, 캐나다 등 영어 사용권 국가의 대학이나 대학원에 입학할 경우 치러야 하는 영어 사용 능력 검정시험이다. TOEFL시험은 미국 New Jersey주의 Princeton에 본부를 둔 ETS(Educational Testing Service)의 주관으로 전세계적으로 시행되고 있으며 5,000여 대학이나 교육기관에서 공인시험으로 인정하고 있다.

＊ What is ETS?
ETS는 Educational Testing Service의 약자다. ETS는 1947년에 설립된 미국 북동부의 New Jersey에 위치한 국가공인 시험 전문 비영리기관(Nonprofit Institution)이다. ETS는 TOEFL 등 영어에 대한 시험뿐만 아니라 미국의 고등학교, 대학교, 대학원 입학에 관련된 영어, 수학, 논리, 전공에 대한 시험을 주관한다. ETS에서 주관하는 대표적인 시험으로는 SAT(미국 대학 입학 능력 평가), GRE(미국 대학원 입학 능력 평가), GMAT(미국 경영대학원 입학 능력 평가), LSAT(미국 법대 입학 능력 평가) 등이 있다. 합격 또는 불합격에 대한 판정은 하지 않으며 단지 해당 시험 분야에 대한 능력만을 평가한다.

2. TOEFL *i*BT란?

2006년부터 전세계적으로 새롭게 시행되고 있는 인터넷 기반의 새로운 토플 시험을 Next Generation TOEFL(차세대 토플) 또는 TOEFL *i*BT(Internet-based Test)라고 한다.

* ＊ TOEFL *i*BT는 2005-2006년에 걸쳐 순차적으로 전세계적으로 시행되었다.
  * ✓ 2005년 9월 – 미국에서 시행
  * ✓ 2005년 10월 – 캐나다, 독일, 프랑스, 이탈리아 등 4개국에서 시행
  * ✓ 2006년 – 한국을 포함, 전세계적으로 시행(한국에서는 2006년 9월 시행)
* ＊ TOEFL *i*BT는 인터넷을 기반으로 ETS에서 지정한 날짜(주로 금요일과 토요일)에 연중 30-40회 정도 시행이 되며, 시험장소가 대폭 확대되어 가까운 곳에서 편리하게 시험을 볼 수 있다.
* ＊ TOEFL *i*BT의 시험 등록은 인터넷, 메일, 전화 등 다양한 매체를 통해 가능하며, 비용은 $140~$170이다.

3 TOEFL *i*BT의 주요 변화

❏ 문법(Structure)이 없어지고 Speaking이 추가

새로운 토플에서는 기존의 structure 평가영역이 사라지고 실제 의사소통 기능을 갖는 통합형 평가 방식 위주의 speaking이 보강되었다.

✽ 이는 문법이나 영어구조에 대한 학습은 중요하지 않고 speaking이 더 중요하다는 의미는 아니다. 우리와 같이 제한된 시간에만 영어에 노출되어 있는 EFL환경에서는 문법과 어휘 등 언어구조에 대한 학습이 필수적이라는 인식에는 이견이 없다. 따라서 새로운 토플체제하에서도 문법학습은 여전히 중요하다고 할 수 있다.

❏ 통합형 문제(Integrated Tasks)의 도입

영어를 사용하는 실제 환경의 구현을 위해 [읽고+듣고+쓰기]와 같은 실제 의사소통 기능을 갖는 통합형 평가 방식(Integrated-Skills Approach)의 문제가 출제된다. 새롭게 도입된 통합형 문제 유형은 다음과 같다.

Read / Listen / Speak
Listen / Speak
Read / Listen / Write

❏ Core Academic Skills Assessment 강화

기존의 영어시험이 제시된 영어문장의 이해도를 주로 평가하는 것이라면 새로운 토플은 note taking, paraphrasing, synthesizing, summarizing 등과 같은 영어로 수업을 진행하는데 필요한 실질적인 능력(Core Academic Skills)을 요구하고 있다.

❏ Reading과 Listening의 난이도는 현재의 CBT와 같은 수준

외형상 새로운 토플에 많은 변화가 있기는 하지만 Reading과 Listening은 대부분 기존에 익숙한 CBT 문제 유형을 그대로 사용하고 있다. 또한 새로운 토플에 등장하는 문장의 구조나 어휘범위, 토픽범위, Writing Topics 등이 기존의 CBT와 동일한 수준이다.

4 TOEFL iBT의 각 영역별 개요

	Reading (독해)	Listening (청취)	Speaking (말하기)	Writing (작문)

구성	• 총 지문 수: 3-5개
	• 총 문제 수: 36-70개
	• 각 지문 당 문제 수: 12-14개
	• 각 지문 당 단락 수: 4-8개
	• 각 지문 당 어휘 수: 약 700단어
		• Conversation: 2-3개
		• Lecture: 4-6개 (Interactive Lecture 2-3개; Academic Lecture 2-3개)
		• Conversation은 2-3분 정도 (400-500단어의 길이), Lecture는 4-5분 정도 (600-800단어의 길이)
		• 2-3개의 Conversation (각 5문제씩)과 4-6개의 Lecture (각 6문제씩)에서 총 34-51문제 출제
			• Independent Speaking (개별 말하기): 2문제
			• Integrated Speaking (통합형 말하기시험): 4문제 (읽고 듣고 말하기 2문제; 듣고 말하기 2문제)
			• Integrated Speaking의 독해 지문은 75-100단어 수준으로 45초의 읽기시간이 주어진다.
			• Integrated Speaking의 듣기 지문은 150-280단어 수준으로 1-2분 정도의 길이다.
			• 총 6문제 출제
				• Integrated Writing (통합형 작문): 1문제(20분 동안 150-225단어 정도 작성)
				  - Integrated Writing의 독해 지문은 230-300단어 수준으로 3분의 읽기시간이 주어진다.
				  - Integrated Writing의 듣기지문은 230-300단어 수준으로 2분 정도의 길이다.
				• Independent Writing (개별 작문): 1문제(30분 동안 최소한 300단어 이상 작성)
				• 총 2문제 출제

시간	총 60-100분 (각 지문당 20분씩)	대략 60-90분 정도(듣는 시간을 제외하고 실제 문제를 푸는데 걸리는 시간은 20-30분)	대략 20분	대략 50분 (Integrated Writing: 20분; Independent Writing: 30분)
문제 유형	(1) Vocabulary Questions (2) Reference Questions (3) Sentence Simplification Questions (4) Factual Information Questions (5) Negative Fact Questions (6) Inference Questions (7) Rhetorical Purpose Questions (8) Insert Text Questions (9) Prose Summary Questions (10) Classifying, Categorizing, and Organizing Information Questions	(1) Main Idea Questions (2) Supporting Detail Questions (3) Organization Questions (4) Organization-Rhetorical Connection Questions (5) Content-Identifying Relationship Questions (6) Content-Linking Questions (7) Stance / Attitude Questions (8) Function-Purpose Questions	(1) Independent Speaking Personal Preference (2) Independent Speaking Paired Choice (3) Reading / Listening / Speaking Campus Situation Topic (4) Reading / Listening / Speaking Academic Course Topic (5) Listening / Speaking Campus Situation Topic (6) Listening / Speaking Academic Course Topic	(1) Reading / Listening / Writing Academic Course Topic (2) Independent Writing based on Experience & Knowledge
특징	• Glossary (어휘사전) 제공: 단어를 클릭하면 해당 단어의 설명이 나타난다. • Review (복습) 기능: 체크한 답과 그렇지 않은 답의 상태를 알 수 있어 그냥 지나간 문제를 확인할 수 있다. • 각 지문의 제목이 제시된다. • 문제는 보통 지문의 순서대로 주어지며, 문제가 왼쪽에, 지문이 오른쪽에 제시된다.	• Note Taking (받아적기) 가능: 듣는 동안에 요점을 종이에 쓸 수 있다. • 강의의 핵심 구문을 모니터 상에 제시한다. • 들은 내용을 그대로 다시 들려주고 푸는 Replay Item을 도입했다.	• Note Taking을 이용해 효율적으로 Speaking Task의 답변을 준비할 수 있다. • Independent Speaking은 일상 생활의 경험에 관한 질문 등 매우 익숙한 토픽에 대한 질문이다. • Integrated Speaking은 읽고 들은 내용을 바탕으로 Speaking Task가 주어진다. • 각 문제당 15-30초 정도의 답변 준비 시간이 주어지고 실제 답변 시간은 45초 또는 60초다.	• Note Taking을 이용해 효율적으로 Writing Task의 답변을 준비할 수 있다. • Independent Writing의 주제는 기존의 CBT TOEFL의 185 Writing Topics와 거의 동일하다. • Integrated Writing은 읽고 들은 내용을 바탕으로 Writing Task가 주어진다.

5 TOEFL iBT의 점수체계

❏ Next Generation TOEFL Scores

Four skill scores

Reading: 0 – 30
Listening: 0 – 30
Speaking: 0 – 30
Writing: 0 – 30
Total score: 0 – 120

※ 각 영역별(Reading, Listening, Speaking, and Writing)로 0-30의 scale로 할당되며 total 120 scale이 만점이다. 또한 성적통지표에는 4개의 영역 점수(four skill scores)와 더불어 total score난이 별도로 표기된다.

※ Score Report는 테스트 후 15일 이후에 온라인에서 확인하거나 우편으로 받아볼 수 있다.

❏ 각 영역별 배점체계

	Reading (독해)	Listening (청취)	Speaking (말하기)	Writing (작문)
구 성	• 보통 문제당 1점의 원점수가 주어진다. • Prose Summary Questions나 Classifying, Categorizing, and Organizing Information Questions 문제 유형은 부분 점수가 부여되는 Partial-Credit Item으로 0-4점 사이의 원점수가 부여된다. • 모든 원점수를 합하여 30점 만점으로 환산한다.	• 보통 문제당 1점의 원점수가 주어진다. • 일부 Supporting Detail Questions 문제의 경우 2점의 원점수가 주어질 수 있다. 이 경우, 해당 문제에 점수기준이 명시되어 있다. • 모든 원점수를 합하여 30점 만점으로 환산한다.	• Scoring Rubrics를 바탕으로 각 문제당 0-4점 사이의 원점수가 주어진다. • 6명의 human raters에 의해 채점된다. • 모든 원점수를 합하여 30점 만점으로 환산한다.	• Scoring Rubrics를 바탕으로 각 문제 0-5점 사이의 원점수가 주어진다. • 2명의 human raters에 의해 채점된다. • 모든 원점수를 합하여 30점 만점으로 환산한다.
문제 수	36-70	34-51	6	2
환산점수	0-30	0-30	0-30	0-30

※ 한국인의 토플 평균 점수는 200-210점(CBT기준)으로 추산된다. 이는 링구아 토플시리즈의 i-TOEFL단계에 해당하는 수준으로 약 5,000-6,000단어 정도의 어휘력을 갖는 것으로 추정하며, 이를 링구아 토플 중급학습자로 분류한다.

※ 보통 미국 대학에서 요구하는 토플 점수는 213점(CBT기준)으로 TOEFL iBT 80점에 해당하는 점수이다.

II. 점수 환산 기준

TOEFL Total Score Comparison

Internet-based Total	Computer-based Total	Paper-based Total
120	300	677
120	297	673
119	293	670
118	290	667
117	287	660-663
116	283	657
114-115	280	650-653
113	277	647
111-112	273	640-643
110	270	637
109	267	630-633
106-108	263	623-627
105	260	617-620
103-104	257	613
101-102	253	607-610
100	250	600-603
98-99	247	597
96-97	243	590-593
94-95	240	587
92-93	237	580-583
90-91	233	577
88-89	230	570-573
86-87	227	567
84-85	223	563
83	220	557-560
81-82	217	553
79-80	213	550
77-78	210	547
76	207	540-543
74-75	203	537
72-73	200	533
71	197	527-530
69-70	193	523
68	190	520
66-67	187	517
65	183	513
64	180	507-510
62-63	177	503
61	173	500
59-60	170	497
58	167	493
57	163	487-490
56	160	483
54-55	157	480
53	153	477
52	150	470-473
51	147	467
49-50	143	463
48	140	460
47	137	457
45-46	133	450-453
44	130	447
43	127	443
41-42	123	437-440
40	120	433
39	117	430
38	113	423-427
36-37	110	420
35	107	417
34	103	410-413
33	100	407
32	97	400-403
30-31	93	397
29	90	390-393
28	87	387
26-27	83	380-383
25	80	377
24	77	370-373
23	73	363-367
22	70	357-360
21	67	353
19-20	63	347-350
18	60	340-343
17	57	333-337
16	53	330
15	50	323-327
14	47	317-320
13	43	313
12	40	310
11	37	310
9	33	310
8	30	310
7	27	310
6	23	310
5	20	310
4	17	310
3	13	310
2	10	310
1	7	310
0	3	310
0	0	310

Range Comparison

Internet-based Total	Computer-based Total	Paper-based Total
111-120	273-300	640-677
96-110	243-270	590-637
79-95	213-240	550-587
65-78	183-210	513-547
53-64	153-180	477-510
41-52	123-150	437-473
30-40	93-120	397-433
19-29	63-90	347-393
9-18	33-60	310-343
0-8	0-30	310

Converting Rubric Scores to Scaled Scores
Speaking Section of the New TOEFL *i*BT Test

Speaking Rubric Mean	Scaled Score
4.00	30
3.83	29
3.66	28
3.50	27
3.33	26
3.16	24
3.00	23
2.83	22
2.66	20
2.50	19
2.33	18
2.16	17
2.00	15
1.83	14
1.66	13
1.50	11
1.33	10
1.16	9
1.00	8
	6
	5
	4
	3
	1
	0

Notes

Evaluation Sheet

Read the evaluation questions and check the level of your delivery. On a scale from 1 to 5 (1=very poor, 2=poor, 3=OK, 4=good, 5=very good), rank your delivery accordingly.

Could you complete your response?	1	2	3	4	5
Is your answer coherent and unified?	1	2	3	4	5
Do you find a sequence in your response?	1	2	3	4	5
How is the use of vocabulary?	1	2	3	4	5
Does your response show grammatical structures?	1	2	3	4	5
How is the use of idiomatic expressions?	1	2	3	4	5
Is your response fluent and smooth?	1	2	3	4	5
Is your pronunciation clear?	1	2	3	4	5
How is the use of stress and intonation?	1	2	3	4	5

Read the evaluation questions and check the level of your delivery. On a scale from 1 to 5 (1=very poor, 2=poor, 3=OK, 4=good, 5=very good), rank your delivery accordingly.

Could you complete your response?	1	2	3	4	5
Is your answer coherent and unified?	1	2	3	4	5
Do you find a sequence in your response?	1	2	3	4	5
How is the use of vocabulary?	1	2	3	4	5
Does your response show grammatical structures?	1	2	3	4	5
How is the use of idiomatic expressions?	1	2	3	4	5
Is your response fluent and smooth?	1	2	3	4	5
Is your pronunciation clear?	1	2	3	4	5
How is the use of stress and intonation?	1	2	3	4	5

Evaluation Sheet

Read the evaluation questions and check the level of your delivery. On a scale from 1 to 5 (1=very poor, 2=poor, 3=OK, 4=good, 5=very good), rank your delivery accordingly.

Could you complete your response?	1	2	3	4	5
Is your answer coherent and unified?	1	2	3	4	5
Do you find a sequence in your response?	1	2	3	4	5
How is the use of vocabulary?	1	2	3	4	5
Does your response show grammatical structures?	1	2	3	4	5
How is the use of idiomatic expressions?	1	2	3	4	5
Is your response fluent and smooth?	1	2	3	4	5
Is your pronunciation clear?	1	2	3	4	5
How is the use of stress and intonation?	1	2	3	4	5

Read the evaluation questions and check the level of your delivery. On a scale from 1 to 5 (1=very poor, 2=poor, 3=OK, 4=good, 5=very good), rank your delivery accordingly.

Could you complete your response?	1	2	3	4	5
Is your answer coherent and unified?	1	2	3	4	5
Do you find a sequence in your response?	1	2	3	4	5
How is the use of vocabulary?	1	2	3	4	5
Does your response show grammatical structures?	1	2	3	4	5
How is the use of idiomatic expressions?	1	2	3	4	5
Is your response fluent and smooth?	1	2	3	4	5
Is your pronunciation clear?	1	2	3	4	5
How is the use of stress and intonation?	1	2	3	4	5

Evaluation Sheet

Read the evaluation questions and check the level of your delivery. On a scale from 1 to 5 (1=very poor, 2=poor, 3=OK, 4=good, 5=very good), rank your delivery accordingly.

Could you complete your response?	1	2	3	4	5
Is your answer coherent and unified?	1	2	3	4	5
Do you find a sequence in your response?	1	2	3	4	5
How is the use of vocabulary?	1	2	3	4	5
Does your response show grammatical structures?	1	2	3	4	5
How is the use of idiomatic expressions?	1	2	3	4	5
Is your response fluent and smooth?	1	2	3	4	5
Is your pronunciation clear?	1	2	3	4	5
How is the use of stress and intonation?	1	2	3	4	5

Read the evaluation questions and check the level of your delivery. On a scale from 1 to 5 (1=very poor, 2=poor, 3=OK, 4=good, 5=very good), rank your delivery accordingly.

Could you complete your response?	1	2	3	4	5
Is your answer coherent and unified?	1	2	3	4	5
Do you find a sequence in your response?	1	2	3	4	5
How is the use of vocabulary?	1	2	3	4	5
Does your response show grammatical structures?	1	2	3	4	5
How is the use of idiomatic expressions?	1	2	3	4	5
Is your response fluent and smooth?	1	2	3	4	5
Is your pronunciation clear?	1	2	3	4	5
How is the use of stress and intonation?	1	2	3	4	5

Evaluation Sheet

Read the evaluation questions and check the level of your delivery. On a scale from 1 to 5 (1=very poor, 2=poor, 3=OK, 4=good, 5=very good), rank your delivery accordingly.

Could you complete your response?	1	2	3	4	5
Is your answer coherent and unified?	1	2	3	4	5
Do you find a sequence in your response?	1	2	3	4	5
How is the use of vocabulary?	1	2	3	4	5
Does your response show grammatical structures?	1	2	3	4	5
How is the use of idiomatic expressions?	1	2	3	4	5
Is your response fluent and smooth?	1	2	3	4	5
Is your pronunciation clear?	1	2	3	4	5
How is the use of stress and intonation?	1	2	3	4	5

Read the evaluation questions and check the level of your delivery. On a scale from 1 to 5 (1=very poor, 2=poor, 3=OK, 4=good, 5=very good), rank your delivery accordingly.

Could you complete your response?	1	2	3	4	5
Is your answer coherent and unified?	1	2	3	4	5
Do you find a sequence in your response?	1	2	3	4	5
How is the use of vocabulary?	1	2	3	4	5
Does your response show grammatical structures?	1	2	3	4	5
How is the use of idiomatic expressions?	1	2	3	4	5
Is your response fluent and smooth?	1	2	3	4	5
Is your pronunciation clear?	1	2	3	4	5
How is the use of stress and intonation?	1	2	3	4	5

초급부터 실전까지 토플교재의 바이블
링구아포럼 TOEFL Series

- 아시아 최초로 2003년부터 미국은 물론 전 세계로 영어 교재와 판권 수출
- 온라인 서점 아마존닷컴 토플 판매 1위 (2003년, 2004년)
- 주니어 토플 개념 정의
- 최초 6단계별 토플 시리즈 개발

링구아포럼의 6단계별 토플 교재 **eBASIC / e / b / m / i / Hooked on / Insider / Test Book**
- eBasic 시리즈를 시작으로 e, b, m, i, Hooked On 순으로 단계가 올라갑니다. 영문 종합서 Insider 와 모의고사집 Test Book이 있습니다.

1단계 — New Edition eBasic Series
중학교 1~2학년 수준으로 토플을 처음 접하는 학습자를 위한 입문 단계로, iBT의 주제와 형식, 문제유형에 입문 수준의 어휘와 문법으로 구성되었습니다.
〈개정판〉

2단계 — New Edition e Series
중학교 2~3학년 수준의 토플 학습자를 위해 개발된 두번째 초급 단계이며, iBT의 주제와 형식, 문제유형에 입문 수준의 어휘와 문법으로 구성되었습니다.
〈개정판〉

  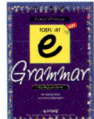 

3단계 — b Series
중학교 3학년 이상의 영어능력을 가진 학습자를 대상으로 개발. 링구아포럼 eBasic, e 시리즈를 학습한 학습자에서부터, 토플을 처음 접하는 대학생/성인들 모두 토플에 적응하고 중급~고급 단계로 진입할 수 있도록 구성 되었습니다.
〈개정판〉

4단계 — m Series
중급 수준(성인 입문)의 토플 학습자를 대상으로 개발. iBT에 등장하는 모든 주제와 문제유형 등을 모두 다루었으며, 실전보다 조금 쉬운 수준으로 연습할 수 있습니다.
〈개정판 출간예정〉

5단계 — New Edition i Series
실제 토플 시험을 준비하는 학습자를 대상으로 개발. 링구아포럼 토플 시리즈의 중/고급단계로, iBT에 등장하는 모든 주제와 문제유형 등을 모두 다루었으며, 실전과 거의 유사한 수준으로 연습할 수 있습니다.

6단계 — New Edition Hooked On Series
실제 토플 시험을 준비하는 학습자를 대상으로 한 고급단계로, iBT에 등장하는 모든 주제와 문제유형등을 모두 다루어, 실전과 동일한 수준으로 연습할 수 있습니다.

STEP TEPS

링구아포럼과 함께
TEPS 실력에 날개를 달자!

- ✓ 학습자들의 영역별 취약 Point 전략 제시
  (빠른 독해 풀이, 청해 파트 오답 유형 분석, 문법 최신 기출 포인트, Collocation 어휘 학습)
- ✓ 초급(basic)-중급(expert)-실전(final) 3단계 구성으로 단계별 학습 가능
- ✓ 경쟁사 교재 대비 최다 연습문제와 실전문제 수록
- ✓ 자세한 해설서 제공으로 독학과 강의에 모두 적합한 구성
- ✓ 최신 기출 경향을 반영한 진단고사와 Actual Test 수록

High Intermediate Course

NEW EDITION
TOEFL® iBT
SPEAKING
Answer Key & Explanations

LinguaForum

Answer Key & Explanations

Part A. Independent Tasks	A2
Part B. Integrated Tasks	A14
Part C. Actual Test	A46
Workbook	A54

PART A Independent Tasks

Task 1 | Personal Preference

❶ Outlining   p. 20

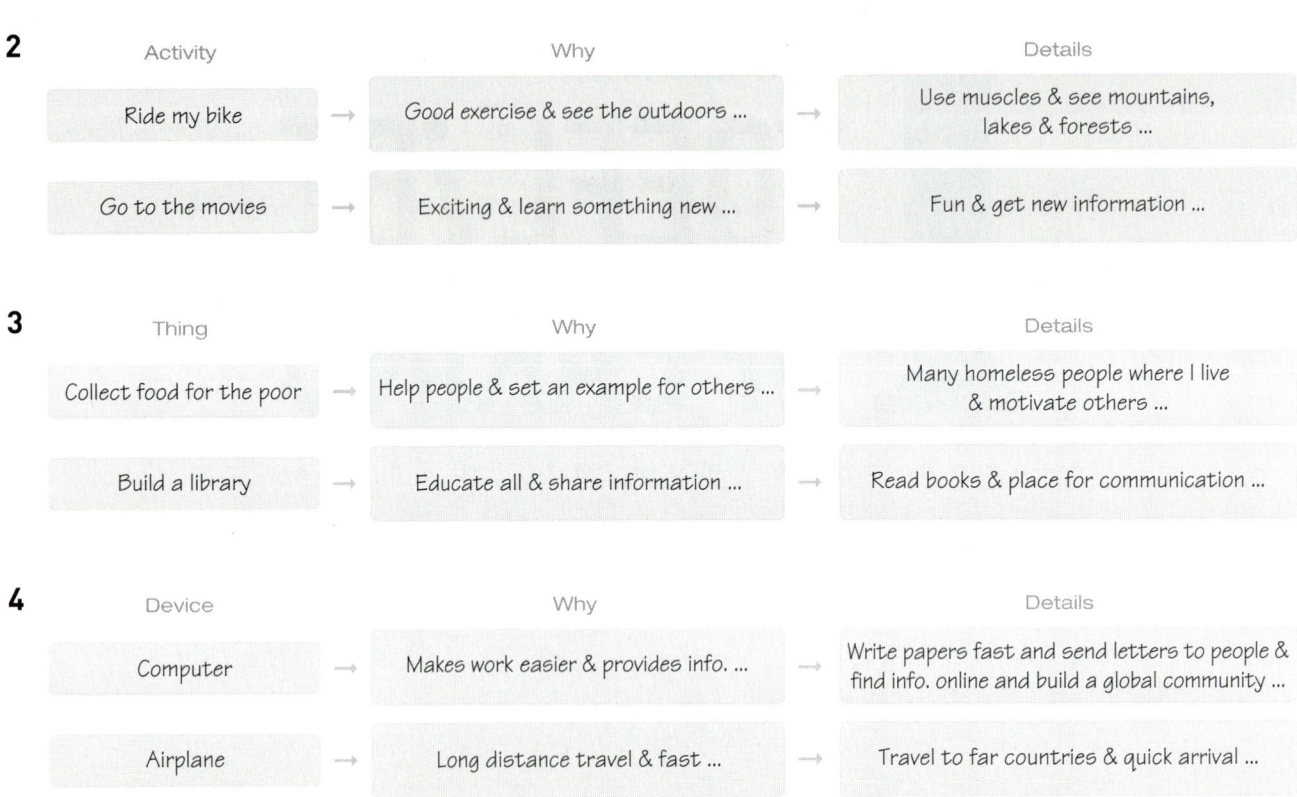

2

Activity	Why	Details
Ride my bike	Good exercise & see the outdoors …	Use muscles & see mountains, lakes & forests …
Go to the movies	Exciting & learn something new …	Fun & get new information …

3

Thing	Why	Details
Collect food for the poor	Help people & set an example for others …	Many homeless people where I live & motivate others …
Build a library	Educate all & share information …	Read books & place for communication …

4

Device	Why	Details
Computer	Makes work easier & provides info. …	Write papers fast and send letters to people & find info. online and build a global community …
Airplane	Long distance travel & fast …	Travel to far countries & quick arrival …

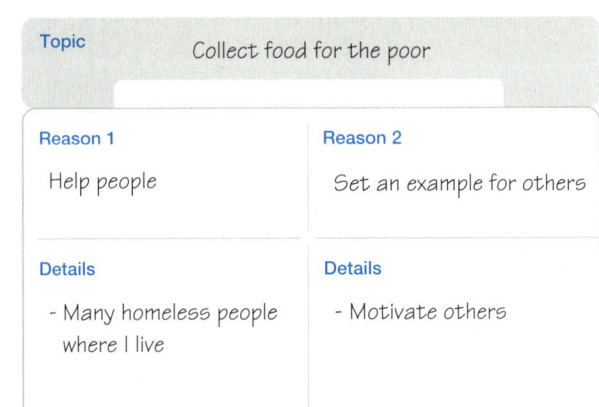

2

Topic: Ride my bike

Reason 1	Reason 2
Good exercise	See the outdoors
Details	**Details**
- Use muscles	- See mountains, lakes, & forests

3

Topic: Collect food for the poor

Reason 1	Reason 2
Help people	Set an example for others
Details	**Details**
- Many homeless people where I live	- Motivate others

4

Topic	Computer	
Reason 1 Makes work easier		**Reason 2** Provides info.
Details - Write papers faster - Can send letters to people instantly		**Details** - Find out anything on Internet - Build a global community

❷ Speaking Grammar   p. 23

2 **Topic** In my opinion, riding my bike is the activity I like to do most on weekends.

   Reason 1 One reason is that it's good exercise.

   Details What I am saying is that I can use my leg muscles and get aerobic exercise while riding my bike.

   Reason 2 The other reason is that I can see the outdoors.

   Details In other words, I can enjoy the beautiful scenery of mountains, small lakes, and forests while riding my bike in the countryside.

3 **Topic** As far as I'm concerned, collecting food for the poor is the least I can do to help them.

   Reason 1 One reason is that this is one of the greatest ways to help people in need.

   Details What I am saying is that there might be many homeless people where I live.

   Reason 2 The other reason is that I can set an example for others.

   Details In other words, I can motivate others to help the poor, and this would greatly enhance our living environment.

4 **Topic** In my opinion, the most helpful device ever invented is the computer.

   Reason 1 One reason is that it made my work easier.

   Details What I am saying is that I can write papers faster, send letters to people instantly, and do math more quickly.

   Reason 2 The other reason is that it provides much information quickly.

   Details In other words, you can get any kind of information online very conveniently. Also, the Internet unites people in a global community.

outdoors 야외의 **communication** 정보 전달 **device** 장치 **arrival** 도착 **muscle** 근육 **motivate** ~의 동기를 주다 **aerobic** 유산소의
scenery 경치, 경관 **conveniently** 편리하게

Practice Questions

p. 26

1 Sample Outlining

Topic	A novel

Reason 1	Reason 2
Imagine being in a different world	Enough free time

Details	Details
- Especially on a beach or in a hotel room	- Learn new words, notice new details as I reread, & never get bored

Sample Response

If I could take one entertainment item with me on vacation, I would take a novel with me because I enjoy reading and I could read it more than once. First, I like to read novels because I can imagine that I'm in a different world. I usually do this when I am on vacation, especially on a beach or in a hotel room. Second, I'd have enough free time to read a book more than once. I will learn new words when I read the book, and I usually notice new details in the story each time I read it, so I never get bored with it. This is why I would bring a book along to entertain me on vacation.

2 Sample Outlining

Topic	My car

Reason 1	Reason 2
Get to places very quickly	I'm in control when driving my car

Details	Details
- Faster than train because it doesn't stop - Prefer driving over walking	- Choose roads I want to travel, take the shorter way to work, & drive around to look at the city

Sample Response

My favorite mode of transportation is my car. There are two reasons why I like to drive my car. The first reason is that I can get to places very quickly in a car. The car is quicker than the train where I live, because it doesn't have to stop to drop off passengers all the time. I also cover more distance by driving than by walking. The other reason is that I am in control when I drive my own car. I get to choose whatever roads I want to travel, so I can take the short way to work or drive around to look at the city. I also feel responsible while driving, because I'm watching my speed and checking my mirrors.

3 Sample Outlining

Topic: When I won a math contest

Reason 1	Reason 2
Result of hard work	Nobody thought I could win

Details	Details
- Wasn't good at math - Studied very hard to improve math skills	- Attitudes of my classmates toward me changed - Gave me confidence in myself

Sample Response

My proudest moment in school was when I won a math contest. I beat more than 10 other students in my grade. I am proud of my achievement because it was the result of much hard work. I had never been very good at math before this contest, and I had poor grades and trouble doing homework. Because of this, I had to study very hard, sometime for three hours a night, just to improve my math skills. I'm also proud of that memory because nobody thought that I could win this contest. When I won, my classmates changed their attitudes toward me. They respected my skill and even asked for my help in math. Knowing this gave me confidence in myself and showed me that hard work is rewarding. This is why winning a school math contest is my proudest moment.

4 Sample Outlining

Topic: Students wear pin-on buttons

Reason 1	Reason 2
Add variety to the school	Make students to be creative

Details	Details
- Many shapes & colors - Funny pictures - More fun for some students	- Students can express opinions & ideas - Relieve students' stress

Sample Response

If I could change one policy at my school, I would allow students to wear pin-on buttons. For starters, these buttons would add variety to the school. They come in many shapes and colors, and many of them have funny pictures or sayings written on them. The variety of all these buttons would make school more fun for a lot of students. Next, wearing these buttons would let students be more creative. These buttons would let students express their opinions and their ideas. They would also let them be creative in how they dress. This would relieve a lot of the frustration that some students in my school feel.

5 Sample Outlining

Topic: My aunt

Reason 1	Reason 2
Has traveled a lot	Fun to speak with

Details	Details
- Has been to countries like India, Italy, and Panama. Learned languages, especially Italian	- Knows a lot of jokes & historical facts - A good listener

Sample Response

An interesting person that I know is my aunt, because she has traveled a lot, and she is fun to speak with. First off, my aunt has traveled a great deal around the world. She has visited distant countries such as India, Italy, and Panama. In her travels, she has learned a little bit of foreign languages – she is actually fluent in Italian. In addition, it is fun to speak with my aunt. She knows a lot of jokes and historical facts. Best of all, though, she is a good listener, for she responds to what I am saying. This is why my aunt is one of the most interesting people I know.

6

Sample Outlining

Topic	Piano	
Reason 1		**Reason 2**
Challenging		Can be played w/ any music
Details		**Details**
- Must play w/ both hands & different notes - Read long sheets of music		- Has many techniques like scales & chords - Play jazz, classical, rock, & gospel

Sample Response

An instrument that I would like to learn to play is the piano. The first reason why I'd like to learn the piano is that it is a very challenging instrument. You have to be able to play with both hands, hitting several different notes quickly or at the same time, and you have to be able to read long sheets of music. However, if you can do it, you will be an excellent musician. Another reason is that a piano can be played with any style of music. It has many techniques, like scales and chords, that can be played in jazz, classical, rock, and gospel. These are all of my reasons for wanting to learn the piano.

7

Sample Outlining

Topic	Civil rights movement in 1960s	
Reason 1		**Reason 2**
Gave everyone equal rights		Non-violence can change people's minds
Details		**Details**
- Let everyone vote - Everyone should be treated equally by government		- People didn't fight back against violence - People got sympathy of Americans

Sample Response

I think an event that was historically important for my country was the civil rights movement. To begin with, the civil rights movement gave Americans equal rights. It changed the policy that only white people could vote, and let Americans of all races vote. This led Americans to believe that everyone should be treated equally by the government. Also, it showed that non-violence can change people's minds. People in the movement didn't fight back using violence, and they got the sympathy of other Americans, convincing them that everyone should live together peacefully. This is why I believe the civil rights movement was historically important for my country.

8

Sample Outlining

Topic	Bill Gates – chairman of MS	
Reason 1		**Reason 2**
Sells lots of programs		Donates lots of money to charity
Details		**Details**
- His prog. is used > any others & comp. is needed for everything		- Gives money to char. in Africa - Can get other people to change lives too

Sample Response

I personally think that a person that has a great influence on people's lives today is Bill Gates. To start, he sells a lot of computer programs, more than anyone else. This means that people rely on him for their computers to work, and computers are needed for almost everything that we do. Next, Bill Gates donates lots of money to charity. He has given billions of dollars to help people in Africa. By using his money and power like this, he can influence others to give too, and this can help everyone. In conclusion, Bill Gates is someone who has a great influence on people's lives today.

---

entertainment 연예, 오락물　**pin-on button** 뺏지　**frustration** 좌절　**non-violence** 비폭력　**donate** 기부하다　**charity** 구호 단체

Vocabulary Study — Daily Expressions

p. 30

- spare time 자유시간
- talent 재능, 소질
- dream job 희망하는 직업
- hiking 도보 여행
- genealogy 계보, 족보
- surfing the Internet 인터넷 하기
- babysitting 아기 보기
- enthusiasm 열성
- attempt 시도
- look up to 존경하다
- a lifetime friend 평생 친구
- study abroad 유학
- go to the theater 영화관 가기
- hang out 외출하기
- egocentric 자기중심적
- ambitious 야심인
- determined 확고한
- hilarious 웃긴
- hasty decisions 급한 결정
- coincidence 우연

- kind-hearted 친절한
- self-assured 자신이 있는
- reluctant 마음이 내키지 않는
- conservative 보수적인
- discern 인식하다
- sluggish 나태한
- insolent 오만한
- stimulate 자극적인
- skilful 숙련된, 솜씨 있는
- thoughtful 생각에 잠긴, 신중한
- vigorous 활력에 넘친, 원기 왕성한
- pleasant 즐거운
- adorable 귀여운, 사랑스러운
- chore 잡일
- beware 주의하다
- vulnerable 상하기 쉬운
- tardy 더딘, 느린
- urgent 다급한, 긴급한, 촉박한
- feel at home 집처럼 편안하다
- stressed out 기진 맥진한

정답 |

A 1. (e)   2. (d)   3. (g)   4. (b)   5. (a)
   6. (f)   7. (h)   8. (c)   9. (j)   10. (i)

B 1. enthusiasm   2. conservative   3. reluctant   4. looked up to   5. egocentric

Task 2   Paired Choice

❶ Outlining   p. 34

2

Eat at home	Why	Details
Where to eat →	Can cook anything, don't have many people around ... →	Less money, make own sauces, no noise, no waiting ...
Eat at a restaurant →	Try delicious food, don't need to waste time ... →	Professional cooks make food, do other things ...

3

Kind of vacation	Why	Details
One 4-mo. summer vac. →	Get a good rest from studying, have time for projects ... →	Have energy after a long vac., work on interesting project ...
Separate shorter vac. →	Have many field trips, visit my relatives ... →	Experience many things, enjoy time with my relatives ...

4

When to work	Why	Details
Work during the day →	Meet friends at night, more energy during the day ... →	Friends work in the day, get more work done during the day ...
Work at night →	Very quiet at night, don't have many customers at night ... →	Don't have many people around, less work to do at night ...

---

2 Topic: **Eat at home**

Reason 1	Reason 2
Can cook anything	Don't have many people around

Details	Details
- Less money - Make own sauces	- No noise - No waiting

3 Topic: **One 4-mo. summer vacation**

Reason 1	Reason 2
Get a good rest from studying	Have time for projects

Details	Details
- Have energy after a long vac.	- Work on interesting projects

Task 2. Paired Choice

4

Topic	Work during the day	
Reason 1		**Reason 2**
Meet friends at night		More energy during the day
Details		**Details**
- Friends work in the day		- Get more work done during the day

❷ Speaking Grammar

p. 37

2 **Topic** I believe that eating at home is better than eating at a restaurant.

  Reason 1 That's because I can cook anything I want in my style if I eat at home.

   Details I mean I can make my own sauces, and it will make a differece in taste though I cook the same dish. And I don't need to spend much money if I eat at home.

  Reason 2 Furthermore, it's much better if I don't have many people around me when I eat.

   Details Especially, I don't like having much noise when I eat. Besides, at restaurants, I sometimes need to wait a long time in line just to be seated. For these reasons I mentioned above, it's better for me to eat at home.

3 **Topic** I would say that one-4-month summer vacation is better than separate, shorter vacations.

  Reason 1 That's because I can get a good rest from studying.

   Details I mean I don't need to worry about studying and I can focus on things I'd like to do for a long time.

  Reason 2 Furthermore, I can have a lot of time for my projects.

   Details Especially if I take a trip to Africa to do a project for my anthropology class, I'd need to spend at least several months to finish it. For these reasons I mentioned above, it's definitely better to have a long summer vacation.

4 **Topic** I believe that working during the day is better than working at night.

  Reason 1 That's because I can meet my friends at night.

   Details I mean most of my friends work during the day. So, we only have time to spend at night. If I work at night, I won't be able to meet my friends at all.

  Reason 2 Furthermore, I have more energy during the day and not as much at night.

   Details Especially during the day, I can get more work done because I have more energy and better concentration.

Anthropology class 인류학 수업   concentration 집중

Practice Questions

p. 40

1 Sample Outlining

Topic	Live with a roommate

Reason 1	Reason 2
I have someone to talk to	Help me take care of my apartment

Details	Details
- Discuss all kinds of things, like schoolwork & sports - Have a new friend	- Split chores like sweeping and dishwashing - Help me pay the rent and utilities

Sample Response

I prefer to live with a roommate because then I have someone to talk to and I have someone who can help me take care of my apartment. First, I enjoy having conversations with people, so a roommate would provide me with good company. We could discuss all kinds of things, like schoolwork and sports, and I would have a new friend. Second, I prefer having a roommate because he can help me take care of my apartment. We can split chores, like sweeping and dishwashing. Not only that, but he could also help me pay the rent and utilities.

2 Sample Outlining

Topic	Do activities on a holiday

Reason 1	Reason 2
Something to discuss with friends	It's a waste of time to sit around and do nothing

Details	Details
- Tell stories about the time I went to the countryside for a picnic or rode my bicycle	- Don't want to waste time watching T.V. - Have a meaningful way of spending time

Sample Response

I prefer to do activities on a holiday rather than just stay home and relax. One reason I prefer doing activities is that I have something to discuss with friends when I do an activity on a holiday. For example, I can tell stories about the time I went to the countryside for a picnic or rode my bicycle down a new trail. Moreover, I believe it is a waste of time to sit around and do nothing, because a holiday is such a good time to do things I want to do. I feel like I waste a whole day when I just sit around and watch TV. In other words, it can be a more meaningful way of spending time if you actually get out of the house.

3 Sample Outlining

Topic	Learning of art

Reason 1	Reason 2
Important in building creativity and social skills	Age is important in learning art

Sample Response

I agree with the opinion that schools should emphasize the learning of art, and there are two reasons why I agree with that opinion. First, learning art is important in building creativity and social skills. Art gives students the opportunity to create something on their own, like a story or a painting. Students can put their ideas in these creations and

A10 i SPEAKING Answer Key & Explanations

Task 2. Paired Choice

Details	Details
- Opportunity for studs. to create something on their own, studs. and teachers can communicate their ideas, can't have this experience when learning science	- Young studs. can find out whether they have talent - It's harder for adults to learn art

communicate their ideas with the teachers, which is something you can't learn when you are studying a bunch of numbers and facts in science. Second, it is important to teach art at an early age. Young students who learn art can find out if they have a talent for it, and they will have more time to develop this talent. If they don't learn about art until they are adults, then it will be harder for them to learn art and develop their skill.

4 Sample Outlining

Topic	More free time & spend less money	
Reason 1	**Reason 2**	
I save more money	Can't enjoy money if you don't have enough time	
Details	**Details**	
- Don't need small things like movies or CDs - Need to save up money for college	- Never get to enjoy stuff you buy, like TVs or computers - Working too much will cause stress	

Sample Response

I prefer to have more free time and spend less money rather than to earn more money and have less free time. The first reason is that I save more money if I spend less. I really don't need a lot of smaller items like movies or albums right now, and those can easily eat up a lot of money. Instead, I need to save up money for college, and I am more careful about saving money when I work less. Another thing is that you can't enjoy your extra money if you don't have enough time to spend it. You may not have enough time to watch all the TV channels you get or all the stuff on your computer if you work most of the time. Not only that, but working too much will cause stress, so you may be too stressed to enjoy your stuff even when you aren't working.

5 Sample Outlining

Topic	Attend as long as they need	
Reason 1	**Reason 2**	
Some studs. need more time	Colleges get benefits	
Details	**Details**	
- Some have jobs & take a few classes - Some do complex school work & must stay longer	- Coll. can use extra tuition for many purposes; improve the quality of education, expand campus, renovate facility, etc	

Sample Response

I would prefer that colleges allow students to attend as long as they need, because some students need to stay in school longer. Some students need more than five years. For example, if they work full-time jobs, they can only take a few classes at one time. Other students may need more time for complex studies, like medicine or engineering. Another reason is that colleges can benefit from such a system. If students who can afford college are given as much time as they need, colleges can use their tuition for many purposes. They can use that money to improve the quality of education, to expand the campus, to renovate facilities, and so on.

6 Sample Outlining

Topic	Determined by several tests	
Reason 1	**Reason 2**	
Give studs. chances for good grades	Studs. learn more from tests	
Details	**Details**	
- Studs. prepare for a little at a time - Studs. learn from past mistakes	- Studs. only study one topic for paper - More likely come to class to study for test	

Sample Response

I prefer that a class grade be determined by several tests for several reasons. One reason is that it gives students more chances to get a good grade. Students can study a smaller amount of information at a time, like a chapter, for each test. Not only that, but they can also learn from their past tests, by reviewing their past mistakes or good essays. This will help them get a better grade each time. Another reason is that a student will learn more from tests. Students will cover one topic for a paper, but they will cover more material for tests. Thus, they will be more likely to show up for class to study for the tests. This is why I believe a class grade should be determined by several tests.

7 Sample Outlining

Topic	Riding in carpools	
Reason 1	**Reason 2**	
Good for the environment	Talk with people	
Details	**Details**	
- Fewer cars on the road & less pollution from cars & less gas uses	- Make new friends - Have fun in the morning	

Sample Response

I prefer to ride in carpools because it is good for the environment and you get to talk with other people. To start off, riding in a carpool is good for the environment. With a carpool, there will be fewer cars on the road and less car fumes polluting the environment. Also, this means that less gas is used, so we don't have to use up as much fossil fuel. Next, in carpools you get to talk to people. This is a great way to make new friends on your way to work. Also, you can have a lot of fun in the morning by talking with people in your carpool. Thus, I prefer to ride in carpools, not alone.

8 Sample Outlining

Topic	Give to starving people	
Reason 1	**Reason 2**	
Cruel to let them starve	Can prevent further problems	
Details	**Details**	
- What if someone starved you? - People have moral obligation to help each other	- Starving people won't resort to violence - They could help other people in society	

Sample Response

I agree that surplus food should be given to starving people. There are two reasons why I believe so. First, it is cruel to let anyone starve if you can feed them. I would never want someone to do that to me. I think that people have a moral obligation to help each other because we all have needs like food and shelter. Secondly, you can prevent further problems by giving surplus food to starving people. People won't have to resort to violence in order to get food if they need something to eat. Instead, they will be able to work or help other people in society. In conclusion, this is why I think surplus food should be used to feed starving people.

Task 2. Paired Choice

chore 잡일   sweeping 청소   renovate 새롭게 수선하다   carpool 합승하다   surplus food 잔여 음식   obligation 의무

Vocabulary Study — Daily Expressions

p. 44

- eat out   외식하다
- trivial   사소한
- go through   경험하다
- preference   선호
- appreciation   감사

- convenient   편리한
- intelligence   지성, 지력
- cost-effective   경제적인
- vice versa   반대로
- hold your horses   인내하다

- prick up your ears   경청하다
- judgmental   비판적인
- expectant   기대를 가진, 기대하는
- awesome   두려움을 느끼게 하는, 무서운
- skeptical   의심이 많은

- self-centered   이기적인
- high-spirited   기쁨 가득한
- anxious   근심스러운
- tip of the iceberg   부분적인
- to make a long story short   간단히 말해서

- prejudiced   편견을 가진
- outdated   진부한, 시대에 뒤진
- endurance   지속성, 내구성
- magnificent   웅장한, 화려한
- educated   교육을 받은, 교양이 있는

- opinionated   독단적인
- passionate   열렬한, 정열적인
- optimistic   낙천주의적인, 낙관적인
- hesitation   망설임, 우유 부단함
- idealistic   이상주의자의, 관념론자의

- outgoing   사교적인
- pathetic   측은한, 불쌍한, 감동시키는
- gifted   탁월한 재능을 지닌
- termination   종료, 종결, 만료
- modify   수정하다

- intervene   간섭하다
- give it a try   시도하다
- come up with   제안하다
- at the end of the day   결국
- long for   간절히 바라다

정답 | A   1. (g)   2. (c)   3. (d)   4. (b)   5. (j)
        6. (e)   7. (a)   8. (f)   9. (h)   10. (i)

B   1. educated   2. optimistic   3. come up with   4. convenience   5. awesome

PART B Integrated Tasks

Task 3 Fit & Explain

Sample Question   p. 60

지문 해석 |
건설 관리과에서 알립니다: 적정한 공간의 부족으로 인하여 도서관 상위 3층의 보수를 위해 재건축을 실시합니다. 앞으로 3개월에 걸쳐 더 많은 서가를 놓을 수 있도록 보다 넓은 공간을 개방하기 위해 해당 층에서 공사가 진행될 것입니다. 안전상의 우려 때문에 건설 관계자 외의 모든 사람들에게 이 공간의 출입을 제한해야 할 것입니다. 해당 층에서 필요한 책이 있는 경우, 학생들은 도서관의 대출반납 데스크에 요청 양식을 제출해야 합니다. 해당 층들은 오늘부터 폐쇄됩니다.

Script 해석 |
남자: Tammy! 야, 잘 지내?
여자: 잘 지내고 있어. 근데 도서관 때문에 좀 짜증이 나.
남자: 아, 상위 3층을 폐쇄한다는 공고 말이야?
여자: 응, 내 말은 단지 책 놓을 공간을 더 만들기 위해 도서관의 일부를 폐쇄할 필요는 없다는 거야. 도서관 지하에 공간이 많이 있고 그곳은 대개 쓰이지 않는 창고잖아. 만일 그곳을 정돈하면 오래된 책들을 거기에 내려다 놓을 수 있어. 그런데 그러지 않고 도서관의 일부를 사용할 수 없게 했잖아. 그래서 학생들은 꼭대기 층에 있는 책들을 필요할 때 구할 수가 없어.
남자: 음, 그 책들을 구할 수는 있어. 단지 대출반납 데스크에서 그 책들을 요청하기만 하면 돼.
여자: 대출반납 데스크에서 책 빌려본 적 있어? 직원들이 어떤 책을 찾는데 시간이 많이 걸릴 수 있고 어떤 때는 네가 원하는 책을 아예 못 찾을 수도 있어. 난 차라리 찾을 수 없는 많은 책보다 찾을 수 있는 적은 수의 책을 갖는 편이 훨씬 낫겠어.

Reading
adequate 충분한, 적당한
restructure 구조를 개선하다
retrieve 회수하다

Listening
basement 지하층
close off 닫다
inaccessible 접근하기 어려운, 도달할 수 없는
extremely 극도로
inconvenient 불편한

❶ Outlining   p. 62

1

지문 해석 |
학생 편의과에서 알립니다: 승객의 증가로 인해 학교측은 학교 버스를 오후 6시 이후까지 운행하기로 결정하였습니다. 이제 버스는 오후 9시까지 운행하며, 이는 늦은 밤에 수업을 듣거나 다른 여러 교내 활동에 참여하는 승객들을 수용하기 위한 것입니다. 이는 어두울 때에 걸어 다니는 보행자가 더 많아지리라는 것을 의미합니다. 이러한 상황에서 위험한 운전을 막기 위해 속도제한이 엄격히 시행될 것이고 교내 교통 법규 위반에 부과되는 벌금도 크게 인상될 것입니다.

Script |
W: Hey, Andy! Are you doing okay?
M: I guess. I'm kind of annoyed by the school's decision to run the buses until nine o'clock, though.
W: Yeah, I heard about that. Do you take the bus?
M: No, I drive up here for class after work.
W: So why does it bother you if they run the buses at night?
M: Because that's when I get off work. If I want to get to class on time, I have to drive quickly down the campus roads to reach my assigned parking space. Now that the buses are running, I can't go as fast as I need to without getting fined. I'll probably be late for class now!
W: Yeah, I can see how that's a problem...
M: Besides, I don't see why they need the buses at night. I never see anyone walking or driving on campus. If you ask me, this new policy is going to hurt drivers more than it will help bus riders.

Reading
accommodate (차로) 운송하다, 태우다
pedestrian 승객
violation 위반

Listening
annoyed 짜증나는, 귀찮은

Script 해석 |

여자: 야, Andy! 잘 지내?
남자: 응 뭐. 학교에서 9시까지 버스를 운행한다는 결정에 좀 짜증이 나.
여자: 응, 그 소식 들었어. 너 버스 타?
남자: 아니, 난 일한 후에 차 운전해서 수업 받으러 와.
여자: 그러면 버스를 밤에 운행하는 게 왜?
남자: 왜냐하면 그때가 내가 일을 마치고 오는 때거든. 수업에 정시에 가려면 내 지정 주차 구역에 가기 위해서 교내 도로를 빨리 운전해서 내려가야 하거든. 버스들이 다니면 난 벌금을 물지 않고는 내가 원하는 만큼 빨리 갈 수가 없어. 난 이제 아마 수업에 늦을 거라구!
여자: 그래, 그게 왜 문제가 되는지 알겠다.
남자: 게다가 밤에 왜 버스가 필요한지 모르겠어. 걸어 다니거나 운전하는 사람 못 봤는데. 내 생각에 이 새로운 정책은 버스를 타는 사람들을 돕기 보다는 운전자들에게 피해를 줄 거야.

Campus Tip!
미국 종합 대학의 경우, 늦은 밤까지 셔틀버스나 택시를 제공해서 밤에 도서관이나 학교 사무실에서 기숙사 혹은 캠퍼스 안에 위치한 아파트로 이동하는 학생들의 편의를 봐 준다.

2

지문 해석 |
독자 의견: 학교측이 오후 6시 이후 기숙사에서 음악을 크게 트는 것을 금지한 것에 대해 감사를 전하고 싶습니다. 아래 로비에서 하루 종일, 심지어 이른 아침까지 음악을 크게 트는 사람들 때문에 저는 공부하는 데도, 잠자는 데도, 심지어 전화 통화하는 데에도 어려움이 있었습니다. 그 소음은 또한 소방 훈련 시의 화재 경보도 들리지 않게 했습니다. 이제 우리는 한밤중에 실제로 화재가 나면 화재 경보 소리를 들을 수 있을 것입니다.

염려하는 학생

Reading
ban 금지하다
drown (소리들) 삼켜 버리다, 없애다
fire drill 소방 훈련

Listening
sympathize 공감하다
blast out 터져 나오다

Script |

M: Janice! What are you up to now?
W: Oh, not much, just reading today's school paper.
M: Hey, did you read that letter supporting the ban on loud music after 6:00 p.m.?
W: Yeah. I can sympathize, but I don't think the ban is going to solve the problem.
M: Oh. How do you figure that?
W: Well, to begin with, it won't stop students from playing loud music during the late morning or afternoon. People are still studying and sleeping at those times, too. Now the music will be blasted out of stereos all at once, before 6:00.
M: Yeah, but doesn't all that noise also drown out the fire alarms?
W: I've never had trouble hearing the fire alarms before. If they aren't loud enough to cut through any other noise in the dormitory, like stereo music or running showers, then it's the school's responsibility to replace them with louder alarms. I mean, if they go off before 6:00, we'll have even more trouble hearing them over all the music.

Campus Tip!
미국 대학의 기숙사에는 학생들의 표현의 자유가 많은 부분 허용된다. 그래서 음악을 크게 틀어놓거나 파티를 하거나 함께 Pizza를 시켜먹으며 대화를 하는 경우도 많다. 학교마다 조금씩은 다를 수는 있겠지만 일반적으로 기숙사 안은 좀 어수선한 면이 없지 않다.

Script 해석 |

남자: Janice, 지금까지 뭐해?
여자: 아, 별거 아니야. 그냥 오늘 학교 신문 읽고 있어.
남자: 야, 오후 6시 이후에 음악 크게 듣지 못하게 하는 것을 찬성하는 편지 읽었어?
여자: 응, 공감이 가긴 하지만 금지하는 것이 문제를 해결하리라고 보진 않아.
남자: 아, 왜 그렇게 생각해?
여자: 글쎄, 우선 그게 학생들이 늦은 아침이나 오후에 음악을 크게 트는 것을 막지는 못할 거야. 사람들은 그 시간에도 공부하고 잠을 자. 이제 여섯 시 전에 한꺼번에 음악이 스테레오에서 터져 나올 거야.
남자: 그래. 하지만 그 모든 소음이 화재 경보도 안 들리게 하지 않아?
여자: 나는 화재 경보를 듣는 데 문제가 있었던 적이 한 번도 없어. 만일 경보가 음악 소리나 샤워 소리 같은 기숙사 안의 다른 소음들을 뚫고 들릴 정도로 충분히 크지 않다면, 더 큰 경보 소리로 바꾸는 것이 학교측의 책임이야. 그러니까 만일 경보가 6시 전에 울리면 우린 음악 소리 너머로 경보 소리를 듣는 데 훨씬 더 많은 어려움을 겪을 거라는 거야.

Reading note

Policy
No loud mus. after 6

Opinion
Agree

Reasons
Mus. was noisy & can't hear fire alarms

Listening note

Opinion
Disagree

Reason 1
Still Loud mus. all at once

Detail 1
- Disrupt people then
- Loud mus. all at once

Reason 2
Had no trouble hearing the fire alarms before/
School's responsibility

Detail 2
- Sch. should replace quiet alarms
- Still can't hear alarms in morning.

❷ Speaking Grammar p. 65

2

Reading note

Policy
No loud mus. after 6

Opinion
Agree

Reason 1
Mus. was noisy & can't hear fire alarms

Listening note

Opinion
Disagree

Reason 1
Still Loud mus. all at once

Detail 1
- Disrupt people then
- Loud mus. all at once

Reason 2
Had no trouble hearing the fire alarms before/
School's responsibility

Detail 2
- Sch. should replace quiet alarms
- Still can't hear alarms in morning.

Policy The school's policy is to ban loud music in the dorms after 6:00 p.m.

Opinion The woman disagrees with the school's decision because she believes the policy would be ineffective.

Reason 1 First, she points out that the ban on loud music in dorms after six will not solve the noise problem.

Details What she means is that students will play all their loud music before six, and this will disturb people who sleep and study during those hours.

Reason 2 Second, she mentions that she has never had trouble hearing the alarms, unlike the writer. Also, she argues that it's the school's responsibility to make sure that they have an effective fire alarm system.

Details For instance, if the school replaces the fire alarms with louder alarms, there won't be any problems.

Task 3. Fit & Explain

Practice Questions

p. 68

1

지문 해석 |

체육과에서 알립니다: 농구 시즌이 돌아옴에 따라 남자 농구팀이나 여자 농구팀 소속이 아닌 사람에게는 교내 경기장 내 탈의실 출입이 금지됩니다. 이러한 정책은 최근에 탈의실이 파손된 데 따른 것입니다. 학교측은 우리 팀을 위해서일 뿐 아니라 방문 팀들을 위해서도 이러한 시설들을 깨끗하고 정돈된 상태로 유지하기 원합니다. 탈의실에 들어가고자 하는 사람은 경비에 의해 건물에서 퇴실 조치될 것입니다.

Script |

W: How are you doing today, Bob?
M: I'm doing okay, although I'm kind of upset about today's announcement.
W: You mean about making the locker rooms off limits?
M: Yeah. It really is unfair. The tuition I pay should allow me to use all of the school's facilities, including the stadium and locker rooms. And I do use them regularly, along with a lot of other students. We shouldn't be punished just because someone vandalized the locker rooms one time.
W: Yeah, but they want to keep the locker rooms clean for the basketball players, people who need to use them.
M: Well, I need to use them, too. I have a gym class at the stadium every day, and I don't live very close to campus. I need to use those locker rooms right after my exercise in order to shower and clean up for a class right after that, and I keep my spare exercise clothes in those lockers.

Script 해석 |

여자: 잘 지내니, Bob?
남자: 잘 지내. 근데 오늘 공고 때문에 좀 화나네.
여자: 탈의실을 출입 금지한다는 그거 말이야?
남자: 그래, 정말 불공평한 일이야. 내가 내는 등록금으로 나는 학교의 모든 시설을 사용할 수 있는 권리가 있어. 경기장과 탈의실도 포함해서 말이야. 그리고 난 그곳을 정기적으로 이용한단 말이야. 많은 학생들도 마찬가지야. 누군가가 탈의실을 한 번 파손했다는 이유만으로 우리가 벌을 받아서는 안돼.
여자: 그래, 근데 학교측은 탈의실을 사용할 필요가 있는 농구 선수들을 위해서 탈의실을 깨끗하게 유지하고 싶어해.
남자: 글쎄, 나도 사용할 필요가 있는걸. 매일 경기장에서 체육 수업이 있고 난 학교에서 그다지 가까이 살지 않아. 난 운동 직후에 바로 다음 수업 때문에 샤워를 하고 깨끗이 씻기 위해서 탈의실을 사용해야 해. 그리고 내 여분의 운동복도 사물함에 보관해야 하고.

Reading
vandalize 파손하다
escort off 퇴실 조치되다

Listening
stadium 경기장
entitle 자격을 주다

Campus Tip!
미국 대학의 경우, 학비를 내면 등록금과 함께 학교시설을 이용하는 비용 (의료보험, Gym, 컴퓨터 lab, etc)이 함께 포함된다.

Reading note

Policy
  The locker rooms will be off limits to anybody who isn't on the basketball teams.

Reason
  Locker rooms being vandalized & keep facilities clean

Details
  - Whoever enters the locker rooms will be escorted off the premises by security.

Listening note

Opinion
  Disagree

Reason 1
  Unfair

Details
  - He pays tuition
  - Make people leave & only one instance

Reason 2
  Uses the locker rooms regularly

Details
  - After gym class, needs to clean up
  - Keep clothes in lockers

Sample Response |

The man is upset by the announcement that the stadium locker rooms will be off limits during basketball season. The first reason why he is upset is that he feels that this policy is unfair. He says that his tuition entitles him to use the locker rooms and any other school facility. He also points out that it's unfair to make people leave the stadium if they use the lockers just because of one instance of vandalism. His second reason for being upset is that he uses the locker room regularly. He showers and changes clothes in the locker rooms because he has a class immediately after gym class, and he lives too far from campus to clean up at home.

2

지문 해석 |

금요일에 도서 할인 판매가 있습니다: 이 공지는 교내 서점이 이번 금요일에 모든 중고 교재를 특가에 판매하는 행사를 연다는 것을 모든 학생들에게 알리고자 하는 것입니다. 판매되는 어떤 품목도 내년의 수업에 필요하지 않을 것입니다. 판매되는 모든 중고 교재들은 30퍼센트 할인되어 가격이 책정될 것이고 이번 특별 판매의 모든 수입은 지역 자선 단체에 기부될 것입니다. 중고 교재를 기증하기를 원하는 학생은 수요일 전에 서점에 들러 주십시오.

Script |

M: Hey, Beth! Are you doing okay?
W: Yeah, I'm alright today. Hey, did you hear about that book sale?
M: Oh, you mean the used book sale where the money goes to charity?
W: Yeah. I don't know about you, but I think that it's a waste of time.
M: Oh, really? How come?
W: Well, none of those books will be needed for classes next year. I guess that's why they decided to sell them at low prices instead of books that students will actually need. I mean, after all, the large majority of people who shop at the book store are just looking for books they need for class. I'd be surprised if anyone actually shows up.
M: Yeah, but it's for a good cause. All the money goes to charity.
W: You know, the college could sell other things if they want to raise money for charity. I mean, if people want to give money to charity, they will give money anyway—they won't buy a bunch of books that they don't need.

Script 해석 |

남자: 야, Beth! 안녕?
여자: 응. 안녕. 야, 도서 할인 행사 이야기 들었어?
남자: 아, 수입이 자선 단체에 기부되는 중고 서적 판매 말이지?
여자: 응, 너는 어떤지 모르겠는데 내 생각엔 시간 낭비 같아.
남자: 아, 정말? 왜?
여자: 음, 그 책들 중 어느 것도 내년 수업에 필요가 없을 거야. 그래서 서점이 학생들이 실제로 필요한 책이 아닌 중고 서적을 싼 값에 팔기로 한 이유라고 봐. 내 말은, 결국 서점에서 책을 사는 대다수의 사람들은 수업에 필요한 책을 찾는다는 거야. 그 행사에 과연 누가 올까 싶어.
남자: 그래, 그렇지만 좋은 의도로 하는 거잖아. 모든 수입이 자선 단체에 기부된다며.
여자: 알잖아. 학교가 자선 기금을 모으고자 한다면 다른 것들을 팔 수 있어. 내 말은, 사람들이 자선 단체에 기부하기 원한다면 어떻게든 기부할 것이라는 거야. 그렇지만 필요도 없는 책을 잔뜩 사지는 않을 거라고.

Reading
reminder 알리는 것, 상기시키는 것
mark down 책정하다, 표시하다

Listening
majority 대다수

Campus Tip!

미국 대학에서는 각 학교부서나 도서관 혹은 서점 등에서 필요하지 않은 물품이나 중고 서적 등을 평일 오후나 주말 오후에 사각 테이블 위에 올려 놓고 판매하는 모습을 어렵지 않게 볼 수 있다. 쓰던 물건이나 상품의 가치가 떨어진 물건 등을 좋은 목적으로 판매하기 때문에 일반적으로 판매율이 높은 편이다.

Reading note

Announcement
The campus book store will be holding a special sale of used books.

Details
- None will be required for classes next year
- 30% discount
- Give to local charities
- Donate your books before Wednesday

Listening note

Opinion
Disagree – Waste of time

Reason 1
Books aren't needed

Details
- Students only buy needed books
- Not many ppl. will show up

Reason 2
Good cause doesn't mean it will work

Details
- School can sell other things
- Students won't buy books for char.

Sample Response |

The woman thinks that the book sale for charity mentioned in the school newspaper is a waste of time. First off, she feels this way because the campus bookstore is selling books that will not be required for classes next year. According to the woman, students will only go to the bookstore for books they need, so there probably won't be many people there. Secondly, the woman thinks the fact that the book sale is for a good cause doesn't guarantee that it is actually going to work. She says that there are other ways to raise money for charity, and people will donate to charity if they want to. But she doesn't think students will buy books they don't need, even if it's for a good cause.

3

지문 해석 |

학과 관리처에서 알립니다: 신입생이 많이 들어옴에 따라 대학 측은 신입생들에게 내년에 3시간짜리 강의를 제공하기로 결정하였습니다. 이 강의는 일주일에 단 하루, 3시간 동안 진행되며, 모든 학부에서 입문 과정의 수업에서 제공될 것입니다. 학교 측은 이 수업을 신입생에게 제공할 뿐이지 필수 과목이 아니라는 점을 강조하는 바입니다. 이는 신입생들이 학과 시간표를 짜는 데 더 많은 선택 사항을 갖게 될 것을 의미할 뿐입니다.

Script |

W: Hey, Aaron. What's up?
M: Not much. Say, did you hear about those new three-hour courses being offered to freshmen?
W: Yeah. I don't know if that's such a good idea.
M: Actually, I think it's a great idea!
W: Really? Do you think freshmen could handle classes that only meet once a week?
M: Absolutely. Some freshmen will need those classes to free up their schedules. For example, they could take all of their classes in one or two days, and then they could use the rest of the week to work on whatever assignments they'd like. This will give them the chance to be more independent.
W: But do you think freshmen can do in-class work for three hours?
M: Well, freshmen don't have to take these classes, but it would be good preparation for those that do take them. Most of those new students will eventually have to take tests that last for several hours, or they will have to give hours-long presentations. This will let them know what that feels like.

Reading
introductory class
입문과정
academic schedule
학과 스케줄

Listening
absolutely 물론이야
free up 자유롭게 하다

Script 해석 |

여자: 야, Aron. 별일 없어?
남자: 응. 있지, 신입생에게 제공되는 새로운 세 시간짜리 수업에 대해 들었어?
여자: 응, 그게 그렇게 좋은 생각인지 모르겠어.
남자: 사실 난 아주 좋은 생각 같아!
여자: 정말? 신입생들이 일주일에 한 번만 하는 수업을 감당할 수 있을 것 같아?
남자: 물론이야. 어떤 신입생들은 스케줄을 자유롭게 짜는 데 그런 수업들이 필요할 거야. 예를 들면 하루나 이틀 동안 모든 수업을 듣고, 주중에 남는 날은 원하는 과제를 하는 데에 사용할 수 있을 거야. 보다 독립적일 수 있도록 기회를 주는 것이지.
여자: 하지만 신입생들이 세 시간 동안 수업을 들을 수 있을 것 같니?
남자: 글쎄, 신입생들은 이 수업을 들어야만 하는 게 아냐. 그렇지만 그 수업을 정말 듣는 학생들에게는 좋은 준비가 될 거야. 대부분의 신입생들은 나중에 몇 시간 걸리는 시험을 쳐야 하거나, 몇 시간 동안 발표를 해야 할 테니까. 이 수업이 학생들에게 그것이 어떤 건지 알게 해 줄 거야.

> **Campus Tip!**
> 미국 대학의 경우, 약 2년간 12학점의 외국어 과정을 포함하여 60학점의 교양교육과정을 이수해야 한다. 이는 모든 학생이 영어, 수학, 과학, 외국어 등과 같은 기본 교양 과목을 이수해야 한다는 뜻이다.

Reading note

Policy
  3-hour courses for freshmen

Reason
  Many new freshmen

Details
  - Courses meet once a week
  - Freshmen don't have to take them

Listening note

Opinion
  Agree

Reason 1
  Gives freshmen more options

Details
  - Can take classes only 2 days a week

Reason 2
  Good preparation for students

Details
  - Will have future tests and talks lasting several hours

Sample Response |

The man thinks that offering three-hour courses for freshmen is a good idea. First, he believes this because he thinks that classes that meet once a week will help students who want to free up their schedule. This will give them the option of having fewer days of classes. He believes that this will teach freshmen to be more independent. Second, he believes that the courses are good preparation. While freshmen don't have to take them, they can get ready for tests or presentations that last for several hours after getting a feel for them in a three hour introductory course.

4

지문 해석 |

독자 의견: 학교측이 주차 스티커를 꼬리표로 바꾸기로 한 데에 불만이 있습니다. 왜 이것이 필요하다고 생각했을까요? 이제 우리는 이 새로운 꼬리표를 백미러에 달아야 하고 그것은 제 시야를 방해합니다. 적어도 예전 스티커는 앞 유리 구석 보이지 않는 곳에 가려져 있었습니다. 아, 그리고 이 꼬리표들은 항상 떨어집니다. 적어도 주차 스티커는 차 창문에 붙어 있습니다!

2학년 학생

Script |

W: Hey, Allen! How's it going today?
M: I'm doing okay. Hey, did you read that letter in the newspaper?
W: What, you mean the one about the parking tags?
M: Yeah! What's up with that guy?
W: What do you mean?

Reading
parking sticker
  주차 스티커
tag 꼬리표
fall off 떨어지다

Listening
vehicle 자동차
whereas ~임에 반하여

M: Well, he loved the old stickers because a driver couldn't see them, but no one else could see them, either. I mean, with the tag, at least a campus cop knows to check for it on your rear view mirror. With the sticker, people would just place it anywhere on the car. It confused campus cops, who looked all over for the sticker.
W: But what about the fact that parking stickers stay in place? Don't the hanging tags fall off all the time?
M: Mine never has. Besides, the hanging tag can be transferred to different vehicles. If your car's broken and you need to park a different one on campus, then you can put your tag on the new car. With a sticker, you can't transfer it to different vehicles. If it's on a car, then you're stuck with that car.

Script 해석 |

여자: 야, Allen! 어떻게 지내니?
남자: 잘 지내, 아, 신문에 실린 독자 의견 봤어?
여자: 뭐, 주차 꼬리표에 관한 거 말이야?
남자: 그래! 걔 왜 그러니?
여자: 무슨 말이야?
남자: 그러니까, 그 사람은 예전 스티커를 무지 좋아했는데 그건 운전자에게 보이지 않기 때문이었어. 하지만 다른 사람도 그걸 볼 수가 없었지. 내 말은, 꼬리표는 적어도 교내 경찰이 백미러를 보면 그걸 확인할 수 있다는 걸 알잖아. 스티커는 사람들이 차 아무데나 그냥 붙이잖아. 그건 교내 경찰들을 혼란스럽게 했어. 스티커를 찾아 온 사방을 봐야 하니까.
여자: 그러면 주차 스티커가 제자리에 붙어 있다는 사실에 대해서는? 매다는 꼬리표는 늘 떨어지잖아?
남자: 내 것은 한번도 안 그랬어. 그리고 매단 꼬리표는 다른 차에도 옮길 수 있어. 만일 차가 고장 나서 다른 차를 학교에 세워야 하면 꼬리표를 새 차에 달 수 있어. 스티커로는 다른 차에 옮길 수가 없어. 만일 스티커가 한 차에 있다면 그 차만 써야 하는 거지.

Reading note

Policy
  Replace car stcks. w/ tags

Opinion
  Disagree

Details
- Tag messes w/ view
- Tag falls off

Listening note

Opinion
  Disagree

Reason 1
  Cmp. cops can find tags

Details
- Drvrs. put stkrs. All over car
- Confused cmp. cops

Reason 2
  Tags can be used on other cars

Details
- Can park with another car on campus
- Stckr. stuck to 1 car

Campus Tip!

일반적으로 종합 대학(National Universities)의 경우 캠퍼스 안에 여러 개의 주차장을 보유하고 있다. 이 주차장을 이용하기 위해서는 한 학기 동안 사용할 수 있는 주차 스티커를 구입해야 한다. 주차 스티커의 가격은 장소와 위치에 다라 다양하다.

Sample Response |

The man disagrees with the published letter and believes that hanging tags are better than parking stickers. His first reason for thinking this is because the parking stickers were difficult to find. The tag may get in the way of the driver's vision, but campus cops know that it is always on the rear view mirror and not anywhere on the car, as the parking stickers were. His second reason for preferring tags is because they can be used on different cars. Even though tags fall off the rear view mirror, they can be transferred to another vehicle if the car someone uses breaks down, whereas stickers were for only one car.

Vocabulary Study — Campus Life

p. 72

- maintenance office 관리 사무실
- off campus 대학 외부
- postgraduate 대학원생
- resident assistant 기숙사 조교
- mid-term test 중간 고사

- audit student 청강생
- loan 대출금
- gymnasium 체육관
- extracurricular activities 과외 활동
- academic year 학과 년도

- student council 학생회
- add/drop form 추가/제외 형식
- academic warning 학사 경고
- admissions committee 입학 위원회
- circulation desk 도서대출 계산대

- inter-library loan 도서관 연계대출
- writing sample 에세이 견본

- tuition 수업료
- transcript 성적증명서
- alumni 동문
- applicant 지원자
- assistant professor 조교수

- final test 기말고사
- handout 프린트물
- withdrawal 수업등록 철회
- job fair 채용 박람회
- academic adviser 지도교수

- advance registration 사전 등록
- study abroad program 해외연수 프로그램
- research paper 리설치 페이퍼
- prerequisite course 필수 과목
- liberal arts 인문학

- undergraduate 대학교 과정
- international student office 국제학생 사무실

정답 |

A
1. (e) 2. (b) 3. (a) 4. (f) 5. (c)
6. (j) 7. (h) 8. (g) 9. (i) 10. (d)

B
1. alumni 2. job fairs 3. academic warning 4. academic adviser 5. off campus

Task 4　General / Specific

Sample Question　　　　　　　　　　　　　　　　　　　　　　　　　　　　　　　　　p. 74

지문 해석 |

역할 갈등: 모든 사람은 살면서 다양한 역할을 수행한다. 한 남자는 아버지이자 남편일 수 있다. 이러한 역할들은 각각 완수해야 하는 일련의 책임을 수반한다. 역할 갈등은 한 역할에 부여된 책임들이 또 다른 역할의 책임들과 직접적으로 충돌할 때 발생하여, 두 역할 모두의 책임을 완수하는 것을 불가능하게 만든다. 역할 갈등은 한 역할의 책임을 포기하는 것으로 해결되어야 한다.

Script 해석 |

오늘 우리는 어떤 사람의 직업적 의무와 개인적인 의무가 충돌하는 상황에 대해 이야기해 보겠습니다. 예를 들어 변호사를 살펴보면, 변호사가 자신의 의뢰인이 기소 당한 범죄에 대해 유죄임을 알 수 있는 경우가 많이 있습니다. 이때, 의뢰인이 최선의 변호를 받도록 하는 것이 변호사의 임무입니다. 이는 의뢰인이 감옥에 가지 않도록 노력해야 함을 의미합니다. 그러나 분명한 것은, 책임 있는 시민으로서 변호사는 범죄자가 자유롭게 되는 것을 돕기 원하지 않는다는 것입니다. 그러면 그가 이 상황에서 어떻게 할 수 있을까요? 대부분의 경우에 변호사는 변호사로서의 의무가 더욱 중요하다고 스스로에게 타이르고, 그의 의뢰인을 자유롭게 해주기 위해 일합니다. 정신과 의사들도 유사하게 어려운 상황을 맞습니다. 정신과 의사의 의무 중 하나는 환자가 그에게 이야기하는 모든 것을 비밀로 하는 것입니다. 하지만 환자가 자신의 정신과 상담의에게 자해를 할 계획이라고 말한다고 가정해 봅시다. 이 경우에도 그 정신과 의사의 직업적인 책임은 이 비밀을 지키는 것이지만, 다른 사람의 안위를 걱정하는 사람으로서 정신과 의사는 누군가에게 그 환자가 자해하는 것을 막도록 이야기하고 싶을 것이 분명합니다. 이 경우에 정신과 의사는 자신의 궁극적 책임은 환자를 보호하는 것이라고 스스로에게 말할 것입니다. 비록 그것이 환자의 신뢰를 저버리는 것을 의미할지라도 말입니다.

Reading
impose 부여하다, 부과하다
contradict 충돌하다
abandon 포기하다

Listening
psychologist 정신과 의사
ultimate 궁극적인, 결정적인

❶ Outlining　　　　　　　　　　　　　　　　　　　　　　　　　　　　　　　　　　　p. 76

1

지문 해석 |

잡식성 동물이 갖는 이점: 잡식성의 동물들은 동물, 식물, 균류, 그리고 분해 물질들을 포함하는 온갖 종류의 유기체를 먹고 산다. 잡식성인 것은 이러한 동물들에게 중요한 이점을 준다. 완전히 육식성인 동물의 몸은 영양 성분을 다른 동물에게서만 흡수할 수 있는 반면, 잡식성인 동물은 먹을 수 있는 어떤 유기 물질도 소화할 수 있는 능력을 갖고 있다. 그래서 잡식성의 동물들은 환경의 변화에 따라 그들의 식량원을 얻을 수 없게 될 경우, 필요한 영양소를 얻는 데 유연성을 갖는다. 만일 어떤 잡식성 동물이 일차적으로는 고기와 채소에 의존한다 해도, 정상적인 식사가 어려워지면 대체 식량원을 이용할 수 있다.

Script |

Let's talk about ways that animals can go extinct. Sometimes animals will go extinct because they can't adapt to subtle habitat changes, like the removal of other species from their environment. For instance, say that the gazelle population of an area suddenly died off from an epidemic disease. This would have dramatic effects on the animals that prey on these gazelles. For instance, large cats that hunt them, like lions, would eventually die off, too. Felines have a digestive system that is designed specifically for digesting meat; without any animals to feed on, they too would become extinct.

Wild dogs, on the other hand, could possibly thrive. Now, wild dogs are also predators, and as such they will primarily eat whatever animals they can hunt down. However, wild dogs can subsist on things like nuts, fruits, and even grass if they absolutely have to. This allows them to survive periods of time when prey are low in number and meat is unavailable. Thus, even if the gazelles died off, the wild dogs in that area could find potential sources of food.

Script 해석 |

동물들이 멸종하는 과정에 대해 이야기해 봅시다. 때로 동물들은 환경에서 다른 종들이 없어지는 것과 같은 서식지의 미세한 변화에 적응하지 못하여 멸종합니다. 예를 들면 가젤 영양류*가 전염병으로 갑자기 전멸했다고 가정해 봅시다. 이는 가젤 영양을 먹이로 하는

Reading
omnivorous 잡식성의
fungi 균류 (s. fungus)
decomposing material
　분해 물질
crucial 중요한
assimilate 흡수하다
flexibility 유연성
sustenance 영양소
environmental change
　환경의 변화
alternative 대체, 대안
disrupt
　어려워지다, 두절되다

Listening
extinct 멸종된
habitat 서식지
epidemic disease
　전염병
digestive system
　소화 체계

동물들에게 심각한 영향을 미칠 것입니다. 예를 들면 가젤 영양을 사냥하는 사자와 같은 큰 고양이과의 동물들도 결국 죽게 될 것입니다. 고양이과의 동물들은 특별히 고기를 소화시키도록 만들어진 소화 체계를 갖고 있습니다. 먹을 동물이 아무것도 없게 된 고양이과 동물들은 같이 멸종하게 될 것입니다.

반면 야생 개들은 살아남을 수도 있습니다. 자, 야생 개들 또한 육식동물이고, 그렇기 때문에 그들이 주로 사냥하는 어떤 동물이든 먹습니다. 하지만 야생 개들은 절대적인 필요가 있을 경우 견과류와 과일, 심지어 풀로 생존할 수 있습니다. 이러한 점 때문에 야생 개들은 먹이의 수가 적고 고기를 얻을 수 없는 시기를 견딜 수 있습니다. 그래서 가젤 영양이 멸종되어도 야생 개들은 그 지역에서 잠재적 식량원을 찾을 수 있을 것입니다.

*가젤 영양류(gazelle): 소목, 소과 가젤속에 속하는 영양류

2

지문 해석 |

비극적 결함: 비극적 결함은 문학 작품이나 극중 인물의 특징으로, 스스로를 파멸로 이끄는 원인이 된다. 인물이 어떤 면에서는 비범하지만, 그의 비극적 결함은 성격의 도덕적인 결함이거나 그가 저지르는 실수이고, 그것은 언제나 그 인물의 성격에 중요한 요소이다. 더욱이 그 인물은 비범하기 때문에 또한 매우 많은 권력을 갖고 있다. 그가 굉장히 많은 권력을 휘두르기 때문에 그의 비극적 결함은 자신에게도, 이야기 속의 다른 인물들에게도 비참한 결과를 가져온다.

Script |

Alright, class, today we're going to talk about one of Shakespeare's greatest dramatic works, *Othello*. Here's the main plot of the story: in medieval Venice, the great general Othello succumbs to jealousy and kills his wife, destroying several other lives in the process. This gruesome ending comes about because of two factors: Othello's passion and his power.

First, passion is what drives all of Othello's actions. His passion makes him a fearsome warrior, which eventually turns him from a slave into a powerful general. His passion also wins the love of his beautiful wife. However, Othello's passion also helps destroy him. Because he loves his wife so intensely, Othello becomes passionately enraged when he mistakenly believes that she is unfaithful to him, and this causes him to kill her. Second, Othello's power brings about the play's grisly ending. Othello's passion by itself would only hurt him. However, he also has a great amount of power, so once his misguided passion corrupts him, he uses this great power for revenge. For instance, in a jealous rage, he uses his soldiers to try to assassinate his former friend. Not only that, but his suicide deprives Venice of a skilled warrior. The absence of this powerful general leaves his country vulnerable to an invading army at the end.

Script 해석 |

자, 여러분, 오늘 우리는 셰익스피어의 위대한 희곡 작품 중 하나인 『오셀로』에 대해 이야기해 보겠습니다. 이야기의 주된 줄거리는 이러합니다. 중세 베니스에서 위대한 장군 오셀로는 질투심에 사로잡혀 부인을 죽이고, 그 과정에서 여러 다른 사람들을 죽이게 됩니다. 이 섬뜩한 결말은 두 가지 요소로 인하여 발생하는데, 그것은 오셀로의 열정과 그의 권력입니다.

첫째, 열정은 오셀로의 모든 행동의 동기입니다. 그의 열정은 그를 무서운 전사로 만들어, 결국에는 그를 노예에서 막강한 장군으로 변모시킵니다. 그의 열정은 또한 아름다운 아내의 사랑을 쟁취합니다. 하지만 오셀로의 열정은 자신을 파괴하는 데도 역할을 합니다. 그는 부인을 너무 강렬하게 사랑해서 부인이 자신을 배신했다고 오해하였을 때 격노하게 되고 이러한 정황이 그로 하여금 부인을 죽이게 합니다.

둘째로는 오셀로의 권력이 극의 소름 끼치는 결말을 야기합니다. 오셀로의 열정 자체는 자신만을 해칠 뿐입니다. 그러나 그는 또한 막강한 권력을 갖고 있어서, 잘못된 열정이 그를 한 번 타락시키자, 그는 이 거대한 권력을 복수에 사용합니다. 예를 들어, 질투심에 격노하여 그는 군인들을 시켜 자신의 옛 친구를 암살합니다. 그 뿐 아니라, 그의 자살로 인해 베니스는 노련한 전사를 잃게 됩니다. 이 막강한 장군의 부재는 결국 그의 나라를 침략군에게 저항할 수 없게 만듭니다.

Reading
- literary 문학 작품
- destruction 파멸
- remarkable 비범한
- essential 중요한
- consequence 결과

Listening
- medieval 중세
- succumb 사로잡히다, 굴복하다
- gruesome 섬뜩한, 소름끼치는
- fearsome 무서운
- grisly 소름끼치는, 무서운
- assassinate 암살하다
- deprive 잃다
- vulnerable 저항할 수 없는, 상하기 쉬운

Reading note

Topic
  Tragic flaw

Main Idea
  Trait that leads character to doom

Listening note

Example 1
  Othello: passion

Details
- Good pas.: O. as general, loves beautiful wife
- Bad pas.: becomes jealous because of wife, kills her

Details	Example 2
- Character is remarkable & powerful - T. flaw is moral flaw or mistake - T. flaw means disaster for others	Otheello : Power **Detail** - Power makes him take wrong revenge on friend - O's power: death means Venice has no gen. left.

Definition The passion and power of Othello is related to the concept of the tragic flaw because these two traits are the tragic flaws that lead to Othello's destruction.

Citation According to the professor, passion is essential to Othello's character because it drives his actions, such as becoming a powerful general and marrying a beautiful woman. However, passion becomes Othello's moral imperfection when it causes him to become jealous and kill his wife.

Explanation The professor continues to show how Othello's case illustrates the tragic flaws by discussing the consequences Othello's excessive passion has in the end. Since he is a remarkable figure with so much power, his tragic flaws have disastrous consequences. For instance, he tries to have his soldiers assassinate his former friend, and his death leaves Venice almost defenseless.

Practice Questions

p. 82

1

지문 해석 |

행동 수정: 행동 수정은 심리요법에서 통제자들이 한 사람의 행동을 변화시키거나 통제하기 위해 사용하는 기법이다. 통제자는 강화와 처벌이라는 두 가지 다른 방법으로 한 사람의 행동을 수정할 수 있다. 강화는 통제자가 원하는 방식으로 행동할 때, 그 사람에게 보상하는 것과 관련된다. 반면, 처벌은 그 사람이 부적절하게 행동하였을 때, 불쾌한 조건들을 가하는 것과 관련된 것이다. 두 가지 행동 수정 방식 모두 사람들이 온갖 종류의 상황과 조건들에 적응하는 데 쓰인다.

Script |

Today we are going to talk about controlling the students in your classroom. Now, you obviously can't tolerate disruptive behavior, or else you will quickly lose control of the class. So what can you do? Well, the most successful thing to do is to reward students for doing their work and maintaining good conduct. For younger students, you can give out candy if they do well on a test. For older students who work hard or behave themselves, you can let them study in the library during in-class work periods. This shows the students that good behavior is rewarded, and many will work accordingly for these benefits.

Now, it is necessary to openly discourage improper conduct in students, so you must establish penalties for students who insist on breaking the rules. A rather dull or tedious punishment will get your more troublesome students to shape up. By not letting an unruly child draw pictures in class, or by uing detention to teenagers who want to get out of school as soon as possible, you will teach them to cooperate. After all, if they don't do things the teacher's way, then they won't get their own way, either.

Script 해석 |

오늘 우리는 여러분 교실의 학생들을 통제하는 것에 관해 이야기할 것입니다. 자, 여러분은 분명 분열을 일으키는 행동을 참지 못하죠, 아니라면 여러분은 곧 교실을 통제할 수 없게 돼 버릴 겁니다. 그렇다면 여러분은 어떻게 해야 할까요? 글쎄요, 가장 성공적인 방법은 학생들에게 그들이 해야 할 일을 하고 바람직한 행동을 유지하는 것에 대한 보상을 해주는 것입니다. 어린 학생들이 시험에서 좋은 성적

Reading
modification 수정
psychotherapy 심리 요법
reinforcement 강화
undesirably 부적절하게

Listening
tolerate 참다, 용서하다
disruptive 분열을 일으키는
tedious 뻔한, 지루한
troublesome 문제 있는
unruly 제멋대로인
detention 못하게 함, 저지

을 거두었다면, 여러분은 그들에게 사탕을 나누어 줄 수 있습니다. 공부를 열심히 하거나 스스로 바르게 행동하는 더 큰 학생들에게는 교실 내 활동 시간 동안 도서관에서 공부하게 해 줄 수 있습니다.

이는 학생들에게 바람직한 행동은 보상을 받는다는 걸 보여주고, 따라서 많은 학생들이 이러한 이익을 얻기 위해 열심히 공부할 것입니다. 그렇다면, 학생들의 부적절한 행동은 공공연하게 그만두게 할 필요가 있으므로, 여러분은 규칙을 계속적으로 위반한 학생들에 대한 벌칙을 마련해야 합니다. 다소 정도가 약하고 뻔한 벌칙은 더 많은 문제 학생들이 생겨 나도록 합니다. 제멋대로인 아이에게 교실에서 그림을 그리지 못하게 함으로써, 또는 가능한 빨리 학교에서 벗어나려고 하는 십대에게 방과 후 남는 벌을 내림으로써 여러분은 그들에게 협력하는 것을 가르칠 수 있습니다. 결국, 그들은 교사의 생각대로 행동하지 않으면, 자신들이 원하는 대로도 하지 못하는 겁니다.

Reading note

Topic
  Behavior modification

Main Idea
  Administrators' technique to change or control a person's behavior.

Details
  - Reinforcement & punishment

Listening note

Example 1
  Reinforcement: reward good students in class

Details
  - For young stu.: give candy if they do well on a test
  - Reward good students in class

Example 2
  Punishment: penalties for bad students

Details
  - Forbid stu. to draw pic.
  - Give detention

Sample Response |

The professor's discussion on rewarding and punishing students relates to the concept of behavior modification. The professor first talks about reinforcement by giving an example of rewarding good students in class. Rewarding students for good behavior, like candy for a good test grade or study time in the library for good conduct, is an example of reinforcement because the teacher desires this behavior and wants the students to keep giving these results. After that, the professor discusses another way of behavior modification, which is punishment, by talking about punishing students for bad behavior. Assigning detention or forbidding children to draw are examples of punishment, which is the application of unpleasant conditions so the students won't repeat bad behavior. Both methods of behavior modification can be used to correct undesirable behavior.

2

지문 해석 |

기회비용: 기회비용은 누군가가 한 가지 상품을 생산하거나 구입하려는 선택을 할 때, 또 다른 상품에 대해서 입어야만 하는 손실이다. 이러한 손실은 물질적인 것 또는 기회적인 것 둘 다가 될 수 있다. 그 사람은 두 가지 선택물을 모두 얻기에는 필요한 자원이 부족하기 때문에, 두 가지 상품 중 선택이 이루어져야만 한다. 그 사람은 그 둘을 모두 얻을 수 없기에, 보통 선택한 상품의 질이나 양이 그것의 전체 기회비용을 능가하는 선택물을 고르게 된다.

Script |

Okay, today we're going to talk about why entrepreneurs carefully study public demand for various goods. Before an entrepreneur can make his fortune, he must decide on what kind of business he'd like to start. Now, when most of these ambitious people start, they can only afford one business. Thus, they must fully consider their options. If they decide to build cars, then they probably won't be able to build houses as well, because both industries are intensive, and either one would take up all of their money, land, or labor. This is where an entrepreneur studies the public demand for goods. He will usually see which industry has the most customers at a certain place or time. Usually, by reaching more customers in a given market, he can make more money. He does this in order to maximize his profits. For example, if he chooses to make cars instead of houses, it's because he feels that he can make enough money selling cars to compensate for the money he loses by not selling houses.

Reading
outweigh 능가하다, 뛰어넘다

Listening
entrepreneur 기업가, 사업주
intensive 집약적, 집중적
maximize 최대화하다
compensate 보상하다

Task 4. General / Specific

Script 해석 |
자, 오늘 우리는 기업가들이 다양한 상품들에 대한 공공의 수요를 신중하게 연구하는 이유에 대해 이야기해 보기로 하겠습니다. 한 기업가는 성공하기 이전에, 어떤 유형의 사업을 시작하면 좋을지에 대해 결정해야만 합니다. 자, 이러한 야심가들은 대부분 처음 시작할 때, 단 하나의 사업을 시작할 여유밖에 되지 않습니다. 따라서, 그들은 자신들이 선택할 수 있는 것들을 면밀하게 고려해 보아야 합니다. 그들이 자동차를 제조하기로 결정하고 나면 주택 건축까지 할 수는 없게 될 것입니다. 왜냐하면 두 산업 모두 집약적이라, 그들의 모든 돈과, 토지 또는 노동력을 둘 중 하나에만 들여야 하기 때문입니다. 이것이 기업가가 상품들에 대한 공공의 수요를 연구하는 이유입니다. 그는 보통 특정한 장소와 시기에 어떤 산업이 최대의 고객을 가지는지를 알게 될 것입니다. 주로, 그는 주어진 시장에서 더 많은 고객을 얻게 됨으로써 더 많은 돈을 벌 수 있습니다. 그는 자신의 이익을 최대화하기 위해 이렇게 합니다. 예를 들어, 그가 집 대신 차를 제조하길 선택했다면 그것은 그가 자동차를 판매함으로써, 집을 판매하지 않음으로써 입게 되는 손해액을 보상하기에 충분한 돈을 벌 수 있다고 생각하기 때문입니다.

Reading note

Topic
Opportunity cost

Main Idea
Someone's losses when choosing to produce or purchase one product over another product.

Details
- The person can't have both options.
- Choose one that is better in quality or quantity

Listening note

Example 1
Entrepreneur starting a business

Details
- Gets to choose one business (has $, land, lab. For 1 business)
- Studies demand for goods: cars & houses
- Decides which bus. has more demand
- Wants choice w/ max. profits
- Profits from cars comp. for not selling houses

Sample Response |
According to the reading passage, opportunity costs are losses in choosing one product over another. The professor explains this concept by giving an example of an entrepreneur who's starting a business. The professor discusses how an entrepreneur must choose one business because he lacks the material resources for multiple businesses. For instance, he cannot build both cars and houses, because he only has enough money, land, and labor for one. Then, the professor mentions that entrepreneurs study opportunity costs because they want the benefits of a chosen product to outweigh the opportunity costs. Thus, if one can make more money selling cars than he would lose by not selling houses, then he'll make cars in order to maximize his profits.

3

지문 해석 |
신경계: 신경계는 본질적으로 신체의 모든 자율/비자율 기관들의 기능과 근육 운동을 조절하는 신경들의 망입니다. 이 계통의 가장 중요한 특징들 중 하나는 신체 기능들을 자율 활동과 비자율 활동으로 구분한다는 것입니다. 생명을 유지하는 데 필수적인 신체 기능들은 자동적으로 신경계에 의해 통제되어, 인간은 본질적으로 그것들을 통제하지 못합니다. 한편 신경계는 인간이 특정 근육들에 대해 의식적 통제를 명령할 수 있게 하기도 합니다. 이는 인간이 유익한 부수적인 과업들을 자기 의지에 따라 수행하도록 해줍니다.

Script |
Humans, like most other animals, have a series of different organs, all used for different tasks. One benefit animals get from this complex set of organs is the division between voluntary actions and involuntary actions. First, many muscle and organ functions, like respiration, heartbeat, and salivation are involuntary. This is because these tasks are necessary, and they must be performed continuously. So, our unconscious mind takes care of that for us. For example, our hearts must pump blood through the body every second. Thus, our brain automatically orders the heart to constantly perform this task so we don't have to always monitor it.
So how, you may ask, does having separate voluntary organic functions help us? Well, this division allows us to concentrate all of our attention on voluntary actions like using our skeletal muscles or five senses. We can move

Reading
regulate 조절하다
biological 생리적인, 생물학적인
auxiliary 부수적인
volition 의지

Listening
respiration 호흡
heartbeat 심장박동
salivation 타액분비
detect 식별하다, 탐지하다
external stimuli 외부 자극
extinguish (불을) 끄다

around or focus our vision on certain objects whenever we must. Because of separate voluntary actions, we can adapt to our environment by detecting and reacting to external stimuli. For instance, you can use all the physical energy you need to see a fire and physically avoid it, or you can also extinguish it, depending on what is necessary.

Script 해석 |

인간들은, 대부분의 다른 동물들처럼 모두 다른 과업들에 사용되는 일련의 다양한 기관들을 가지고 있습니다. 동물들이 이처럼 복잡한 일련의 기관들을 가지는 것에서 얻게 되는 한 가지 장점은 자율 활동과 비자율 활동 사이의 구분이라는 것입니다. 먼저, 호흡, 심박동, 그리고 타액 분비 같은 많은 근육/기관 기능들은 비자율적입니다. 이는 이러한 활동들이 필수적이고 계속적으로 수행되어야만 하기 때문입니다. 따라서, 우리의 무의식적인 정신은 우리를 대신해 그것을 관장합니다. 예를 들어, 우리의 심장은 매 순간 혈액을 신체 곳곳으로 공급해야만 합니다. 따라서 우리 뇌는 심장에게 끊임없이 이 과업을 수행하도록 자동적으로 명령하여, 우리가 항상 그것을 감시할 필요는 없습니다.

그렇다면 여러분들은 개별적인 자율기관 기능들을 갖는 것이 우리에게 이로운지 물을 수 있습니다. 자, 이 영역은 우리가 골격근이나 오감의 사용 같은 자율 활동들에 주의를 집중시킬 수 있게 해주는데요. 우리는 필요할 때, 여기저기 돌아다니거나 혹은 우리 시각의 초점을 특정 물체들에 둘 수 있습니다. 각각의 자율 활동들 덕택에 우리는 외부 자극을 식별하고 반응함으로써 우리 환경에 적응할 수 있습니다. 예를 들면, 우리는 불을 발견하고 신체적으로 그것을 피하기 위해 필요한 모든 신체적 에너지를 사용할 수 있습니다. 혹은 필요에 따라 그 불을 끌 수도 있습니다.

Reading note

Topic
Nervous system

Main Idea
NS regulates vol. & invol. bio. functions

Details
- Divides functions into vol. & invol.
- Nec. functions are auto.
- Org. has consc. control over some musc.
- Vol. control is helpful

Listening note

Example 1
Involuntary functions: resp., heart, saliv.

Details
- Tasks are nec.
- Unconsciously done
- Don't have to monitor them

Example 2
Voluntary functions: skel. musc., 5 senses

Details
- Free to focus on vol. func.
- Can adapt to ext. env.
- Ex. Avoid or put out fire

Sample Response |

The professor's discussion about voluntary and involuntary organic functions in humans demonstrates the functioning of the nervous system. First, the professor mentions that involuntary functions of organs are separated from the voluntary functions. This is because involuntary functions are needed to stay alive, so people don't have to constantly monitor actions like heartbeat, respiration, and salivation. Thus, humans have no control over these automatic functions. Second, the professor explains that this division between different functions helps people because they can voluntarily perform actions to adapt to their environment, such as moving, focusing eyesight, and avoiding fires. These are auxiliary tasks we consciously control, so we can choose to do them whenever we need to.

4

지문 해석 |

단기 기억: 단기 기억은 인간 기억의 한 부분으로, 적은 양의 정보를 단시간 동안 저장하는 데 쓰인다. 단기 기억에 저장된 정보는 누군가에게 즉시로 사용 가능하지만 소멸과 간섭이라는 두 가지 다른 방식을 통해 사라질 수 있다. 소멸은 단기 기억 내의 자주 사용되지 않는 정보가 점차 사라지는 것이다. 간섭은 새로운 정보를 습득하거나 암기하는 것으로 단기 기억이 차단되는 것이다.

Task 4. General / Specific

Script |
Today, we're going to talk about some of the mental techniques people use to remember information. By adjusting the scope and quantity of learned information, people are able to remember more facts for longer periods of time.

First, people can remember facts more easily if they are able to apply them in repetitious exercises. Like regular exercise for the muscles, constantly reviewing a piece of information will prevent its removal from the memory. For example, when you study for a chemistry exam, you can remember the order of elements on a periodic table by constantly reviewing it until recalling it is as natural as remembering the alphabet.

Second, people also remember facts better if they don't try to learn too much information at one time. Instead, they thoroughly examine one piece of information until they know it, and then build upon that knowledge with other facts. For example, they won't try to memorize the elements while studying chemical reactions. This will only confuse them, and they'll forget everything about both subjects.

Reading
vanish 사라지다
decay 소멸
interference 간섭

Listening
repetitious 반복적인
thoroughly 철저하게
chemical reaction 화학 반응

Script 해석 |
우리는 오늘 사람들이 정보를 기억하기 위해 사용하는 정신적인 기법 몇 가지에 대해 이야기해 보겠습니다. 사람들은 습득한 정보의 범위와 양을 조절함으로써 더 많은 정보를 더 오랜 시간 동안 기억할 수 있습니다.

첫째로, 사람들이 정보들을 반복적인 연습에 적용할 수 있다면, 더욱 쉽게 그것들을 기억할 수 있습니다. 규칙적인 근육 운동처럼, 지속적으로 하나의 정보를 복습하는 것은 그것이 기억으로부터 사라지는 것을 막을 수 있습니다. 예를 들어 여러분이 화학 시험을 위해 공부를 할 때, 주기율 표의 원소 순서를 알파벳처럼 자연스럽게 떠올릴 수 있을 때까지 계속해서 복습함으로써 기억해 낼 수 있습니다.

두 번째로, 사람들이 너무 많은 정보를 한꺼번에 습득하려 하지 않는다면, 더 잘 기억할 수 있습니다. 대신에 사람들은 하나의 정보에 대해 알 때까지 그것을 철저하게 검토한 다음, 그 지식을 다른 사실들과 함께 축적시킵니다. 예를 들면, 사람들은 화학 반응을 학습하면서 동시에 원소들을 외우려 하지는 않을 것입니다. 이는 그들을 혼란스럽게 할 뿐이며, 두 가지 주제에 관한 모든 것을 망각하게 할 것입니다.

Reading note

Policy
  Short term memory

Opinion
  Stores small bits of info. for short time

Reason
  - S-term memory is easily avble.
  - Decay: S-term dis. If not applied
  - Interference: Dis. If new info is learned

Listening note

Example 1
  Decay: repeatedly apply s-term info. Ex) Study per. table until it's like alphabet

Details
  - Applications keep s-term memory fresh
  - Prevents decay of s-term memory

Example 2
  Interference: study one thing at a time. Ex) don't study elem. & chem. reactions at once.

Details
  - Too much info at once can be confusing
  - Can cause interference & block s-term mem.

Sample Response |
The professor's discussion about ways to study for a chemistry exam relates to short term memory because these ways help prevent the disappearance of information from short term memory, which stores a little information for a short time. The professor begins by discussing how applying facts in repetitious exercises, like constantly reviewing the periodic table, will retain information in the short term memory. This prevents the decay of short term memory that isn't repeatedly applied. Second, the professor discusses how studying one piece of information at a time will prevent confusion and forgetting facts, such as trying to study both elements and chemical reactions at once. This is an example of how to prevent interference, where too much new information blocks retention in the short term memory.

Vocabulary Study — Lectures   p. 86

Psychology

- intuition 직감
- amnesia 기억 상실
- retarded 지능 발달이 늦은
- empathy (남에 대한) 공감, 감정 이입
- insight 통찰력
- egocentric 자기 중심적인
- illusion 환각
- cognition 인지
- insanity 광기
- impulse 충동

Business/ Economics

- acquisition 획득
- facilitate 촉진시키다
- conflict 충돌, 싸움
- enthusiasm 열의
- socialize 사교적으로 활동하다
- subsidize (원조를 얻어) 일정액을 지불하다
- tariff 관세
- welfare 복지
- monopoly 독점
- prosperity 번영

Biology

- replicate 복제하다
- absorb 흡수하다
- stimulate 흥분시키다
- inhibit 억제하다
- bipolar 양극의
- deprive (사람, 물건, 권리 등을) 빼앗다
- discriminate 차별하다
- cacophony 불협화음
- velocity 속도
- receptive 수용하는

Art & Literature

- catharsis 카타르시스, 정화법
- explicit 명쾌한, 숨김없는
- spontaneous 자연히 일어나는, 자발적인
- fallacy 착오, 오류
- inference 추론
- extrinsic 외부의
- resentment 분노
- suppress 억제하다, 숨기다
- integrity 정직, 청렴
- manifest 명백한

정답 | **A** 1. (d)   2. (f)   3. (h)   4. (a)   5. (j)
         6. (i)   7. (g)   8. (c)   9. (b)   10. (e)

B 1. discriminate   2. spontaneous   3. facilitate   4. replicate   5. integrity

Task 5 Problem & Solution

Sample Question   p. 88

Script 해석 |

남자: 안녕, Helen! 오늘 기분 어떠니?
여자: 괜찮아, 그런데 문제가 좀 있어.
남자: 어? 그래, 그게 뭔데?
여자: 응, 이 영어 논문 마감이 금요일까지인데 인용에 사용할 어떤 책을 찾아야 해. 문제는 도서관에 이 책이 없다는 거야. 그래서 정말 어떻게 할지 모르겠어.
남자: 그렇다면, 한 가지 제안이 있는데. 넌 근처 서점에서 그 책을 구입할 수 있다는 거야. 학교 안팎에는 네가 찾고 있는 책이 있을 만한 서점들이 많이 있거든. 네가 그걸 사면 넌 책장에 메모를 할 수도 있을 거야.
여자: 그래, 하지만 난 새 책 한 권에 돈을 쓰고 싶진 않거든.
남자: 네가 할 수 있는 또 다른 선택은 인터넷에 접속해 그 책에서 발췌된 지문들을 찾을 수 있는지 보는 거야. 다양한 책들에서 몇 장의 페이지나 혹은 이따금씩 전체 단원들까지도 제공하는 학문용 웹사이트들이 많거든. 거기엔 아마 네가 논문을 위해 필요로 하는 정보들이 있을지도 몰라. 게다가, 그건 아무런 비용도 들지 않는다구.
여자: 지금 당장은 어떻게 해야 할지 정말 모르겠다.

quotation 인용
nearby 근처의

 Outlining   p. 90

1

Script |

W: Justin! It's good to see you! How are you today?
M: I'm actually kind of stressed out by a class project.
W: What kind of project is it?
M: Well, I have to interview a professor for my Teacher's Education class. I set up a meeting with my history professor, but it turns out that he's on a field trip today. This project is due in a week, and it's going to be a lot of work writing up the interview. What can I do?
W: I suppose that one option for you is to interview him later. I'm sure that he can find time in his schedule, and it will give you more time to prepare your questions. Plus, you can work on the rest of your project in the meantime.
M: Yeah, but THAT is a lot of work.
W: Well, you could also set up an interview with a different professor. I know that there are several professors who could do one today. Now you might have to change a lot of your questions, but you'd have more time to work on the project next week.
M: Let me think about it.

Teacher's Education class 교사 교육학 수업
field trip 현장학습

Campus Tip!
미국 대학에서는 경험을 통한 학습을 중요시 하는 경향이 있어서 research paper, team projects, interview projects 등과 같이 직접 경험을 통해 학습 할 수 있도록 한 과목에 많게는 두세 개의 프로젝트가 진행되기도 한다.

Script 해석 |

여자: Justin! 만나서 반갑다! 잘 지내지?
남자: 나 사실 수업 프로젝트 때문에 좀 스트레스를 받고 있어.
여자: 무슨 프로젝트인데 그래?
남자: 응, 내가 듣는 교사 교육학 수업 때문에 교수님을 한 분 인터뷰해야 하거든. 우리 역사 교수님과 만나기로 약속을 잡아 놓았는데, 그 분이 오늘 현장학습 중이라는 걸 알았어. 이 프로젝트는 일주일 후에 마감이야, 그리고 인터뷰를 기술하는 건 큰 일일 텐데. 어떻게 해야 하지?
여자: 내 생각에 한 가지 선택은 네가 나중에 그 분을 인터뷰하는 거야. 그는 분명 자신의 스케줄에서 틈을 낼 수 있을 거고, 넌 질문들

을 준비할 수 있는 시간이 더 생기게 되는 거지. 게다가, 넌 그 동안에 나머지 프로젝트 일을 할 수도 있어.
남자: 그래, 하지만 그건 일이 많다구.
여자: 그렇다면 넌 다른 교수님과의 인터뷰를 잡을 수도 있어. 내가 알기론 오늘 네가 인터뷰할 수 있는 교수님이 여러 분 계셔. 그럼 넌 네 질문들을 바꿔야만 하겠지. 하지만 다음 주엔 프로젝트에 전념할 시간이 더 많이 생기잖아.
남자: 거기에 대해 생각해 봐야겠다.

2

Script |

W: Oh, hi, Harvey. Are you doing alright today?
M: Yeah, I guess.
W: Hmm. It sounds like something's bothering you. What's the matter?
M: It's the college newspaper. I'm the editor this semester, and the guy who writes our movie reviews is going to quit soon. It will take a couple of weeks to replace him, and I don't know what to do until then.
W: I've got an idea. Why don't you split movie-reviewing duties among your staff? Have one writer do the movie review one week, another writer do it the next week, and so on. If everyone does a little extra work, you'll still have a movie review each issue.
M: It could work, although everyone on the newspaper staff is pretty busy.
W: Oh, well, here's something else you can do. You could reprint the movie reviews that are published in the city newspaper. Now, it will probably cost some money to get the city newspaper's permission. I don't know how much, but newspapers do it all the time. Plus, none of your reporters would have to do any extra writing.
M: Yeah, this will be a tough choice.

bother 곤란하게 하다, 괴롭히다
movie-reviewing duty 영화평론 업무
permission 허가

Campus Tip!
미국에서는 학생들이 어려서부터 일을 하는 것을 자연스럽게 생각한다. 대학에 가면 학생들을 위한 일자리가 수도 없이 많다. 그래서 원하기만 한다면 정부가 지원하는 work study program 혹은 internship 그 외 teaching assistant, library student assistant, dormitory staff 등으로 여러 방면에서 수업과 병행하여 부분적인 직장 생활을 경험할 수 있다. 또한 글 쓰는 것에 소질이 있다면 editor로도 일할 수 있는 기회는 언제든 열려있다.

Script 해석 |

여자: 오, 안녕, Harvey. 오늘 기분 괜찮지?
남자: 응, 그런 것 같아.
여자: 음, 뭔가 널 곤란하게 하는 일이 있는 것 같은데. 무슨 일이야?
남자: 대학신문 때문이야. 내가 이번 학기 에디터인데, 우리 신문에 영화 평론을 쓰는 남자가 곧 그만둘 거야. 그를 대체할 사람을 찾으려면 2~3주는 걸릴 텐데, 그때까지 난 어떻게 해야 할지 모르겠어.
여자: 내게 생각이 있어. 너희 직원들끼리 영화 평론 업무를 나누어서 하면 어떻겠니? 한 주는 한 작가가 영화 평론 일을 하게 하고, 그 다음 주는 다른 작가가 하는 식으로 계속 가는 거야. 모두가 조금씩 추가 업무를 한다면, 매번 발행되는 신문에 영화 평론이 계속 실릴 수 있겠지.
남자: 그것도 좋겠지만 신문반의 모든 직원들이 매우 바쁜걸.
여자: 오, 그렇다면 네가 할 수 있는 게 또 하나 있어. 넌 도시 신문에 발행된 영화 평론들을 다시 실을 수도 있어. 음, 아마 도시 신문의 허가를 얻는 데 비용이 좀 들 거야. 얼마만큼인지는 모르겠지만 신문사들을 매번 그렇게 하더라구. 게다가 너희 기자들 중 아무도 추가 집필을 하지 않아도 되고 말이야.
남자: 그래, 이것 참 어려운 선택이다.

Listening note

Problem
  Movie reviewer quits sch. paper
  - Will take a few weeks to replace

Solution 1
  Split duty among staff
  - Diff. writer does review each wk. Extra work for staff

Solution 2
  Reprint reviews from city paper
  - Cost $ to reprint reviews. No extra work

Reasons
  1) Students are not professional writers – Extra work could hurt their studies
  2) Can find a new reporter soon – Won't cost too much

Task 5. Problem & Solution

❷ Speaking Grammar   p. 94

2

Problem The man's problem is that the writer who reviews movies for the paper is quitting.

Solutions The woman suggests that he split the movie reviews among the staff or pay a fee to reprint movie reviews from the city newspaper. I think that he should pay to reprint other movie reviews.

Reason I think the second solution is better because students aren't professional reporters, and they have other obligations besides the newspaper. The extra work could hurt their studies. Another reason is that it will only be a few weeks before the editor can replace the movie reviewer. This won't cost too much, and there are probably many students who want the position. They can probably find a replacement quickly.

Practice Questions   p. 96

1

Script |

M: Hey, Lisa, how are you doing?
W: Um, not too good today.
M: Oh? What's the matter?
W: Well, my computer broke down last night, and the repair shop said that it will take about a week to fix it. The trouble is that I have to take an online test by tomorrow, so I need to find a computer I can use tonight.
M: Hmm. You could go to the library. They have several computers that are available for students, and using them doesn't cost anything. The only problem is that there is a one-hour time limit on computers.
W: Well, I suppose I could go to the library, but I don't know exactly how much time I'll need to take the test.
M: You know, you could also try this Internet café they have in town. They charge you a small fee for every hour you use one of their computers, but, as long as you pay, you can stay online for however long you'd like.
W: Hmm. I'm a little short on money right now, so I'll have to think about it.

repair shop 수리점
internet café 인터넷 카페
afford ~할 여유가 있다

Campus Tip!

일반적으로 대학의 학생이라면 컴퓨터를 사용할 수 있는 장소는 상당히 많을 것이다. 다만 소규모의 학교일 경우 컴퓨터 사용을 1시간 또는 2시간으로 제한하여 모든 학생이 컴퓨터를 함께 사용할 수 있도록 돕는 규칙을 만들어 놓고 컴퓨터실을 운영한다. 하지만 대부분의 학교에서 컴퓨터를 사용하는 것은 크게 문제가 되지 않는다.

Script 해석 |

남자: 안녕, Lisa. 잘 지내지?
여자: 음, 오늘 기분이 별로 안 좋아.
남자: 어? 무슨 일인데?
여자: 글쎄, 내 컴퓨터가 지난밤에 고장이 났는데, 수리점에서 그걸 고치는 데 일주일 정도 걸릴 거래. 문제는 내가 내일 온라인 테스트를 하나 봐야 돼서 오늘 밤에 쓸 수 있는 컴퓨터를 구해야 한다는 거야.
남자: 흠. 너 도서관에 가면 되잖아. 거기엔 학생들이 이용할 수 있는 컴퓨터가 여러 대 있고 이용하는 데 전혀 돈이 들지 않아. 단 한 가지 문제는 컴퓨터들에 한 시간이라는 시간 제한이 있다는 거지.
여자: 글쎄, 도서관에 갈 수는 있는데, 내가 그 시험을 보는 데 정확히 얼마만큼 시간이 걸릴지 모르겠어.
남자: 있잖아, 넌 시내에 있는 그 인터넷 카페를 이용할 수도 있을 거야. 컴퓨터 한 대를 사용하는 데 매 시간마다 얼마간 요금을 내야 할 테지만, 네가 돈만 낸다면 네가 사용하고 싶은 만큼 인터넷에 접속해 있을 수 있다구.
여자: 흠. 나 지금은 돈이 별로 없어서 그건 좀 생각해 봐야겠다.

Listening note

Problem
Computer broke down
- Online test tom.

Solution 1
Use library comp.

Solution 2
Go to I-net café

Reasons
1) No time limit - Test might take longer than 1 hr.
2) Can do other things too

Sample Response |

The woman's problem is that her computer broke down and she has to take an online test by tomorrow. She can either take the test during a one-hour session on the library computer, or she can go to an Internet café and use one of their computers. I think that it is better for her to go to an Internet café. First, there's no time limit if she uses the Internet café. It's possible that the test takes longer than one hour, and if that is the case, she will be in trouble when she is using a library computer. If she uses the Internet café, she'll have as much time as she can afford, so she certainly will finish the test. Moreover, she can use the extra time for things like e-mail or research. If her computer is broken for a week, then she'll need more than an hour.

2

Script |

W: Jack! It's good to see you again. What have you been up to lately?
M: Not too much. I'm kind of worried about my housing situation, though.
W: Oh? How come?
M: Well, I just found out that my dormitory will be closed for about a week for major repairs. The school moved me into a temporary room that's a mile away from my early morning class. I'm afraid I can't walk to class in time.
W: Well, you could go to bed earlier so you can wake up earlier. If you give yourself an extra half hour in the morning, you could easily walk to class before it begins. Plus, you'd get some good exercise.
M: I guess, but I usually have homework that keeps me up late.
W: Well, you know, you could take the bus to class. It costs about two dollars to ride, but it wouldn't even take five minutes to reach your class. You might even be able to sleep later than usual.
M: Yeah, although I need every dollar I can spare right now. I suppose I'll have to choose one option or the other.

Script 해석 |

여자: Jack! 다시 만나게 돼서 정말 반가워. 여태까지 어떻게 지냈니?
남자: 별일 없었어. 다만 숙소 문제 때문에 좀 걱정이 돼.
여자: 어? 왜?
남자: 저기, 내 기숙사가 대대적인 수리 때문에 일주일간 폐쇄될 거라는 걸 알게 됐거든. 학교측은 날 임시 숙소로 옮겨 주었지만, 거긴 내가 아침 일찍 듣는 강의실에서 1마일이나 떨어진 곳이야. 걸어서 제시간에 수업에 도착할 수 있을지 걱정돼.
여자: 그럼, 넌 더 일찍 잠자리에 들어서 더 일찍 일어나면 되잖아. 아침에 네게 30분이 더 주어진다면, 수업이 시작하기 전에 문제없이 걸어올 수 있을 거야. 게다가 너에게 상당히 좋은 운동이 될 거고.
남자: 그럴 테지만 난 보통 늦게까지 해야 할 과제가 있는걸.
여자: 그렇다면, 있잖아, 수업에 버스를 타고 올 수도 있어. 타려면 2달러 정도 들긴 하지만 수업에 도착하는 데 5분도 걸리지 않을걸. 넌 아마 평소보다 늦게까지 잘 수도 있을 거야.
남자: 그래. 하지만 난 지금 당장 한 푼도 아쉬운걸. 두 가지 중 하나는 선택해야 하겠지.

---

temporary room
임시 숙소

eventually 결국은

Campus Tip!

미국 대학에서는 대학교에 갓 입학한 저학년일 경우 나이가 아직 어리기 때문에 기숙사 생활을 의무화 하고 있는 학교가 대부분이다. 그 이유는 21세가 되지 않는 학생이 학교 밖 아파트에서 생활을 하다 보면 여러 가지 위험한 요소가 있기 때문이다. 부모를 떠나 17-18세의 나이에 대학에서 혼자 생활해야 하기 때문에 학교측에서는 어느 정도 어린 학생들을 보호해야 할 의무가 있기 때문이다.

Task 5. Problem & Solution

Listening note

Problem
Dorm closed for repairs
- Temp. house is mile from class & may be late for class

Solution 1
Wake up earlier

Solution 2
Take bus

Reasons
1) Good exercise – Get faster and stronger & It will take less time eventually
2) Save money by not taking bus – Save almost $10/ week

Sample Response |

The man's problem is that he has been moved to temporary housing and he can't walk from there to his morning class in time. The woman suggests either he get up early in the morning to give himself more walking time or pay to take the bus. I prefer that the student get up earlier to give himself more walking time. I prefer that solution because he would get some good exercise from the long walk, and he would get faster and stronger. Thus, he could eventually cover the distance in much less time. Also, the student will save some money by not taking the bus. It's two dollars each ride, so in one week he'd save ten dollars.

3

Script |

M: Hey there, Cindy! Did you have a good weekend?
W: I wish I could say I did. Unfortunately, I got a letter that said my scholarship would be cancelled next year.
M: Oh, I'm sorry.
W: Yeah, I really needed that scholarship. Without it, I don't know how I'm going to pay for my classes.
M: Well, you could apply for a government loan. The government has plenty of programs that lend out money to students with good grades. What's great is that you wouldn't have to pay them back until after you graduate from college.
W: Maybe, but I might not be able to find a job right after I graduate.
M: Another option is to work as a professor's assistant. You could ask one of your professors to hire you next year as an aide, doing things like reading student papers and doing research. You work a lot and don't get paid much, but the real benefit is that the college won't charge you academic fees if you work for a professor.
W: Yeah, but I'll be working a lot on classes next year. I'll have to think about this.

Script 해석 |

남자: 아아, Cindy! 주말 잘 보냈니?
여자: 그랬으면 좋겠는데, 불행히도 내 내년 장학금이 취소될 거라는 편지를 받았어.
남자: 오, 안됐다.
여자: 그래, 난 정말 그 장학금이 필요했는데. 그게 없으면 난 어떻게 수업료를 지불해야 할지 모르겠어.
남자: 음, 넌 정부기관 대출을 신청할 수 있을 것 같은데. 정부에는 성적이 좋은 학생들에게 돈을 대출해 주는 프로그램이 많아. 정말 좋은 건 네가 대학을 졸업한 후가 될 때까지 그 돈을 갚지 않아도 된다는 거야.
여자: 그렇겠지. 하지만 졸업한 후 바로 직장을 구할 수 없을지도 모르잖아.
남자: 또 한 가지 선택은 교수님의 조교로 일하는 거야. 네 교수님들 중 한 분에게 내년에 널 학생들의 논문을 읽고 연구를 하는 조수로 고용해 달라고 부탁드릴 수 있어. 많은 일을 하고 급여는 그리 많지 않지만, 실직적인 혜택은 네가 교수님을 위해 일하면 대학 측은 네게 학비를 청구하지 않는다는 거지.
여자: 그래, 하지만 난 내년에 수업 때문에 바쁘게 공부하고 있을 텐데. 이건 생각해 봐야겠다.

---

unfortunately
불행하게도

government loan
정부기관 대출

Campus Tip!

미국 대학에 입학할 때, 대부분의 학생들이 장학금을 받고 대학에 입학한다. 학교뿐만 아니라 여러 장학단체와 개인들이 장학금으로 학교를 후원하기 때문에 미국에서는 장학금을 받을 수 있는 확률이 아주 높다. 비단 미국인들을 위한 것이 아닐 뿐더러 국제학생(International student)을 위한 장학금 또한 적지 않다. 다만 장학금을 유지하기 위해서는 학교에서 요구하는 성적을 유지해야 하며 책임 있는 학교생활을 해야 한다. 장학금을 받지 못하는 학생들은 많은 경우 정부나 은행을 통한 단체에서 지원하는 대출금(Loan)을 받게 되는데 이는 졸업 후 10년 혹은 20년 동안 조금씩 상환할 수 있도록 되어있다.

Listening note

Problem
Scholarship cancelled
- Need sch. for classes next year

Solution 1
Apply for laon
- Gov. loans $ for college
- Pay back after grad.

Solution 2
Work as prof. assistant
- Grade papers, do research
- Don't have to pay for classes

Reasons
1) If gov. loan → must pay money back & may not find a good job after graduation.
2) Assistant → valuable job experience – chances of finding a job after graduation.

Sample Response |

The problem is that the student's scholarship for next year has been canceled. The man advises her either to apply for a government loan or to work as a professor's assistant in order to pay for classes. I think she should take a job as a professor's assistant. First, if she got the government loan, she would have to pay the money back after graduation, and she shouldn't do that unless she knows she can find a good job. As an assistant, she wouldn't have to pay for classes. Second, she will get valuable job experience by working as a professor's assistant. This will increase her chances of finding a good job after graduating. In short, I think that working as a professor's assistant is the better solution.

4

Script |

W: Hey, Antoine! What's up?
M: Hey, nothing much. But I've been kind of bothered by something these past couple of days.
W: Really? What's bothering you?
M: I've got to do a special writing project next semester if I want to graduate from my program. I just don't have any idea what I want to do, but I need to decide quickly.
W: Well, I can suggest something. The college newspaper is looking for some reporters to cover sporting events on the weekends. All you would have to do is go to a football or baseball game every weekend and write a short article about it by Monday.
M: Yeah, but that might take up all of my free time on the weekends.
W: Oh, then another thing you could do is a special research project. You would write a fairly long paper for one of your professors over the course of a semester. At the end, you would do a presentation on it before a committee of other professors. It's more work, but you could do your writing whenever you wanted to.
M: I don't know. I'll think about which one I'd rather do.

Script 해석 |

여자: 안녕, Antoine! 잘 지내?
남자: 아, 별일 없어. 근데 나 요 며칠 어떤 일 때문에 좀 성가셔.
여자: 정말? 널 성가시게 하는 게 뭐야?
남자: 내가 듣는 수업 과정을 끝마치려면, 다음 학기에 특수 작문 프로젝트를 해야만 해. 어떻게 해야 할지 정말 모르겠는데, 빨리 결정해야 해서.
여자: 그럼, 내가 뭣 좀 제안할게. 학교 신문사는 주말에 스포츠 이벤트를 취재할 기자들을 몇 명 구하고 있어. 넌 매주 축구나 야구 경기에 가서, 월요일까지 거기에 대한 짧은 기사를 쓰면 되는 거야.
남자: 그런데 그 일은 주말 내 자유시간을 모두 빼앗아 버릴걸.
여자: 오, 그렇다면 넌 또 특별 연구 프로젝트를 할 수도 있어. 넌 네 교수님들 중 한 분을 위해 한 학기 그 과목에 대해서 꽤 긴 논문을 쓸 수도 있어. 마지막엔 다른 교수님들의 위원회 앞에서 프레젠테이션을 할 거야. 일이 많지만 넌 네가 원할 땐 언제든지 작문을 할 수 있다구.
남자: 모르겠다. 어느 걸 하는 게 나은지 생각해 봐야겠어.

---

fairly 꽤
committee 위원회
defense
답변하다, 항변하다

Task 5. Problem & Solution

Listening note

Problem
Idea for writing project
- Needs proj. to graduate

Solution 1
Write for paper
- Cover sports events
- Work every weekend

Solution 2
Special research paper
- Present it at end of sem.
- Long paper, more work
- Can write any time you want

Reasons
1) Less work than research paper – Only 1 article a week
2) Fun thing to do – As much fun as anything else he could do & won't take up the whole weekend

Sample Response

The man's problem is that he must do a special writing project next semester in order to graduate. The woman suggests that he could either write about weekend sporting events for the college newspaper or write a special research paper for one of his professors. Between the two options, I prefer the first one, which is to write about weekend sporting events. One reason is that it's less work than the research paper. He'd only write an article every weekend instead of doing lots of research for a paper and defense over a whole semester. Another reason is that he would get to do something fun every weekend, like watching a football or baseball game. This would be as much fun as anything else he could do, and it wouldn't take up all of his time on the weekend.

Vocabulary Study — Campus life   p. 100

- syllabus 강의 개요
- snack bar 매점
- override 정원수 초과 수강신청
- assignment 과제
- credit hours 수강시간
- curriculum 교과 과정
- lab 실험실의 줄임 말
- dean 학부장
- probation 근신 기간
- course withdrawal 수업 철회
- matriculation 입학 허가
- college catalog 대학 요람
- study lounge 공부하는 휴게실, 대합실
- tenure 종신 재직권
- distance learning 원거리 수업
- advisor 지도교사

- coed 남녀공학
- minor 부전공
- tuition hike 수업료 인상
- term paper 리포트
- GPA 성적
- sorority 여학생 클럽
- pop quiz 갑자기 보는 퀴즈
- intercollegiate sports 대학 대항 경기
- pass/fail grade 통과/낙제 성적
- placement service 직업 소개
- practicum 실습과목
- professor/academic rank 교수 평가 제도
- semester 학기
- shuttle service 셔틀버스 서비스
- plagiarism 표절
- work-study 공부하며 일하는 제도

정답 | A 1. (f) 2. (d) 3. (h) 4. (g) 5. (a)
         6. (j) 7. (b) 8. (c) 9. (i) 10. (e)
      B 1. coed   2. sorority   3. a term paper   4. override   5. placement service

Task 6 Summary

Sample Question
p. 102

Script 해석 |

우리는 고전 음악을 생각할 때, 거대하고 복잡한 관현악단을 떠올리는 경향이 있습니다. 그렇다면, 관현악단이 어떻게 그렇게 큰 규모로 성장하게 되었는가를 여러분들 중 몇 명이나 궁금하게 여기나요? 자, 우리가 알고 있는 현대의 관현악단은 과거 400년에 걸쳐 점차적으로 발전되어 왔습니다. 그러나 두 가지의 발전이 현대 관현악단의 초기 발달에 도움을 주었는데요. 하나는 오페라의 도입이었고, 다른 하나는 진공관의 발명이었습니다.

17세기 초, 오페라는 인기 있는 악극의 한 형태가 되었습니다. 오페라가 있기 이전, 유럽의 많은 부유한 가문들이 사적인 공연을 위해 악단들을 고용했지만 이들은 매우 작은 단체였습니다. 오페라가 생겨났을 때 작곡가들은 극장 관객들을 위해 곡을 쓰기 시작했고, 이는 더 많은 수의 악기뿐만 아니라 이 악기들을 위해 쓰여진 구체적인 곡 부분까지도 필요로 했습니다. 이탈리아 작곡가인 끌라우디오 몬테베르디는 처음으로 매우 큰 규모의 관현악단들을 조직하여, 그들에게 연주할 특정 부분들을 할당해주었던 한 사람입니다. 이는 후기 작곡가들을 위한 하나의 기준을 확립해 주었고, 그들은 계속해서 자신이 쓰는 오페라를 위해 관현악단의 규모를 늘여갔습니다.

진공관과 같은 새로운 발명품들도 역시 현대 관현악단의 팽창을 야기했습니다. 18세기 초, 금관 악기들에 진공관이 접목 되었습니다. 이는 음의 높낮이를 바꾸는 것을 용이하게 하여, 연주가들에게 새로운 범위의 음색을 갖추어 주었습니다. 진공관은 결국 트럼펫, 코넷, 튜바와 같이 여러 발전된 금관 악기들의 사용을 불러왔습니다. 이러한 모든 새 악기들이 현대 관현악단에 추가되어, 더 많은 수의 악기뿐만 아니라 소리의 광범위한 다양함을 갖추게 해 주었습니다.

performance 공연
theatrical 극장의
instrument 악기
pitch 소리, 음

Outlining
p. 104

1

Script |

In our discussions about how people use water, some of you might be wondering exactly how we get water in the first place. Well, water is not only abundant, but also is constantly distributed all over the earth in a never-ending cycle. Throughout this cycle, two power sources help spread water and refresh all the different water sources. Those sources are solar radiation and geothermal activity.

First, solar radiation helps distribute water from sea to land by creating precipitation. Solar radiation heats up the world's seas, causing water from the surface to rise into the air. Now, the warm water vapor spreads all above the earth, throughout the atmosphere. Here, it loses its heat to the colder air surrounding it, forming precipitation such as rain or snow. This precipitation will scatter frozen and liquid water all over the planet, using abundant ocean water to moisturize the dry earth.

Second, geothermal activity distributes water from the bottom of the ocean to the top of the ocean. Magma leaks out of holes in the ocean floor, radiating heat in the deep waters. Of course, this heated water will rise to the ocean's surface. Meanwhile, colder water sinks, and this rising and falling of ocean water causes currents, like the one in the North Atlantic Ocean. Currents such as this one form a giant global current that redistributes water to every ocean on the planet.

distribute 공급하다
radiation 태양 복사열
geothermal 지열의
precipitation 강수
atmosphere 주변
moisturize 수분을 공급하다
magma 마그마

Script 해석 |

사람들이 물을 어떻게 사용하는가에 대한 우리의 토론에서, 여러분들 중 몇몇은 우리가 정확히 어떻게 물을 얻는가에 대해 우선적으로 매우 궁금하게 여길 것입니다. 자, 물은 풍족할 뿐 아니라 끊임없는 순환을 통해 계속적으로 지구 곳곳에 공급되고 있습니다. 이 순환의 전 과정에는 두 가지 동력원이 물의 보급을 도와, 다양한 모든 수자원들이 다시 채워지게 합니다. 이 동력원은 태양 복사열과 지열 활동입니다.

먼저, 태양 복사열은 강수를 일으켜 바다에서 육지로 물이 공급되는 것을 돕습니다. 태양 복사열이 지구의 바다를 가열시켜, 수분이 표면에서 공기 중으로 상승하도록 합니다. 이제, 그 따뜻한 수증기는 대기를 통해 지상 곳곳으로 퍼집니다. 여기서 그 수증기는 주변을 둘러싼 차가운 공기에 열을 빼앗겨, 비나 눈과 같은 강수가 형성되는 것입니다. 이러한 강수는 풍부한 해수를 이용하여 건조한 대지에 수분을 공급하도록, 지구상 전역에 결빙되거나 액체 상태의 수분을 뿌립니다.

두 번째로, 지열 활동은 물을 해저로부터 해양의 상부로 고루 분포시킵니다. 해양 밑바닥 구멍에서 새어 나오는 마그마는 심층수에 열을 발산시킵니다. 물론, 이 가열된 물은 해양 표면으로 상승하게 되죠. 동시에 차가운 물은 가라앉게 되는데, 이 같은 해수의 상승과 하강이 북대서양 해류와 같은 해류의 원인이 되는 것입니다. 이와 같은 해류들은 지구상에 있는 모든 해양에 물을 재분포하는 지구 전체 거대한 조류를 형성합니다.

2

Script

As we talk about seed plants today, we should note how plants with flowers have a reproductive advantage over seed plants that don't have flowers. This advantage can be attributed to two features that only flowering plants have: flowers and fruits. These two features increase flowering plants' chances of getting fertilized and of successfully spreading their seeds.

First, the flowers on these plants use animals to actively distribute their pollen. The color, scent, and shape of these plants' flowers attract bees, birds, and other animals that feed upon the nectar inside. While feeding on the nectar, these animals rub against the flowers and get grains of pollen on their bodies. By rubbing against the flowers, they also spread pollen from other plants as they move from flower to flower. This actively scatters pollen grains among flowering plants, giving them more chances to fertilize their seeds.

Second, flowering plants grow fruits, and these help transport their seeds over a larger area. How does this work? Again, it relies on animals. Any animal that feeds on fruits or nuts, like bears or monkeys, also consumes the seeds of flowering plants. As the animals travel long distances from the plant, they drop seeds in their excrement and scatter them over a wide distance around the plant. This dispersal increases the chances a seed has of finding soil that can nurture it and eventually growing into an adult plant.

reproductive 생식적
attribute ~이라 여겨지다
feature 특징
fertilize 비옥하게 하다
scent 향기
transport 이동하다
excrement 배설물
dispersal 분산

Script 해석

오늘 우리가 종자식물에 대해 이야기하면서, 어째서 꽃을 가진 식물들이 그렇지 않은 종자식물들에 비해 생식에 있어 한 가지 장점을 가지는가에 주목해야 합니다. 이 장점은 꽃을 피우는 식물들만이 가지는 두 가지 특징에 의한 것이라고 여겨지는데, 그것은 꽃과 열매입니다. 이 두 가지 특성은 꽃식물이 수분이 되고 성공적으로 씨를 뿌릴 수 있는 기회들을 증가시켜 줍니다.

먼저, 이러한 식물들의 꽃은 자신들의 화분을 활발하게 퍼뜨리기 위해서 동물들을 이용합니다. 이러한 꽃들의 색깔, 향기 그리고 모양은 벌이나 새, 또는 그 안의 화밀*을 먹고 사는 다른 동물들을 끌어들입니다. 화밀을 먹는 동안 이 동물들은 꽃들과 접촉하게 되고, 몸에 꽃가루 알갱이들을 묻히게 됩니다. 또한 그들은 꽃에서 꽃으로 이동하면서 그 꽃들과 접촉해 꽃가루를 퍼뜨리게 됩니다. 이는 꽃식물들에게 활발하게 꽃가루가 뿌려지도록 해서, 그들이 씨앗을 수분시키는 더 많은 기회를 얻게 해 주는 것입니다.

두 번째로, 꽃식물은 열매들을 맺는데, 이는 그 씨앗들이 더 넓은 지역으로 이동하게 해줍니다. 어떻게 이런 일이 가능할까요? 말했다시피, 동물들에 의존하는 것입니다. 곰이나 원숭이처럼 열매나 견과류를 먹고 사는 동물들은 그 꽃식물의 씨앗도 섭취하게 됩니다. 동물들은 그 식물에게서 멀리 떨어진 곳까지 가서, 그들의 배설물로 씨앗들을 배출하는 방식으로, 식물 주위에서 멀리 떨어진 곳에 그것들을 뿌려 놓게 됩니다. 이러한 분산은 하나의 씨앗이 영양분을 얻을 수 있는 토양을 찾아, 결과적으로 성체*식물로 성장할 수 있는 기회들을 증가시켜 주는 것입니다.

*화밀 (nectar): 꽃의 꿀샘에서 분비하는 꿀
*성체 (adult plant): 동식물이 다 자라서 생식 능력이 있는 것을 말함

Listening note

Main Idea
Flowers & fruits
- Flow. plants have reproductive adv.
- Better chance at fert. & planting

Example 1
Flowers

Details
- Nectar attracts animals
- Pollen rubs on bees, birds
- Animals rub pollen on other flowers
- Actively scatters pollen

Example 2
Fruits

Details
- Fruits attract animals
- Bears, monkeys eat & digest seeds
- Scatter seeds in droppings
- Seeds cover wider area

❷ Speaking Grammar   p. 108

2

Main Idea The professor discusses how flowers and fruits give flowering plants a reproductive advantage over non-flowering plants.

Example 1 First, flowers increase flowering plants' chances of getting fertilized. The professor states that flowers attract animals like birds and bees that feed on their nectar. These animals rub against flowers and get pollen grains on their skin while feeding, actively spreading pollen from flower to flower and helping fertilize the different seeds.

Example 2 Second, fruits increase a flowering plant's chances for spreading seeds. The professor discusses how fruits attract different animals and help spread fertilized seeds. Animals like bears and monkeys, which feed on these fruits, will swallow the seeds and scatter them along the ground in their excrement. This spreads the seeds out across a larger area and gives them a better chance of becoming plants.

Practice Questions   p. 110

1

Script |

When consumers have to choose between two different brands of the same product, they usually look at which product costs less. Most of the time, however, the prices of these products are roughly the same. So what can consumers do when this is the case? Well, when choosing between similarly priced products, consumers will normally compare the overall quality of the products, and they tend to base their choice on two factors: reliability and external appearance.

First, consumers will evaluate the reliability of a product. This means that before people buy something, they want to make sure that the item will serve its purpose for a reasonable amount of time. Look at cars, for instance. If you buy a car, your primary concern is that it will safely transport you to work and your home, so you want to make sure that it runs properly. You also want to make sure that it will last you a long time, because you'll lose money if you have to replace a car that doesn't work very well.

Second, external appearance will affect a consumer's choice. Sometimes a consumer will prefer an appealing or fashionable product, even if the product is more expensive or less reliable. For example, take sports cars. Not only do sports cars cost a lot of money, but they also require a lot of maintenance. However, they are very popular with many consumers because they are fashionably designed. Many consumers want to impress other people by driving around in a sports car.

roughly 거의, 대략
reliability 신뢰도
maintenance 유지 (비용)
fashionably 세련되게

Task 6. Summary

Script 해석 |

소비자들은 다른 두 브랜드의 같은 제품 사이에서 선택을 해야 할 때, 보통 어떤 제품의 가격이 더 저렴한지를 살펴봅니다. 하지만 대부분, 이러한 제품들의 가격은 거의 같습니다. 그렇다면 이 경우에 소비자들은 어떻게 할까요? 자, 비슷한 가격의 제품들 중에 선택을 할 때, 소비자들은 보통 그 제품들의 전체적 질을 비교해 보고, 두 가지 요소에 근거해서 선택하는 경향이 있습니다. 이는 신뢰도와 외형입니다.

첫째로, 소비자들은 제품의 신뢰도를 평가할 것입니다. 이는 사람들이 물건을 구입하기 전에 그것이 합당한 기간 동안, 그 용도를 충족시키는가를 확인하기 원한다는 것을 의미합니다. 그 예로 자동차를 살펴 봅시다. 여러분이 차를 구입하기 원한다면, 주요 관심사는 그 차가 여러분을 직장과 집까지 안전하게 데려다 줄 것인가 하는 것이므로, 그것이 제대로 달리는가를 확인하고 싶어합니다. 또한 여러분은 그것을 오래 사용할 수 있는가를 확인하고 싶어합니다. 왜냐하면 여러분이 제대로 작동하지 않는 자동차를 교체해야 한다면, 손해를 보게 되는 것이기 때문입니다.

두 번째는 외형이 소비자들의 선택에 영향을 끼친다는 것입니다. 때때로 어떤 소비자는 더 비싸고 덜 신뢰가 가더라도, 매력적이고 세련된 상품을 선호할 것입니다. 그 예로 스포츠카를 들어 봅시다. 스포츠카는 가격이 비쌀 뿐 아니라 유지비도 많이 듭니다. 하지만 디자인이 세련되기 때문에 많은 소비자에게 매우 인기가 있습니다. 많은 소비자들은 스포츠카를 타고 돌아다니면서 다른 사람들의 관심을 끌기 좋아합니다.

repair shop 수리점
internet café 인터넷 카페
afford ~할 여유가 있다

Listening note

Main Idea
2 factors in choosing products
- Reliability & external appearance

Example 1
Reliability

Details
- Prod. should serve purp. For long time.
  Ex) Car should go to work & home safely
- Lose $ replacing bad car

Example 2
External appearance

Details
- Appealing or fashionable prod.
  Ex) Sports cars pop. b/c of fash. design
- May take looks over reliability

Sample Response |

According to the lecture, reliability and external appearance help determine the product a consumer buys when his options cost about the same. As the professor first states, a product's reliability shows the consumer that it can serve its purpose for a necessary length of time, such as a car that runs properly and safely gets someone to and from work. If a product isn't reliable, then a person would lose money replacing it, such as a car that doesn't work very well. The professor follows up by saying that external appearance will affect a consumer's choice by offering an appealing or fashionable product. The professor shows how sports cars with fashionable designs are popular, even though they cost more and require more maintenance than other cars.

2

Script |

Reading novels may be a long and complex process, but writing one is far more difficult. So, what makes someone go to all this trouble to write? Well, I'd like to discuss two sources of motivation for writers. One is sublimation, or the desire to creatively express repressed personal desires. The other is activism, or the deliberate attempt to transform society for the better.

Let's take a look at sublimation, a psychological process in which a person redirects impulses like love or anger into energy for a creative pursuit, such as art or science. Here, motivation is caused by internal forces. Writers who use sublimation are usually coping with frustration over not being able to fulfill their impulses. For instance, the medieval Italian poet Dante loved a woman named Beatrice, but she died before he could ever express his love to her. Instead, he created epic poetry where Beatrice is turned into an angelic being that gives Dante moral instruction.

motivation 동기
sublimation 승화
deliberate 의도적인
impulse 충동
corruption 부정부패

Now, another source of motivation is activism, or the desire to improve society. For activist writers, motivation would be caused by external forces, like, say, poor working conditions or government corruption. The writer hopes to address these social, political, and economic troubles in order to make people aware of them and perhaps even fix them. For instance, the modern American writer John Steinbeck, who wrote novels about the troubles facing migrant workers in the United States. This helped raise concern among Americans, and the government eventually tried to help these migrant workers.

Script 해석

소설을 읽는 것은 하나의 길고 복잡한 과정입니다. 하지만 소설은 쓰는 것은 훨씬 더 어렵습니다. 그렇다면 누군가가 이러한 모든 어려움을 겪으면서까지도 글을 쓰는 이유는 뭘까요? 글쎄요, 전 작가들에게 있어 동기의 원천이 되는 두 가지에 대해 논의하고 싶습니다. 그 하나는 '승화'로, 억압된 개인적 욕망들을 창조적으로 표출하고자 하는 욕망입니다. 또 다른 한 가지는 행동주의, 혹은 사회를 더 바람직하게 바꾸고자 하는 의도적인 시도를 말합니다.

'승화'에 대해 살펴보자면, 그것은 한 인간이 사랑과 분노와 같은 충동들을 창조적인 활동을 위한 에너지로 전환하는 심리적인 과정입니다. 여기에서는 내적인 힘들에 의한 동기화가 일어나는 것입니다. '승화'를 이용하는 작가들은 주로 자신들의 충동적 욕구를 만족시키지 못하는 데 대한 좌절을 다룹니다. 예를 들어, 중세의 시인 단테는 베아트리체라는 한 여성을 사랑했었는데, 그가 그녀에 대한 사랑을 미처 표출하기도 전에 그녀는 죽고 말았습니다. 대신에, 그는 베아트리체가 단테에게 도덕적인 가르침을 주는 천사로 변모한 대서사시를 창조해 냈습니다.

자, 동기화의 또 다른 원천은 행동주의로, 사회를 개선하고자 하는 욕구입니다. 행동주의자인 작가들에게 있어, 동기화는 말하자면 열악한 근무 조건이나 정부의 부정 부패와 같은 외적인 힘들에 의해 유발되는 것입니다. 작가는 이러한 사회적, 정치적, 경제적인 문제들에 이의를 제기하여, 사람들로 하여금 그것들을 인식하고 심지어는 바로잡게 만들길 원합니다. 예를 들어, 현대 미국 작가인 존 스타인벡은 미국의 이주 노동자들이 직면하는 문제들에 관해 소설을 썼습니다. 이는 미국인들 사이에서 관심을 불러 일으켰고, 정부는 마침내 이러한 이주 노동자들을 돕기 위해 노력했습니다.

Listening note

Main Idea
Motivation for writers
- Sublimation: int. forces & Activism: ext. forces

Example 1
Sublimation

Details
- Redirection of love, anger, etc. → creative pursuits
- Dante couldn't share love w/ Beatrice
- Wrote poetry (B. as angel)

Example 2
Activism

Details
- Act. Writer → imp. society
- Raise awareness of social prob. → fix prob.
- Steinbeck wrote about mig. workers

Sample Response

According to the lecture, sublimation and activism have motivated writers to create literature by inspiring them to use internal and external forces for creative energy. The professor first states that sublimation is the redirection of love, anger, and other impulses into creative pursuits, usually done out of frustration. She discusses the poet Dante as an example to explain this. Dante wrote epic poetry that had Beatrice as an angel. Beatrice was a girl that died before Dante could express his love for her. Next, the professor discusses activism by talking about activist writers who want to improve society. According to the professor, they write novels in order to address a social problem, like poor working conditions or government corruption. Through their activism, writers hope to fix these problems. As an example of activist writers, the professor talks about John Steinbeck, who wrote novels about migrant workers.

3

Script |

Today we are going to look at how small companies can use advertising to gain success. Let me give you an example: Eleven Speed Bicycles. Three years ago, this local company took a risk and spent money on advertising. It is now one of the top manufacturers of bicycles and bicycle equipment in the nation, and they owe it all to two crucial marketing techniques: direct advertisement and indirect advertisement.

First, there was direct advertisement. Eleven Speed Bicycles used direct advertisement to let people know about their bicycles. This means that the company directly addressed people with information about their products, such as the products' prices and features. Some examples of the company's use of direct advertisements were the television commercials and newspaper ads they would release about, oh, say, once a month, just so people would at least be familiar with the products' names and then maybe buy them.

Second, there was indirect advertisement. The bicycle company eventually began to use indirect advertisement to help sell their bicycles. This kind of advertising is less obvious than direct advertising. Through indirect advertising, the company made their bicycles visible without providing any specific details about them. For instance, a television show once had an Eleven Speed Bicycle displayed in a character's garage because Eleven Speed paid the show's producers to include it. This technique subtly raised viewers' awareness of the bikes Eleven Speed Bicycles manufactures.

manufacturer 제조회사
equipment 장비
commercial 광고
awareness 인식

Script 해석 |

오늘 우리는 작은 회사들이 성공을 거두기 위해서 어떻게 광고를 활용할 수 있는가에 대해 살펴볼 것입니다. 제가 '일레븐 스피드 자전거'의 예를 하나 들도록 하죠. 3년 전 이 지방의 작은 회사는 위험을 무릅쓰고 광고에 돈을 투자했습니다. 그 회사는 현재 국내 최고의 자전거와 자전거 장비 제조회사 중 하나인데요, 그들은 이 모두를 두 가지 중요한 마케팅 기술 덕택이라 여기고 있습니다. 그것은 바로 직접광고와 간접광고입니다.

먼저, 직접광고란 것이 있었습니다. '일레븐 스피드 자전거'는 사람들이 자신들의 자전거에 대해 알게 하기 위해 직접광고를 이용했습니다. 이는 그 회사가 직접 사람들에게 제품 가격이나 특징들 같은 제품 정보를 직접 알렸다는 것을 의미하죠. 그 회사가 직접광고들을 이용한 몇 가지 예는 텔레비전 광고들과 그리고 어, 예를 들어, 한 달에 한 번 정도 발행되는 신문 광고들이었고, 사람들은 최소 그 제품에 익숙해져 나중엔 그것을 사곤 했을 것입니다.

두 번째로 간접광고가 있었는데요. 그 자전거 회사는 결국 자전거 판매를 돕기 위해 간접광고를 사용하기 시작했습니다. 이 종류의 광고는 직접광고보다는 덜 두드러지는 방법인데요. 간접광고를 통해서, 그 회사는 제품에 대한 어떠한 구체적인 세부사항도 제공하지 않고 자신들의 자전거를 눈에 띄게 만들었습니다. 예를 들어, 어떤 TV쇼에서 한번은 주인공의 차고에 진열된 일레븐 스피드 자전거를 보여주었습니다. 이는 일레븐 스피드 측이 프로듀서들에게 그것이 나오게 하도록 대가를 지불했기 때문이었습니다. 이러한 기술은 교묘하게 일레븐 스피드 자전거가 제조하는 자전거들에 대한 시청자들의 인식을 높이게 되었습니다.

Listening note

Main Idea
2 Kinds of advertising
- 11 Speed Bikes took risk on ads & now a top bike comp.

Example 1
Direct advertisement

Example 2
Indirect advertisement

Details
- Dir. address. people w/ info
- Ment. prices & qualities
- 11 Spd. Used tv & paper ads

Details
- Less obvious
- Make prod. visible w/o info
- Put bikes in tv shows

Sample Response |

The professor discusses two kinds of advertising, which are direct advertising and indirect advertising. He explains how they contribute to the success of a small company by giving an example of a bicycle company named Eleven Speed Bicycles. First, the professor talks about how Eleven Speed Bicycles used direct advertising, or openly giving people information about their product. This means that the company released commercials and newspaper ads that described their products' prices and qualities. Next, the professor talks about indirect advertising, or less obvious ways of raising public awareness. One method Eleven Speed Bicycles used was paying a television show to show their bikes in a character's garage, making the bikes visible without providing any specific information about them. Viewers thus still became aware of the bikes and perhaps bought them.

4

Script |

Today we are going to discuss some causes of the American Revolution. Now, as we all know, before the United States existed as a country, its eastern shores were colonies of Great Britain. The relationship between Britain and its colonists began to grow increasingly hostile in the late eighteenth century, and there were two principal causes for this hostility: the desire for more land, and taxation without representation.

First, the American colonists had a desire for more land. There was plenty of western farmland to settle, as well as space for new communities, but the, uh, British government had just signed a treaty with other nations that prohibited western expansion. The British didn't want to risk starting a war with the native tribes or their allies, so, in order to move westward without any restrictions, many colonists began to realize that they would have to break ties with the British government.

Second, there was taxation without representation. The British government introduced new taxes on products it exported to the colonies, like tea and stamps, and this angered the colonists because they could not vote for statesmen to represent them in the British parliament. The colonists felt that it was unfair that they did not have any say as to which laws would be forced upon them. Thus, most colonists felt that they should start their own government and elect officials who could best represent the interests of the colonists.

representation 대표
prohibit 금지하다
expansion 개간, 확장
westward 서부로
restriction 제약
taxation 과세
parliament 정부

Script 해석 |

오늘 우리는 미국 독립 전쟁의 몇 가지 원인들에 대해 논의해 보겠습니다. 자, 우리 모두가 알고 있듯, 미국이 하나의 나라로 존재하기 이전, 동부 해안 지역은 대영제국의 식민지들이었습니다. 18세기 말, 영국과 식민지들과의 관계는 점점 적대적으로 발전하기 시작했고, 이러한 적개심에는 더 넓은 토지에 대한 열망과 '대표 없는 과세'라는 두 가지 주요 원인이 있었습니다.

첫째로, 미국 식민지들에게는 더 넓은 토지에 대한 열망이 있었습니다. 비록 서부에는 새로운 공동체를 형성할 공간뿐 아니라, 정착할 수 있는 농경지가 많았지만, 영국 정부는 서부 개간을 금지하는 다른 나라들과의 협정에 막 사인한 후였습니다. 영국은 원주민 부족들이나 동맹국들과 전쟁을 하는 위험을 원치 않았고, 많은 식민지들은 아무런 제약도 없이 서부로 이주하기 위해서는 그들이 영국 정부와 승부를 내야만 한다는 것을 깨닫기 시작했습니다.

두 번째는 '대표 없는 과세'였습니다. 영국 정부는 차와 우표 같은, 식민지들로 수출되는 상품들에 부과되는 새로운 세금들을 도입시켰고, 이는 식민지들을 분노하게 만들었습니다. 왜냐하면 그들은 영국 의회에서 그들을 대표할 정치가에게 투표할 수 없었기 때문입니다. 식민지들은 자신들에게 강요될 법들에 대해 어떠한 발언권도 없다는 것이 부당하다고 느꼈습니다. 그래서 대다수의 식민지들은 자신들만의 독자적인 정부를 출범시키고, 식민지들의 이익을 가장 잘 대변할 관리들을 뽑아야 한다는 것을 깨달았습니다.

*대표 없는 과세 (taxation without representation): 식민지는 본국 의회에 대표를 보내고 있지 않기 때문에 본국 정부는 식민지에 과세할 권리가 없는데도, 영국 정부는 식민지를 대상으로 과세를 징수하려 함

Listening note

Main Idea
2 factors fro American Revolution
- Desire for more land & taxation w/o representation

Example 1
American desire for land

Details
- Col. wanted more west. land
- Brit. signed treaty w/ west. tribes
- Col. would have to break ties

Example 2
Taxes w/o representation

Details
- New Brit. taxes on tea & stamps
- Col. couldn't vote for Parliament reps.
- Mad cause couldn't vote on tax & laws

Task 6. Summary

Sample Response |
The professor discusses two factors that helped cause the American Revolution. Those two factors were the desire for more land and taxation without representation. The professor first discusses how American colonists desired to settle western land for farms and communities, but the British had signed treaties with native tribes and their allies that prohibited any such expansion. Thus, colonists began breaking ties with England. The professor then talks about the second factor, taxation without representation. According to the professor, taxation of goods like tea and stamps also stirred up hostility because the colonists had no representation in parliament. This meant that they had no say in what taxes and laws were put into effect, so many wanted to start a government where everyone would be represented.

Vocabulary Study   Lectures   p. 114

Psychology
- assertive   단언적인, 단정적인
- cynical   의심하는, 냉소하는
- panic   공황
- phobia   병적 공포
- subconscious   잠재 의식의
- agnosia   인지불능증
- delusion   현혹된 상태
- extroverted   외향적인
- perception   지각, 인지
- stimulus   자극물, 흥분제

Business/ Economics
- transaction   업무, 거래, 매매
- accumulation   축적, 적립
- patent   특허, 인가
- privilege   특권
- portable   휴대용의, 운반할 수 있는
- device   궁리, 계획
- equivalent   동등한, 동의의
- continuity   지속성
- substitution   대체, 대용
- monopoly   독점, 전매

Biology
- adaptation   적응
- ferment   발효시키다
- optical   시력의
- plasticity   가소성, 유연성
- sequence   순서, 차례
- gravity   중력, 지구 인력
- particle   소량
- reinforce   보강하다, 강화하다
- enlargement   증대, 확대
- capture   포획하다, 획득하다

Art & Literature
- aesthetic   미학의
- absurd   이치에 맞지 않는
- applied art   응용 예술
- evoke   (기억, 감정)을 불러 일으키다
- paradox   역설
- probability   가능성
- literate   읽고 쓰는 능력, 교육받은
- tangible   만질 수 있는
- allegory   이야기, 풍유 소설, 비유담
- calligraphy   서법, 능필, 필적

정답 | A   1. (h)   2. (d)   3. (e)   4. (g)   5. (b)
              6. (f)   7. (j)   8. (a)   9. (c)   10. (i)
         B   1. cynical   2. adaptation 3. monopoly   4. reinforce   5. transaction

PART C Actual Test

Actual Test 1

p. 120

1

Sample Response |
My favorite item of clothing is my trench coat because it is both practical and fashionable. First, my trench coat is practical, and it helps me out in all kinds of situations. For instance, it has deep pockets that I can carry a small umbrella or book in, and it keeps me dry and warm when needed. Second, my trench coat is fashionable, and all of my friends also wear trench coats. We generally wear them with casual clothes or business suits because trench coats complement any outfit. Also, I've noticed more and more people wearing them lately.

2

Sample Response |
I agree with the opinion that a company should only promote people who work hard. There are two reasons why I agree with that opinion. The first one is that employees that work hard have earned promotions as a reward. They do everything expected of them, and they produce profitable results, whereas someone who has worked for a long time might not. The other reason is that people who work hard will help their companies if promoted. Because they are efficient workers, they can help other workers be more efficient, too. Companies profit even more by promoting diligent and competent employees.

3

지문 해석 |
주거 관리과에서 알립니다: 안전에 대한 우려가 증가함에 따라, 대학 당국은 다음 학기부터 기숙사실 내 개인 전자레인지 소지를 허가하지 않을 것입니다. 이 방침은 전자레인지가 기숙사실 내에서 가연성 물체들에 불을 붙게 하여, 화재를 일으킬 가능성이 있다는 이유로 통과되었습니다. 다음 학기에 기숙사실 내에서 발견되는 어떠한 전자레인지도 기숙사 사감에게 압수될 것이며, 소유자는 100달러의 벌금형에 처해집니다.

Script |
W: Hey, Lyle! Are you having a good day?
M: Yeah. I'm a little annoyed after hearing that the college is going to ban personal microwaves, though.
W: You know, I think that it's a pretty good idea.
M: Really? How come?
W: Well, there are students living here who keep pretty flammable materials in their rooms. For instance, I'm currently on a floor with a lot of art majors, and they keep all kinds of oil-based paints in their rooms. If someone burned their food and it started a fire, then that fire could easily spread throughout the floor and even the building.
M: Yeah, but why are they going to charge students a fine if they take away our microwaves? That seems unnecessary.
W: Well, if you have enough money for a microwave, then you've got enough money to pay the fine. It would definitely save you a lot of money if you didn't have a microwave in the first place, though. Plus, it would be safer for everyone.

Script 해석 |
여자: 얘, 라일! 잘 지내?
남자: 응, 근데 학교 측이 개인용 전자레인지를 금지할 거라는 걸 들으니 좀 화가 나.
여자: 있지, 난 그게 정말 좋은 아이디어라 생각해.
남자: 정말? 어째서?

여자: 응, 여기엔 불에 잘 타는 물건들을 방에 두고 있는 학생들이 살고 있어. 예를 들자면, 난 지금 많은 미대 학생들과 같은 층에 있는데, 걔들은 온갖 종류의 유성 페인트들을 방에 둔다구. 만약 누군가가 음식을 태워서 불이 난다면 그 불은 쉽게 그 층 전체로, 심지어 건물 전체로 번질 수 있어.

남자: 그래, 그런데 왜 우리의 전자레인지를 압수해 가면서 학생들에게 벌금을 부과하려는 거지? 그건 불필요해.

여자: 글쎄, 만약 네가 전자레인지를 하나 살 만한 돈이 있다면, 그 벌금을 낼 돈은 충분히 있겠지. 애당초 네가 전자레인지를 가지고 있지 않았다면, 넌 확실히 많은 돈을 절약하는 게 될 거야. 게다가 그게 모두에게 안전할 거라구.

Sample Response |

The woman thinks that the announced banning of personal microwaves from dorm rooms is a good policy. She gives two reasons to support this. First, she agrees that microwaves could ignite flammable materials, such as the painting materials used by the art majors on her dorm floor. She also mentions that burning food could possibly do this and start a fire. Second, the woman believes that the fine imposed after microwaves are confiscated would prevent students from bringing them in the first place. She thinks that students can pay the fines, but they can avoid having to do so by not having microwaves, thus making things safer.

4

지문 해석 |

시력 장애: 다양한 시력 장애 중 가장 흔한 상황은 굴절 장애와 관련이 있다. 굴절 장애는 눈의 형태가 완전한 구 형태가 아니라서 빛을 똑바로 구부리지 못할 때 발생한다. 안구의 망막은 우리가 받는 신호를 이미지로 형성하는 과정을 담당하는 막이다. 광선이 눈 한 가운데에 부딪히고 망막에 도달하지 못하면, 사람은 가까운 곳에 있는 물체만 볼 수 있게 된다. 만약 빛이 망막 너머로 넘어가면 먼 거리에 있는 물체만 명확하게 보인다. 이러한 장애는 유전적 성질과 관련이 있지만 교정 과정을 통해서 치료할 수 있다.

Script |

Let's say you have a driver who complains of not being able to see road signs 5~10 meters away, but can clearly see what is immediately ahead of them. Ten to one, they suffer from myopia, a common refractive disorder that you all probably know as near-sightedness. With myopia, far-away images tend to be blurry and out of focus. Headaches and eye strain caused by squinting are common discomforts for those with this disorder.

Let's take another hypothetical driver ... and this driver has the opposite problem. He can see the road ahead of him clearly, but he has to squint to see the speedometer that's right in front of his face. In this case our driver suffers from hyperopia, or far-sightedness. Uh, the symptoms are pretty similar to those of myopia, headaches, eye strain ... Uh, but this time, these discomforts are caused by squinting to see nearby objects, rather than ones far away.

So, you see, class, having good eyesight is essential to being able to function properly in the everyday world. Without perfect or good eyesight, we won't be able to clearly see objects within or beyond our peripheral vision. However, corrective surgery and prescription eyewear have become available to people suffering from such conditions.

Script 해석 |

바로 앞에 있는 것은 또렷하게 잘 볼 수 있지만 5~10미터 앞에 있는 도로 표지판은 잘 안 보인다고 불평하는 운전자가 있다고 생각해봅시다. 열에 하나는 근시라고 알고 있는 굴절 장애를 겪고 있는 것입니다. 근시가 있으면 멀리 있는 물체가 흐려 보이고 초점이 맞지 않습니다. 이 장애를 가진 사람은 대개 두통이나 눈을 찌푸림으로 인한 눈의 피로라는 불편을 겪습니다.

또 다른 운전자를 생각해 볼까요. 이 운전자는 정반대의 문제를 가지고 있습니다. 도로의 먼 곳은 또렷하게 보이지만 코앞에 있는 속도판을 보기 위해서는 실눈을 떠야 합니다. 이런 경우는 원시를 겪는 것입니다. 증상은 근시와 마찬가지로 두통이나 눈의 피로 등입니다. 그렇지만 이 경우는 먼 것을 보려고 하는 것보다는 가까운 것을 보기 위해 눈을 찌푸리기 때문에 오는 것이죠.

그렇기 때문에, 여러분, 좋은 시력은 일상 생활에서 올바르게 기능할 수 있게 해주는 중요한 요소입니다. 완벽하거나 좋은 시력 없이는 가까운 곳이나 주변 시야를 넘는 곳에 있는 물체를 잘 볼 수 없게 됩니다. 그러나 이런 경우에 있는 사람들이 사용할 수 있는 시력 교정 수술이나 의사가 처방한 안경들이 존재합니다.

Sample Response |

According to the reading, the most common condition among various vision problems is refractive disorders which occur when the shape of the eye is not a perfect sphere and can't bend light properly. The professor discusses drivers who suffer from myopia and drivers who suffer from hyperopia to illustrate refractive disorders. The professor says that the drivers who suffer from myopia, also known as near-sightedness experience headaches and eye strain when looking at far-away images. Also, the drivers who suffer from hyperopia, also known as far-sightedness, experience similar discomforts when looking at nearby objects. The professor emphasizes the importance of having good eyesight. However, he also mentioned that these refractive disorders can be treated through corrective surgery and prescription eyewear.

5

Script |

M: Hey, Melanie! How's it going?

W: Oh, hi. I'm doing okay, I guess.

M: It sounds like something's wrong. What's up?

W: Well, I'm writing a paper for my history class, but I can't find any good research materials at our school library. I even went to the public library and the local bookstore, but I can't find anything! I don't know what to do.

M: Well, something that you can do is find sources on the Internet. You can go through different online journals and books, using the ones your professor recommended. Now, a lot of those sites charge you money for a membership, but you'll have unlimited access to their resources.

W: Yeah, but I don't know if I want to buy an online membership just for a research paper.

M: Well, if you don't, then you can always request the books from a different college. The librarians can track down any materials that are currently available at other academic libraries and have them transferred here at your request. Now, you won't get them for about a week or two, but it won't cost you anything.

W: I don't know. I'll give both choices some thought.

Script 해석 |

남자: 야, 멜라니! 어떻게 지내니?

여자: 오, 안녕. 난 잘 지내는 것 같기도 하고.

남자: 그건 뭐가 곤란한 일이 있는 것처럼 들리는데. 무슨 일이야?

여자: 응, 역사 과목 논문을 쓰려 하는데, 우리 학교 도서관에선 괜찮은 연구 자료들을 못 찾겠어. 심지어 공공도서관과 시내 서점에도 가 봤지만 어떤 것도 찾아낼 수 없었어! 어떻게 해야 할지 모르겠어.

남자: 음, 인터넷으로 자료를 찾아볼 수도 있잖아. 교수님이 추천한 사이트들을 이용해서 다양한 온라인 저널들과 책을 훑어볼 수 있다구. 상당수의 이런 사이트들이 회원 가입을 위해 돈을 청구할 테지만, 넌 그 자료들에 무한대로 접근할 수 있을 거야.

여자: 그래, 하지만 난 연구 논문 하나를 위해 온라인 멤버십을 구입하고 싶진 않은걸.

남자: 글쎄, 그렇다면 넌 다른 대학에서 언제든지 그 책들을 구할 수 있어. 네가 요청하면 도서관 사서들이 현재 사용 가능한 다른 대학 도서관의 자료들을 추적해서 여기로 옮겨올 수 있다구. 1~2주 동안은 그것들을 손에 넣을 수 없겠지만 아무 비용도 들지 않아.

여자: 모르겠다. 두 가지 선택 다 생각 좀 해 봐야겠어.

Sample Response |

The problem is that the woman needs good research materials for her history paper, but she can't find any at the nearby libraries or bookstore. Her options are purchasing a membership for an online resource or waiting for research materials from other libraries. I prefer that she purchase a membership for an online resource. For one thing, she'll have the material immediately, but if she requests the books, then she will have to wait about one or two weeks, which is precious studying time. Second, she will have unlimited access to materials online, and she could use them for future assignments. With the library, she would have to request different books each time and wait for them for several days.

6

Script |

Today, we are going to look at one of the worst episodes in the history of the United States: the Civil War. The Civil War between the Northern and Southern states was the bloodiest conflict ever fought in America. Now, a lot of you are probably asking, what ultimately led to this violent conflict? Well, there were two main factors behind it: growing opposition to slavery and cultural differences between Northern and Southern states.

First, there was a growing opposition to slavery. Slavery in the Southern states had been controversial in America decades before the Civil War, but opposition to it was growing increasingly fierce. For instance, several escaped slaves told stories about the horrors of captivity, and these accounts gained much sympathy from people in the Northern states. Sometimes opposition to slavery led to bloodshed, as both slaves and free people led violent revolts against slave-owners.

Second, there were cultural differences between the Northern and Southern states. These differences between the North and the South had existed since the beginning of the United States, but they grew more divisive right before the war. For instance, the Southern states wanted to create their own laws and be left alone by the federal government, whereas the Northern states wanted consistent federal laws for all the states. Also, the South wanted to rely on agriculture as an economic system, whereas people in the North, where industry was the main economic system, wanted to industrialize the South. Eventually, both sides felt that the only way to achieve their goals was through violent force, and this is what started the Civil War.

Script 해석 |

오늘 우리는 미국 역사상 최악의 에피소드 중 하나인 남북전쟁에 관해 살펴보도록 하죠. 북부와 남부 주들 간에 벌어진 남북전쟁은 미국에서 여태까지 가장 피비린내 나는 전쟁이었습니다. 그런데, 여러분들 중 다수는 이렇게 묻습니다. 무엇이 궁극적으로 이 격렬한 전쟁을 일으켰냐고요. 글쎄요, 그 뒤에는 두 가지 주요 요인이 있었습니다. 노예제도에 대한 커져가는 반대와 북부와 남부 주들 간의 문화적 차이라는 거죠.

먼저, 노예제도에 대한 반대가 점점 심해졌습니다. 남부 주들의 노예제도는 남북전쟁이 일어나기 몇 십 년 전부터 논란이 되어 왔지만, 그것에 대한 반대가 점점 격심해져 가고 있었습니다. 그 예로, 탈출한 여러 노예들이 노예 기간 동안 의 참혹함에 대해 이야기했으며, 이러한 이야기들은 북부 주들 사람들로부터 많은 동정을 얻었습니다. 노예제에 대한 반대는 종종 유혈 사태를 야기시켰고, 노예들과 자유인 모두 노예 소유자들에 대항하여 격렬한 폭동들을 일으켰습니다.

두 번째로 북부와 남부 주들 간에 문화적 차이가 있다는 것이었습니다. 북부와 남부 간의 이러한 차이점들은 미합중국의 초기부터 존재해 왔지만, 남북전쟁 바로 직전 더욱 불화를 일으키는 요소가 되었습니다. 예를 들면, 북부의 주들은 모든 주들에 대해 일관적으로 적용되는 연방법을 원했던 반면, 남부의 주들은 자신들만의 독자적인 법을 제정하기 원하여 연방 정부로부터 분리되기를 원했습니다. 또한 남부는 경제 체제로서 농업에 의존하길 원했지만, 공업이 주요 경제 체제였던 북부 사람들은 남부를 산업화하길 원했습니다. 결국 양쪽 모두 자신들의 목표를 달성하는 유일한 방법은 폭력을 통해서라 생각했고, 이것이 남북전쟁을 일으킨 것입니다.

Sample Response |

According to the professor, growing opposition to slavery and cultural differences between the Northern and Southern states led to the American Civil War by intensifying tensions that already existed between the North and South. First, Southern slavery grew more controversial and became more strongly opposed in the Northern states as escaped slaves began to tell stories about the horrors they had endured in the South. Many bloody revolts also occurred, making matters worse. Second, there were many cultural differences between the Northern and Southern states that would drive them to fight. For instance, Southern states wanted their own laws, while Northern states wanted everyone to abide by federal laws. Additionally, Southern states favored agriculture, while the North wanted to expand its industries to the South.

Actual Test

p. 128

1

Sample Response |
I regret never being in any high school plays because I wanted to know the students in drama class and I wanted to overcome my fear of performing. First, I wanted to make friends with drama students. They were creative and not afraid of telling people what they thought. Because the drama class put on all the plays, I could've met them by acting in one. Second, I have a fear of performing that I'd like to overcome. I want to be able to give speeches or tell jokes without stuttering, and acting would've helped that. However, this fear prevented me from trying out for a high school play. In short, these are reasons why I regret not being in a school play.

2

Sample Response |
I agree that all students should graduate from high school at the same time. There are a couple of reasons why I believe so. To start off, schools have an easier time when all students graduate together. It is easier to maintain everyone's student records and organize classes if everyone goes to high school for the required number of years. Not only that, but this better prepares students for college. Even if someone is smart, he may not be mature enough to start college. Having him stay with a certain class will help him build relationships and develop the maturity needed for college.

3

지문 해석 |
독자 의견: 저는 학교가 이제 더 이상 오후 6시 이후에 학생들이 자기 개들과 캠퍼스를 산책하는 것을 허락하지 않는다는 것에 얼마나 화가 났는지를 알리기 위해 편지를 씁니다. 근처에 개를 데리고 산책할 수 있는 유일한 공원이 대학 캠퍼스인데, 저는 6시가 되기 전까지는 강의실에서 나오지 못합니다. 대학 측은 이 방침을 조금 바꾸어, 사람들이 자신들의 개에게 목줄을 채우도록 하게 하는 건 어떨까요? 그렇게 하면 캠퍼스도 안전하고 사람들도 자신의 개와 함께 여기서 걸어도 될 것입니다.

우려하는 독자로부터

Script |
M: What's going on, Tammy?
W: Not much. I'm just reading this letter in the school newspaper.
M: Oh, is that the one where the student's angry about no dogs being allowed on campus? I can't believe that person is so upset.
W: Really? Why can't you believe it?
M: Well, for one thing, the university doesn't force anyone to take classes until 6:00 p.m., and there are plenty of streets where people can walk their dogs. The university's policies aren't going to be convenient for EVERYBODY.
W: Yeah, but why doesn't the college just require dogs to wear leashes?
M: Because some owners just tie their dogs up to trees or benches and leave them there for a while, and the dogs still bother people. The college just doesn't want people to leave their dogs here all day, so I think it's easier for everyone if dogs have to be off campus by 6:00.

Script 해석 |
남자: 무슨 일이야, 태미?
여자: 별일 아닌데. 그냥 학교 신문에 난 이 편지를 읽고 있었어.
남자: 아, 그 캠퍼스에 개를 허용하지 않는다는 데 화가 난 독자의 편지 말이야? 그 사람이 그토록 화를 내는 게 어처구니가 없어.
여자: 정말? 왜 그걸 이해하지 못하니?
남자: 글쎄, 한 가지 이유는, 대학 측은 누구에게도 오후 6시까지 수업을 듣도록 강요하지 않는다는 거야. 그리고 사람들이 자기 개를 데리고 산책할 수 있는 길거리도 많고 말이야. 대학 방침이 모든 사람들에게 다 편리하진 않은 거라구.
여자: 그래, 하지만 대학이 그냥 개들에게 목줄을 채우도록 하는 건 어떨까?
남자: 몇몇 주인들이 자기 개를 나무나 벤치에 묶어서 얼마 동안 그냥 내버려 두기 때문에 사람들에게는 계속 방해가 된다구. 대학 측은 사람들이 자신들의 개를 하루 종일 여기에 두는 걸 원치 않아. 그래서 난 6시까지 개들이 캠퍼스 밖으로 나가게 되면, 모든 사람에게 더 편할 거라고 생각해.

Sample Response |

The man disagrees with the letter writer, who is upset about no dogs being allowed on campus after six. The man gives two reasons for his opinion. The first one is that the man feels the university's rules can't be convenient for everyone. He argues that no one has to take classes until six and there are other places to walk dogs, which are less convenient but possible. He also says that the new policy is safer than leashes. He argues that leashes won't make the campus safer because dogs that stay there all day bother people. Thus, dogs should be kept off campus altogether. This is why the man disagrees with the writer's complaint.

4

지문 해석 |

학습된 무기력: 학습된 무기력은 한 인간이 반복적으로 불쾌한 경험들에 노출되어 와서, 이러한 과거 경험들의 결과로 자신이 모든 불쾌한 상황들에서 무력하다고 느끼는 심리적인 상태입니다. 그 인간의 초기 경험은 정말 그가 통제할 수 없었을 것이며, 이러한 불쾌한 상황들에 지속적으로 노출되는 것이 그로 하여금 수동적이고, 자신의 운명에 체념하게 해 왔던 것입니다. 이것의 결과로 그의 방어적인 행동은 소멸되어, 그가 실제로 통제할 수 있는 미래 상황들에 대해서도 본능적으로 무기력해지게 되는 것입니다.

Script |

In today's class we are going to talk about abusive relationships. Psychological studies about these types of relationships show that people who were abused as children tend to end up in abusive relationships as adults, too. For instance, let's say that a woman who was abused as a child is now married to an abusive husband. Why doesn't she try to end it? After all, as a grown woman, she should be able to take care of herself. She can escape from her husband, or she can find ways to defend herself, right? So why doesn't she try to end this abusive relationship?

Well, as a girl, she came to believe that she would never be able to escape abuse. Being a young child, she could not physically defend herself against such treatment, and she wasn't able to escape her abuser's custody. After a while, the girl eventually gave up any hope of ending this abusive relationship. Once she adopted this attitude, it stuck with her for the rest of her life. It doesn't matter whether or not she has power now; if she doesn't believe she can escape an abusive relationship, then she probably won't—because she only knows how to be a victim.

Script 해석 |

오늘 수업에서 우리는 학대 받는 관계에 대해 이야기하도록 하겠습니다. 이러한 유형의 관계들에 관한 심리학적 연구는 어린 시절에 학대 받았던 사람들이 어른이 되어서도 학대 받는 관계를 지속하는 경향이 있다는 것을 보여 줍니다. 예를 들어 어린 시절에 학대를 받았으며, 지금 학대하는 남편과 결혼한 한 여성에 대해 이야기해 봅시다. 그녀는 왜 그것을 끝내려고 하지 않는 걸까요? 결국, 한 성인 여성으로서, 그녀는 자기 자신을 돌볼 수 있어야 합니다. 그녀는 남편에게서 달아나거나 자신을 방어할 방법들을 찾을 수도 있죠, 맞요? 그렇다면 그녀는 왜 이같이 학대 받는 관계를 끝내려고 하지 않는 걸까요?

자, 소녀일 때, 그녀는 자신이 학대로부터 절대 벗어날 수 없다고 믿게 되었습니다. 어린 아이였기 때문에 그녀는 이같은 처우로부터 신체적으로 자신을 방어할 수가 없었고, 학대자의 구속에서 벗어날 수 없었습니다. 얼마 후, 그녀는 결국 학대 관계를 끝내는 어떤 희망도 포기해 버렸습니다. 한번 이러한 태도를 취하자, 그것은 그녀의 남은 평생 동안 고착되어 버렸습니다. 이제 그녀가 힘이 있건 없건 그게 문제가 아닙니다. 그녀는 학대 받는 관계에서 벗어날 수 있다고 믿지 않는다면, 아마 그렇게 할 수 없을 것입니다. 왜냐하면 그녀는 희생자가 되는 법만을 알기 때문입니다.

Sample Response |

The professor's discussion about women who get abused as both children and adults is an example of the concept of learned helplessness. In the beginning of the lecture, the professor provides an example of a woman who suffered child abuse and marries an abusive husband. The professor emphasizes that she doesn't defend herself or flee her husband, even though she's an adult with control. This ties into the idea that learned helplessness causes people to view all situations as uncontrollable because they couldn't control past unpleasant situations. Later on in the lecture, the professor directly addresses learned helplessness by stating that the woman had no control as a child and eventually gave up any hope of ending an abusive relationship, so she can't escape because she only knows victimization.

5

Script |

W: What's up, Harry? Are you doing okay?
M: Yeah, except I found out that I've got to get credit for two semesters of foreign language classes before I graduate next year. The trouble is this: all of the foreign language classes next year are full!
W: Oh, I'm sorry. That sounds like a pretty tough situation.
M: Yeah. I'm just not sure what I'm going to do about this.
W: Well, I've got an idea. You can take a foreign language class over the summer. For about two months, you would sit in class for about three hours, but this one class would cover a full year of foreign language credit.
M: Hmm. It sounds good, but I don't know about taking a class during the summer...
W: You know, another thing that you could do is take a foreign language test before you graduate. If you pass the test, you won't have to take any foreign language classes at all. You would have to study a lot for it, and you'd be on your own. However, you wouldn't have to go to school during the summer.
M: It looks like this is going to be a tough choice to make.

Script 해석 |

여자: 기분이 어때, 해리? 잘 지내고 있는 거야?
남자: 응, 단 한 가지 내가 내년에 졸업하기 전까지 외국어 수업 두 학기를 이수해야 한다는 걸 빼면 말이야. 문제는 내년에 모든 외국어 수업들의 정원이 다 찼다는 거지.
여자: 오, 안됐구나. 정말 곤란한 상황인 거 같다.
남자: 그래. 이 일을 정말 어떻게 해야 할지 모르겠어.
여자: 어, 내게 생각이 하나 있는데. 넌 여름 동안에 외국어 수업을 들을 수도 있잖아. 약 두 달 동안 3시간 남짓 교실에 앉아 있을 테지만, 이 수업 하나로 일 년 동안의 외국어 수업 학점을 모두 채울 수 있다구.
남자: 흠. 좋은 생각이긴 한데, 여름 동안에 수업을 들어야 한다는 게 좀 그렇다.
여자: 그럼 말이야, 네가 졸업하기 전에 외국어 시험을 치르는 방법도 있어. 그 시험을 통과하게 되면, 넌 어떤 외국어 수업도 들을 필요가 없어진다구. 그걸 위해선 공부를 열심히 해야 하고, 그건 책임인 거지. 하지만 넌 여름 동안에 학교에 나갈 필요는 없을 거야.
남자: 이건 결정하기 힘든 선택인 거 같아.

Sample Response |

The man's problem is that he must take two semesters of foreign language courses next year in order to graduate, but there are none available next year. The woman suggests two options, which are to take a daily three-hour foreign language course over the summer or to take a foreign language test before graduating. I think he should take the summer course because he will have help and it won't last long. First, he will have the help of the instructor and an assigned textbook to learn the material, whereas he would have to study on his own for the test. Second, he would only have to take it over the summer. Even though each class is three hours long and he'll work during the summer, it would be quicker than studying for months.

6

Script |

Okay, class, today we will discuss something that's always been a serious threat to agriculture: soil erosion. Soil erosion is the gradual displacement of soil by natural forces. While soil erosion is responsible for many geological features on land, it has also destroyed fertile farmland. So, how do agricultural communities try to prevent soil erosion? Well, most of them try two different methods: setting up physical barriers and preserving vegetation.

First, setting up physical barriers can help prevent erosion. Physical barriers set up on farmland absorb or deflect natural agents of erosion, like wind and water. For instance, some farmers plow ditches into their fields. These ditches funnel and catch extra water from rainstorms, preventing extra runoff from washing away the soil. Not only does this prevent rainwater from washing away the soil, but it also helps water to seep into the ground.

Second, preserving vegetation is another method farmers use to prevent erosion. See, plants act as a cover against heavy rainwater, and they obstruct surface runoff, slowing down water that erodes the soil. Not only that, but the deep roots of plants also hold the soil in position, preventing it from being washed away. This is why many agricultural communities reforest areas by planting new trees and protecting grasslands from grazing animals, like cattle and sheep. Some farmers also use mulch, a mixture of grass, leaves, and other organic material that acts as a protective barrier against wind and water. Not only does mulch deflect rainwater, but it also preserves moisture in the soil.

Script 해석 |

자, 여러분, 오늘 우리는 농업에 늘 심각한 위협이 되어 온 토양 침식에 관해 논의해 보도록 하겠습니다. 토양 침식은 자연적인 힘에 의한 점진적인 토양의 이동 현상입니다. 토양 침식은 대지의 많은 지리적 형세의 원인이 되는 한편, 비옥한 농경지를 파괴하기도 합니다. 그렇다면 어떻게 농업 공동체들이 토양 침식을 막을 수 있을까요? 글쎄요, 그들은 대부분 두 가지 다른 방법을 시도합니다. 물리적인 방벽을 세우는 것, 또는 초지를 보존하는 것입니다.

먼저, 물리적 방벽을 세우는 것이 침식을 막을 수 있습니다. 농경지에 세워진 물리적 방벽은 바람이나 물 같은 자연적인 침식의 힘을 흡수하거나 빗나가게 합니다. 예를 들어, 어떤 농부들이 자신들의 농지에 쟁기로 도랑을 파 놓습니다. 이 도랑들은 폭풍우로 인한 여분의 물이 도랑으로 흐르게 하고 물길을 잡아주어, 땅에 흐르는 빗물에 토양이 씻겨 내려가는 것을 막아줍니다. 이는 토양이 빗물에 씻겨 내려가는 것을 막을 뿐 아니라 물이 지면에 스며들도록 합니다.

두 번째로, 농부들이 침식을 막기 위해 사용하는 또 다른 방법은 초지 보존입니다. 식물은 세찬 빗물에 대한 보호막구실을 하며, 지표면의 빗물의 흐름을 방해하여 물이 토양을 침식시키는 속도를 느리게 합니다. 그뿐만 아니라, 식물의 깊은 뿌리는 토양을 제자리에 고정시켜, 씻겨 내려가는 것으로부터 막아 줍니다. 이는 많은 농업 공동체들이 여러 지역에 새로운 나무를 심어 숲을 재조성하고, 소와 양과 같은 동물들이 풀을 뜯는 것으로부터 목초지를 보호하는 이유입니다. 또 어떤 농부들은 풀과, 잎사귀 그리고 다른 유기물의 혼합물로서 바람과 물에 보호막 구실을 하는 뿌리 덮개를 이용하기도 합니다. 뿌리 덮개는 빗물을 비껴 가게 할 뿐만 아니라, 토양 속의 수분을 보존시켜 주기도 합니다.

Sample Response |

According to the lecture, physical barriers and preserving vegetation can prevent soil erosion by blocking rainwater that washes soil away and by holding soil together. The professor first mentions that physical barriers like ditches both catch extra rainwater in grooves and allow water to seep into the soil. Thus, many farmers plow ditches in their fields to funnel rainwater and prevent it from washing away the soil. The professor then discusses the presence of vegetation. Plants cover the soil against rainwater and hold the soil together with deep roots, preventing excessive erosion. People will plant new trees in forests, protect grasslands from grazing, and use organic mulch as a barrier for these reasons.

Workbook

1. Independent Task Skills

Exercise 1. 뜻이 비슷한 단어 p. 138

A
- 2. problem
- 3. debate
- 4. true
- 5. understand
- 6. convenient
- 7. total
- 8. journey
- 9. unable
- 10. reason

B
- 2. cost
- 3. healed
- 4. decide
- 5. effective
- 6. between
- 7. decision
- 8. doubt
- 9. improve
- 10. appropriate / good

Exercise 2. 모양·발음이 비슷한 단어 p. 140

A
- 2. desert
- 3. besides
- 4. causal
- 5. precede
- 6. extend
- 7. transform
- 8. classic
- 9. humane
- 10. decreased
- 11. source
- 12. imminent
- 13. continual
- 14. persecute
- 15. terrific

Exercise 3. 능동 vs. 수동 p. 142

A
- 2. OK
- 3. OK
- 4. confusing
- 5. depressing
- 6. OK
- 7. OK
- 8. excited
- 9. OK
- 10. inspiring

B
- 2. interested in
- 3. moving
- 4. pleased with
- 5. satisfying
- 6. shocking
- 7. surprised
- 8. terrifying
- 9. disappointed
- 10. exhausted

Exercise 4. 함께 쓰는 단어 p. 144

A
- 2. relieve stress, suffer from stress, cope with stress, prevent stress
- 3. lose a job, get a job, keep a job, look for a job, have a job
- 4. make a noise, shut out noise, can't stand the noise, prevent noise
- 5. cause damage, prevent damage, suffer damage, have damage

1. Independent Task Skills

    6. keep a secret, have a secret, tell a secret
    7. have a disease, suffer from a disease, prevent disease
    8. make an appointment, get an appointment, have an appointment, keep an appointment
    9. make friends, lose a friend, get a friend, become friends, meet a friend, have a friend
  10. have a heart, lose one's heart, break one's heart

B
- **2.** relieve stress
- **3.** look for a job
- **4.** shut out noise
- **5.** cause damage
- **6.** keep / have a secret
- **7.** suffer from a disease / have a disease
- **8.** lost my heart

C
- **2.** tells
- **3.** take / have
- **4.** make
- **5.** made
- **6.** make
- **7.** reached
- **8.** improve

Exercise 5. 숙어 (Phrasal Verbs)   p. 147

A
- **2.** carry on with
- **3.** blows up
- **4.** run out of
- **5.** speak up for
- **6.** breaks down
- **7.** get over
- **8.** put up with

B
- **2.** (A) 키우다   (B) (문제를) 꺼내다
- **3.** (A) 포기하다   (B) 끊다
- **4.** (A) (소리, 열 등을) 줄이다   (B) 거절하다
- **5.** (A) 체크아웃 하다   (B) 확인하다

Exercise 6. 콩글리쉬 (Broken English)   p. 148

A
- **2.** (A)   **3.** (A)   **4.** (B)   **5.** (B)

B
- **2.** refer to
- **3.** wear
- **4.** on the house
- **5.** with their parents looking out for them

C
- **2.** This way, I could learn from my friends how to study.
- **3.** A telescope gives us a closer look at the universe.
- **4.** There are many advantages to riding a bicycle instead of driving a car.
- **5.** It is important for adults to say good things about their spouses in front of their children.

Exercise 7. 풀어말하기 p. 150

A
2. most of the people in a group
3. to damage public property deliberately
4. to make something worse
5. buildings
6. someone who is walking along a street
7. money that is given to someone to pay for their education
8. impossible to reach
9. to give money to an organization to help people in need
10. the cutting or burning down of trees in an area

B
2. (A) expense
   (B) the amount of money you spend
3. (A) archeology
   (B) the study of ancient societies by examining their buildings, tools, etc.
4. (A) plagiarism
   (B) the act of using another person's words as if they were one's own
5. (A) reward
   (B) to give something to someone because the person has done a good thing
6. (A) potential
   (B) the possibility that someone or something has
7. (A) interaction
   (B) a process by which two things affect each other
8. (A) humidity
   (B) the amount of water contained in the air
9. (A) chronic
   (B) continuing for a long time
10. (A) innovation
    (B) a new idea or invention

Exercise 8. 동사의 패턴 p. 152

A
2. regard 3. explain 4. discuss 5. caused

B
2. calling 3. (should) take 4. to read 5. playing

C
2. from 3. to 4. to 5. to

1. Independent Task Skills

D 2. avoid writing
3. convince, that
4. tell, when to
5. like, to conduct
6. requires, to have/carry
7. argue, over
8. ask, about

Exercise 9. 부사절이 포함된 문장   p. 154

A 2. while   3. so that   4. Whether
5. unless   6. that   7. until
8. even though

B 2. Where polar bears come from, the climate is also ideal for walruses and seals.
3. The price of land near the lake has fallen since they discovered deposits of toxic chemicals in the area.
4. The oranges will freeze and the crop will be destroyed if there is an early frost.
5. There was a 10-car pile up because the snow storm caused zero visibility.

C 2. Although I've never been here before, this place seems familiar.
3. Because there was so much traffic, I took the bus instead of driving yesterday.
4. My sister and I have a lot of things in common, so we get along very well together.
5. I'd rather live in my own country than live abroad because I have my family and friends here.

Exercise 10. 명사절이 포함된 문장   p. 156

A 2. where   3. that   4. where
5. that   6. that   7. when
8. whose   9. wherever

B 2. Where the actress is to be married won't be revealed until tomorrow.
3. I can't believe that woman has not stopped talking!
4. What is talked about in the meeting will not be made public.
5. They now know why the world's climate is warming.

C 2. more students would join the program
3. what he ate that made him sick
4. that standing in front of a working microwave can cause cancer
5. whose priorities were more important
6. where the criminal hid the money stolen from the bank

Exercise 11. 형용사절이 포함된 문장   p. 158

A
2. The area
3. The car
4. the book
5. a car
6. the year
7. A child
8. An artist

B
2. that really causes the problem
3. who must bear the responsibility of maintaining family unity
4. that really offended me
5. where they made their nests
6. when their children marry and move away from home

C
2. whom
3. where
4. when
5. when
6. that
7. which
8. whose

D
2. that provides unlimited cultural experiences like museums, plays, and operas
3. who plays in the English Premier League
4. who is often described as a feminist writer
5. (that) I want to do this year

Exercise 12. 둘 이상의 종속절이 포함된 문장   p. 160

A
2. Which career you choose will determine the classes that you decide to take.
3. When Dad's favorite football team wins, he brags to friends who don't like that team.
4. Let's see the movie you told me about after we eat dinner.
5. This building, which was constructed a hundred years ago, will endure whatever conditions weather can create.

B
2. Whoever wants a ticket must wait until the vendor arrives.
3. Even though it will rain today, students want to go on a picnic because they think it will be fun.
4. Students who had low grades need extra lessons that would be helpful.
5. The factory that makes cars is where most people in town work.

C
2. As she read the book, Mary learned how fractions work.
3. What his uncle said was very clever, although the joke that he told was a little obscure.
4. I am scared of driving because of a car wreck I got in when I was young.
5. Unless my cousin changes his mind, you'll have to travel with whomever you can find.
6. The road that we want to take is where these two streets separate.
7. While the children are asleep, let's set out the presents that we bought for them.
8. Whatever you want to discuss until the teacher arrives is fine.
9. Whether the professor approves of your project or doesn't, you can be proud of the great effort that you've made so far.
10. Some scientists are convinced that global warming is due to human activity, while others believe it's caused by natural factors.

2. Integrated Task Skills

Exercise 1. 비슷한 말(Synonym)로 바꾸어 말하기   p. 164

A
2. The growing tension between Russia and America threatened peace.
3. Now, who knows what the different causes of the bubonic plague were?
4. I've spent all of my money on fees for classes.
5. All creatures must use water to survive.
6. Can you find my dorm on that campus map?
7. I got a lot of books from the library.
8. If you sweat too much during gym, drink some water.

B
2. I had a fight with my roommate, and now she won't talk to me.
3. Freud thought that our dreams show our deepest desires.
4. You have a lot of freedom in a democracy, but you must use it carefully.
5. The collection of dust in the air creates clouds.

C
2. I can't meet with you tonight because I have band practice.
3. I hope the professor ends class early because I have a long drive.
4. Parking your car in this area isn't allowed.
5. Atoms are the most basic pieces of matter.

> **녹음 내용**
> 1. Interstellar travel may be limited, but it can give us crucial information.
> 2. I can't hang out with you tonight because I have band rehearsal.
> 3. I hope the professor dismisses us early because I have a long commute.
> 4. Parking your vehicle in this area is prohibited.
> 5. Atoms are the most fundamental units of matter.

Exercise 2. 문장 구조를 바꾸어 말하기   p. 166

A
2. stinging tentacles as a defense mechanism
3. a difficult assignment yesterday
4. was assassinated at Ford's Theater
5. from cosmic dust clouds compressing
6. go to an orientation next week
7. required to take the graduation test
8. was that the sun orbited the earth

B
2. You may choose from a variety of available meal plans.
3. Congress must have a two-thirds majority to override a presidential veto.

4. Many scientists believe that a meteorite made the dinosaurs go extinct.
5. You can move into the dorm next Tuesday.

C 2. Mosquitoes are a great health risk because they carry diseases.
   3. Next Friday's dance was canceled becasue of repairs to the dance hall.
   4. Add all of the numbers when you determine an average.
   5. I go to the student lounge whenever I complete my homework.

   녹음 내용
   1. Once every week, there will be a student council meeting.
   2. Because they act as carriers for diseases, mosquitoes pose a great health risk.
   3. Due to repairs to the dance hall, next Friday's dance has been canceled.
   4. When you determine an average, make sure that you add all of the numbers.
   5. Whenever I finish my homework, I head down to the student lounge.

Exercise 3. 내용을 단순화시키기 p. 168

A 2. gets only one vote
   3. is too far away
   4. whisper to each other in calculus class
   5. once connected
   6. cause nightmares
   7. used in World War II
   8. good preparation for tests

B 2. Turtles have shells for protection.
   3. Metaphors compare two things to each other.
   4. Jonathan Swift made fun of people's actions.
   5. This essay is long and difficult.

C 2. My World History class meets too early.
   3. You can hand out fliers on campus.
   4. Not all volcanoes erupt.
   5. My mail hasn't arrived yet.

   녹음 내용
   1. With the Treaty of Versailles, combat among nations fighting in World War I ceased.
   2. I am barely awake during World History, which is held at 8:00 in the morning!
   3. Distributing fliers on campus is allowed by the university.
   4. While many volcanoes are quite active, there are some that remain dormant.
   5. I've checked my mailbox many times today, and I'm always left empty-handed.

Exercise 4. 다양한 Paraphrase　　　　　　　　　　　　　　　　　　　　　　　p. 170

A　2.　Lunch is canceled on Friday afternoons since no one's on campus. The campus is vacant on Friday afternoons, so lunch is unavailable.

　　　3.　Columbus found North America while sailing for India. In the course of sailing to India, Columbus stumbled upon North America.

　　　4.　Citric acid can clean surfaces and heal cells.
　　　　　Cleaning surfaces and healing cells can be done with citric acid.
　　　　　Citric acid has many uses, like cleaning surfaces and healing cells.

　　　5.　Fraternity members have to keep its secrets.
　　　　　When a person is admitted into the fraternity, he or she has to pledge to keep its secrets.
　　　　　Anyone who joins the fraternity has to promise to keep its secrets.

B　2.　Class presidents have a lot of power.
　　　　　A person gains substantial authority once elected class president.
　　　　　The candidate who becomes class president will acquire real authority.
　　　　　When elected class president, the victor will assume considerable power.

　　　3.　College radio DJs must work around their classes.
　　　　　As an announcer for the college radio station, one must perform one's duties without neglecting one's academic work.
　　　　　Working around class schedules is required of college radio DJs.
　　　　　College disc jockeys must schedule their broadcasts around their classes.

　　　4.　The Cherokee tribe developed its own alphabet and published a newspaper.
　　　　　A Native American tribe that developed its own alphabet and published a newspaper was the Cherokee.
　　　　　The Cherokee nation created its own alphabet and published a newspaper.

　　　5.　Due to an oncoming thunderstorm, softball practice has been called off.
　　　　　Softball practice was canceled due to a storm.
　　　　　The certainty of rain prompted the cancellation of softball practice.
　　　　　Due to rain, softball practice has been canceled.

C　2.　One convention of older English drama was performance of female roles by males.
　　　　　Men once portrayed women in English plays.
　　　　　Women characters in English drama were once played by men.
　　　　　In older English plays, the female roles would be filled by male actors.

　　　3.　Pie charts are suitable for showing different percentages.
　　　　　If percentages need to be specified, then a pie chart is appropriate.
　　　　　Pie charts are a good choice for showing different percentages.

　　　　　녹음내용
　　　　　1.　Notebooks for chemistry lab sessions are available in the bookstore.
　　　　　2.　In English drama, women characters used to be played by men.
　　　　　3.　If you need to show different percentages, then a pie chart is a good choice.

Exercise 5. 기호·약어 사용하기   p. 172

A
2. plants make oxy. + give nutr.
3. dist. b/w earth & jup. > dist. shut. can fly
4. can't make b.ball team b/c ht. < 6 ft.
5. fin. paper by Fri. noon → pass class
6. farms can't prod. crops b/c drought. ~ usu. close down
7. pub. works may bnft. ← purch. by corp.
8. lost bag → go to class w/o book
9. fat. food esp. red meat → heart dis. risk↑
10. art dept. shows stud. art Wed. ← get cash for art ctr.

B
2. big Euro. fig. were clergy e.g. Martin Luther
3. sch.ship ≠ loan b/c loan's repaid w/ int.
4. shp. coat = wool ~ stand. cold
5. org. labor ← stop ab. work prac.

녹음 내용
1. I ride my bike to class because I want to lose some weight.
2. Some important European figures–Martin Luther, for example–were members of the clergy.
3. A loan isn't the same as a scholarship because you have to pay back the loan, with interest.
4. Sheep's coats are made of wool, so they can withstand cold weather.
5. Labor became organized as a way to stop abusive work practices.

Exercise 6. 중요한 내용 찾기   p. 174

A

1.
Topic	Development of Sputnik satellite
Main idea	development of Sputnik satellite = important
Supporting idea	1) big turning pt. in tech. race b/w Russia & America
	2) 1st obj. launched into orbit around earth → inspired desire to explore space

지문 해석 |
스푸트니크 위성의 개발은 2차 세계 대전 이후 가장 중요한 사건 중 하나였다. 첫째, 그것은 러시아와 미국 간 기술 우위 경쟁에 있어서 커다란 전환점이었다. 그뿐 아니라 스푸트니크 위성은 지구 주위의 궤도로 발사된 첫 번째 물체로서 역사에 기록되었다. 이 새로운 사건은 우주를 보다 깊게 탐사하고자 하는 의욕을 북돋우는 데 도움이 되었다.

2.
Topic	Crusades
Main idea	Crusades had influence on Europe
Supporting idea	brought new ideas in sci. & phil. from ME → led to Renaissance

2. Integrated Task Skills

지문 해석 |

중세 유럽인들은 예루살렘을 지배하던 무슬림들로부터 예루살렘 도시를 되찾기 위한 시도로 십자군 전쟁을 일으켰다. 수세기 동안 여러 차례의 시도가 이루어졌지만 어느 것도 그리 성공적이지 않았다. 그러나 십자군 전쟁에서 돌아온 기사들이 중동으로부터 과학과 철학의 새로운 사상을 도입했다. 이 새로운 사상은 르네상스로 이어졌고 그로 인해 예술과 과학이 발전했다.

3.

Topic	Blank verse = poetry where each line has 10 syll. + no rhyme scheme
Main idea	Brit. writers used blank verse b/c it was poetic & believable
Supporting idea	1) fit into natural rhythm of spoken E
	2) lack of rhyme ? sound like normal speech

지문 해석 |

16세기의 대부분의 영국 작가들이 극에서 사용한 한 가지 형태는 무운시였다. 무운시는 매 행이 10음절로 이루어지고 압운* 형식이 없는 시이다. 영국 작가들은 주로 무운시를 사용했는데 왜냐하면 그것이 구어체 영어의 자연스러운 리듬에 맞았기 때문이고 또한 압운이 없음으로 해서 시가 더 보통의 말처럼 들렸기 때문이다. 그래서 그것은 시적이면서 동시에 현실적이었다.

*압운 (rhyme): 일정한 자리에 같은 음 또는 비슷한 음을 규칙적으로 배치하여 운율적인 효과를 내는 것

Exercise 7. 대화 듣고 Note-taking 하기   p. 176

A   1.

W: needs phys. grade ?
M: opt. 1 = teach class, just once
W: opt. 1 > resp. wanted
M: opt. 2 = extra labs = more work, less resp.

Script |

W: Ryan, I've got to bring my grade up in physics. The trouble is that I don't know what to do for extra credit.
M: Well, one thing you could do is teach a lesson. Some professors will allow you to teach a class, and you only have to do it once.
W: I don't know if I want that much responsibility on my shoulders.
M: You could also do some extra physics labs. It's more work, but you would have lab partners who would share the responsibility.

Script 해석 |

여자: Ryan, 나 물리학에서 성적을 올려야 해. 문제는 추가 점수를 위해 무엇을 해야 할지 모른다는 거야.
남자: 글쎄, 한 가지 방법은 강의를 하는 거야. 어떤 교수님들은 강의실에서 수업을 하도록 허락해 주실 거야. 그리고 한 번만 하면 돼.
여자: 내가 그렇게 많은 책임을 감당할 수 있을지 모르겠어.
남자: 별도의 물리 실험을 할 수도 있어. 그건 일이 더 많겠지만, 책임을 분담할 실험 파트너가 생길 거야.

2.

M: meet. for int. stud. = fun
W: only int. stud. can go
M: int. stud. must go; open to all stud. & fac.
    some stud. e.g. man get ex. credit for soc. studies class

Script |
M: Did you hear about that meeting for international students? I think that I'd like to go to that. It looks like it's going to be fun.
W: But I thought that you had to be an international student to do that.
M: Well, international students have to go to that meeting. Actually, it is open to any student or faculty member who would like to attend. Plus, some students, like me, will get extra credit for their social studies classes if they go.

Script 해석 |
남자: 교환 학생들 모임에 대해 들었니? 나 거기 가고 싶어. 재미있을 것 같아.
여자: 하지만 거기에 가려면 교환 학생이어야 하는 줄 알았는데.
남자: 글쎄, 교환 학생들은 그 모임에 꼭 가야 하는 거고. 사실은 참가하고 싶은 학생이나 강사진 누구에게나 열려 있어. 게다가 나 같은 몇몇 학생들은 거기에 가면 사회 과목에서 추가 점수를 얻게 돼.

3.
M: f.ball game canc. b/c rain; sch. won't ref. man's mon.
W: opt. 1: get rain-delay tick. ~ next game free
M: not sure
W: opt. 2: apply tick. to tuit. → class fee↓

Script |
M: I can't believe the football game got cancelled because of rain. Now these tickets I have aren't any good, and the school won't refund my money.
W: Well, you know, you can take them to the student activity office and have them marked as rain-delay tickets. That way you would get into the next football game for free.
M: I don't know about that.
W: Well, since you're a student, you could apply it toward your tuition. That would lower the cost of your class fees a bit.

Script 해석 |
남자: 비 때문에 축구 경기가 취소되었다니 믿을 수 없어. 이제 내가 가진 이 입장권은 유효하지 않아. 그런데 학교에서 환불을 안 해줘.
여자: 그럼, 있잖아, 학생 활동 사무실에 그걸 가져가서 우천으로 연기된 표라고 표시를 받을 수 있어. 그렇게 하면 다음 축구 경기에 무료로 입장할 거야.
남자: 글쎄.
여자: 음, 넌 학생이니까 그걸 네 등록금으로 요청할 수 있을 거야. 그건 네 수업료를 조금 낮춰 줄 거야.

Exercise 8. 강의 듣고 Note-taking 하기   p. 179

A   1.
Outsource = move jobs to foreign nat.
Why? b/c pay foreign lab. < US lab.
1) for. min. wage < US min. wage
2) in for. nat. e.g. China & India many lab. comp. for few jobs → work for less money

Script |
Recently, many American corporations have been outsourcing, or moving large numbers of jobs to foreign nations. Why do they do this? Well, they don't have to pay foreign laborers as much as they have to pay American laborers. One reason is that the foreign country's minimum wage is likely to be lower than the American minimum wage. Another reason is that large countries like India and China have many laborers competing for limited jobs, so lots of people are willing to work for less money.

Script 해석 |
최근에 많은 미국 기업들이 아웃소싱, 즉 대규모의 일자리를 해외로 옮기는 일을 하고 있습니다. 왜 이렇게 할까요? 음, 외국인 노동자들에게는 미국 노동자들에게 지불해야 하는 만큼 임금을 많이 주지 않아도 됩니다. 한 가지 이유는 외국의 최저임금이 미국의 최저임금보다 더 낮은 경우가 많습니다. 또 다른 이유는 인도와 중국 같은 큰 나라에서는 한정된 일자리를 얻기 위해 많은 노동자들이 경쟁하고 있고, 그래서 많은 사람들이 더 적은 돈을 받고도 일을 하려고 하죠.

2.

> some ch. have phys. traits not in par.
> - e.g. ch. w/ blue eyes has par. w/ brn. eyes
> blue eye = recessive gene; blocked rec. gene not seen
> rec. gene not blocked → rec. phys. trait shows
> - e.g. ch. inh. blue eye & no brn. eye

Script |
Now, you might wonder, why do some children have physical features not found in either of their parents, such as a blue-eyed child with two brown-eyed parents? Well, genes for blue eyes are recessive. People can have recessive genes but won't show the trait if another gene blocks it. Someone may carry the gene for blue eyes, but won't display the trait if a brown-eye gene blocks it. However, if a child inherits a blue-eye gene that isn't blocked by a brown-eye gene, then he or she will have blue eyes.

Script 해석 |
자, 여러분은 갈색 눈의 부모에게서 난 파란 눈의 아이와 같이, 왜 어떤 아이들은 부모 중 누구에게서도 발견되지 않는 신체적인 특징들을 갖는지 궁금할 것입니다. 음, 파란 눈의 유전자는 열성입니다. 사람들은 열성 유전자를 가지고 있으면서도 다른 유전자가 그것을 가로막으면 그 특징을 나타내지 않을 수 있습니다. 어떤 사람은 파란 눈의 유전자를 가지고 있을지 모르지만 만일 갈색 눈의 유전자가 그것을 차단하면 파란 눈의 특징을 보이지 않을 것입니다. 그러나 만일 아이가 갈색 눈의 유전자에 가로 막히지 않은 파란 눈의 유전자를 물려받으면 파란 눈을 가질 것입니다.

3.

> Platinum = prac. e.g. conv. for car
> plat. brks. dn. bad gas to good gas e.g. turns nitr. diox. to nit. & oxy.
> plat. chem. rea. w/ gas on mol. lvl.

Script |
I am sure most of you know that platinum is a valuable metal because of its rarity. However, did you know that it also has some practical uses? For instance, most of you use platinum as a converter when you drive your car. Car engines produce harmful gases, and platinum breaks them down into harmless gases. For instance, platinum converts nitrogen dioxide into nitrogen and oxygen. It does this by chemically reacting with the gases emitted by the engine, taking them apart on a molecular level.

Script 해석 |
백금이 희소성 때문에 귀중한 금속이라는 사실은 여러분 대부분이 알고 있을 것이라 생각합니다. 그러나 백금이 지닌 실용적인 몇 가지 용도도 알고 있나요? 예를 들면 여러분이 자동차를 운전할 때 대부분은 백금을 컨버터로 사용합니다. 자동차 엔진은 해로운 가스를 만들어 내는데, 백금이 그 유해 가스를 분해하여 무해한 가스로 만듭니다. 일례로 백금은 이산화질소를 질소와 산소로 바꿉니다. 백금은 엔진에 의해 방출되는 가스와 화학적으로 반응하여 가스를 분자 단위에서 분해함으로써 이러한 작용을 한답니다.

Exercise 9. 주제(Main Idea) 찾기   p. 180

A

1. In the likely event of rain, the graduation ceremony will be moved from the football field to the gymnasium, where there will be less room and light.

지문 해석 |
기상 예보에 따르면 이번 토요일에 교정에 비가 내릴 가능성이 매우 높다고 합니다. 토요일에 야외에서 졸업식이 있으므로 비가 오지 않기를 바랍니다. 만일 비가 오면 식은 축구장에서 체육관으로 옮겨야 할 것입니다. 유감스럽게도 그렇게 되면 앉을 공간이 적을 것이고 조명이 더 어두울 것입니다.

2. Improper trimming of nails can lead to ingrown nails that curve and cut into the surrounding flesh, increasing the risk of infection.

지문 해석 |
머리카락과 마찬가지로 손톱과 발톱은 지속적으로 자라서 잘라내야 한다. 하지만 이러한 손톱 발톱을 때맞춰 자르지 않으면 안으로 자랄 수 있다. 즉, 손발톱이 휘어서 손가락이나 발가락 주위의 살 속으로 자랄 수 있다. 안으로 자란 손발톱은 주위의 살로 파고들 수 있고 그 부분을 세균에 감염되기 쉽게 하고 어쩌면 감염을 일으킬 수도 있다.

3. Sigmund Freud believed that dreams represent secret wishes that someone isn't aware of having, and he believed that dreams must be symbolically interpreted to reveal these wishes.

지문 해석 |
꿈을 생각할 때 우리는 말이 안 되는 이상한 이미지를 떠올릴지 모른다. 하지만 지그문트 프로이트는 꿈이 말이 된다고 주장했다. 그는 어떤 사람의 꿈이 사실은, 너무나 비밀스러워서 본인이 갖고 있는지조차 모를 수도 있는 바람을 나타내는 상징이라고 생각했다. 프로이트는 그렇다면 어떤 사람의 숨겨진 바람이 무엇인지 이해하기 위해 꿈이 상징적으로 해석되어야만 한다고 주장했다.

B

1. Any group that wants to use campus facilities for meetings must first apply at the Office of Student Affairs.

Script |
So, you said that you would like to start a bird-watching group that meets in a classroom, right? Well, I'm not sure if you were aware of this, but any group that wants to use any campus facilities for meetings must receive permission from the university first. You can do this by filling out an application at the Office for Student Affairs.

Script 해석 |
자, 교실에서 만나는 새 관찰 모임을 시작하고 싶다고 했었지? 그런데 알고 있는지 모르겠지만, 모임을 위해 교내 시설을 이용하고자 하는 단체는 우선 학교로부터 승인을 받아야 해. 학생 사무처에서 신청서를 작성하면 돼.

2. Wind occurs when a cool, heavy air mass shifts air pressure to a warm, light air mass, resulting in equal air pressure for both masses.

Script |
How does wind form? Well, there are air masses of different temperatures all over the planet. Warm air will be lighter and have low pressure, whereas heavier cool air will have high pressure. When a high pressure mass encounters one with low pressure, then air pressure will shift from high to low—this is wind. This shift continues until both masses have equal air pressure.

Script 해석 |
바람은 어떻게 생성될까요? 음, 지구 곳곳에는 다양한 온도의 공기 층이 존재하고 있습니다. 따뜻한 공기는 보다 가볍고 저기압인 반면 더 무겁고 찬 공기는 고기압을 띠죠. 고기압의 공기층이 저기압 층과 만나면 기압은 높은 곳에서 낮은 곳 으로 이동합니다. 이것이 바람입니다. 이러한 이동은 두 공기층이 같은 기압을 가질 때까지 계속됩니다.

3. The student learned that a student identification card is needed to purchase photocopies and that it can be used to purchase anything sold by the college.

Script |
When I tried to copy some pages on the library's photocopier, I realized that the printer wouldn't take my coins. Apparently, you have to purchase credit on your student identification card and pay for photocopies with that. However, the good thing is that this card can be used to purchase anything sold by the college, so you don't have to bring cash when you're here.

Script 해석 |
도서관 복사기에서 몇 페이지를 복사하려고 했을 때, 저는 기계에 동전을 넣을 수 없다는 것을 알았습니다. 보아하니 학생 증에 적립되는 포인트를 구매해서 그것으로 복사비를 지불해야 하는 것 같습니다. 하지만 좋은 점은 이 카드가 학교측에서 파는 것은 무엇이든 구입할 때 사용될 수 있다는 것입니다. 그래서 교내에서는 현금을 갖고 다닐 필요가 없습니다.

Exercise 10. 뒷받침 내용(Supporting Points) 찾기

A

1. Summmary B

지문 해석 |
아마 주차장 앞에 왜 그렇게 많은 스쿨버스들이 있는지 궁금하실 겁니다. 대학 방문 수업이 있어서 그렇습니다. 지역 중학교의 학생들이 보통 대학이 어떤 곳인지 볼 수 있도록 이 학교를 둘러보기를 원했습니다. 아이들을 보는 것은 재미있지만 이 주변에 주차하는 것은 정말 문제입니다. 그러니까 스쿨버스들이 주변의 모든 주차 공간을 차지했기 때문에 저는 교정 반대편으로부터 내내 걸어야 했습니다.

2. Summmary A

지문 해석 |
만일 당신이 다음 학기에 졸업을 할 것이고 졸업 후에 어떤 일을 하고 싶은지 확신이 없다면 이번 주말에 열리는 직업 박람회에 가야 합니다. 이 직업 박람회는 여러 회사와 분야를 대표하는 사람들이 참가합니다. 이 대표들은 당신이 공부하고 있는 분야와 관련된 직업에 대해 당신과 이야기할 것입니다. 하지만 분명히 해야 할 것은 수요일까지 당신의 모든 학생 정보가 담긴 신청서를 작성해야 한다는 것입니다. 특히 당신의 전공과 관심 있는 업종을 기록해야 합니다.

B

1. Summmary A

Script |
I'm sure that you all know the female kangaroo is famous for the pouch she uses to carry her young offspring. While it is most noted in kangaroos, this pouch is actually a distinguishing feature of all marsupials. Marsupials give birth to their offspring rather quickly, but these offspring need more time to feed from their mother than other mammals do. Thus, marsupials have these outer pouches to carry and protect their offspring while they feed them.

Script 해석 |
여러분 모두 암컷 캥거루가 어린 새끼를 넣고 다니는 데 사용하는 주머니로 유명하다는 것을 알 것이라 생각합니다. 이 주머니는 캥거루에게서 가장 유명하지만 사실 모든 유대류* 포유동물의 구별되는 특징입니다. 유대류 포유동물은 새끼를 비교적 빨리 낳지만 이들 새끼들은 다른 포유동물들보다 어미에게서 더 오랫동안 수유를 해야 합니다. 그래서 유대류 포유동물들은 새끼를 먹이는 동안 새끼를 넣고 다니며 보호하기 위해 이 외부의 주머니가 있습니다.

*유대류(marsupial): 원시적인 태생 포유동물로 새끼가 발육이 불완전한 상태로 태어나 보통 어미의 배에 있는 육아낭 속에서 젖을 먹고 자란다.

2. Summmary B

Script |
Today, we'll discuss the American bison. More than a century ago, bison were very numerous. They grazed almost everywhere in North America, and they provided Plains Indians with food, clothing, and other basic necessities. However, American hunters began hunting bison for commercial purposes, and drove this animal to the brink of extinction. The population dwindled to such low numbers that the US government thought about protecting them. However, the government wanted to drive the Plains Indians off their land, so bison hunting continued in order to deprive the Indians of their main food source.

Script 해석 |
오늘 우리는 아메리카 들소에 대해 이야기 할 것입니다. 백여 년 전에 들소들은 매우 많았습니다. 들소들은 북미의 거의 전 지역에서 풀을 뜯어먹었습니다. 그리고 들소들은 인디언들에게 먹을 것과 입을 것 그리고 다른 기본적인 필요들을 공급해 주었습니다. 하지만 미국의 사냥꾼들이 들소를 상업적인 목적으로 사냥하기 시작했고, 이 동물을 멸종의 위기에 이르게 했습니다. 들소의 수가 너무 낮은 수치로 줄어들어서 미국 정부는 들소들을 보호하는 것을 고려했습니다. 하지만 당국은 인디언들을 그들의 땅에서 몰아내기 원했습니다. 그래서 들소 사냥은 인디언들의 주요 식량원을 박탈하기 위해 계속 되었습니다

Exercise 11. 노트 보고 요약하기(독해)   p. 184

A

1. Manifest Destiny was the belief that America's conquest of North America was destined, inevitable, and morally right. Americans used Manifest Destiny as an excuse to settle Western farmland and drive off native tribes who already lived there.

지문 해석 |
19세기 말에 미국에서는 방대한 규모의 서부 땅을 어떻게 이용할 것인지에 대해 논쟁이 있었다. 많은 미국인들은 이 땅에 정착하여 그곳을 농사에 사용하기 원했지만 이미 서부에서 살고 있는 여러 다양한 원주민 부족들이 있었다. 그래서 미국인들은 '명백한 사명'이라는 개념을 내놓았다. '명백한 사명'은 미국인들이 그들 사회가 북미를 다스릴 운명이라고 믿는 것인데, 그리하여 서부를 정복하는 것이 불가피한 일이고 도덕적으로도 옳다고 믿었다. '명백한 사명'은 결국 원주민들을 그들의 고향 땅에서 몰아내는 명분이 되었다.

2. When tectonic plates grind against each other, they can strain and suddenly slip, causing earthquakes on the earth's surface. The intensity of earthquakes can destroy cities, like San Francisco, which are located near plate boundaries.

지문 해석 |
지구의 지각은 여러 개의 구조판들로 이루어져 있고, 이 판들은 지각의 바로 아래에 있는 마그마 층 위에 떠다닌다. 이때이 판들의 경계는 지속적으로 서로를 마모시키고 때로는 마모되는 중에 밀려나 갑자기 미끄러져서 지표를 흔드는 에너지 파동을 방출한다. 이것이 지진이다. 지진은 매우 강해서 많은 손실을 유발할 수 있다. 그 결과 샌프란시스코와 같이 맞물리는 판의 경계 근처에 위치한 몇몇 도시들은 지진에 의해 거의 완전히 파괴되었던 적이 있다.

B

1.

> insider trading: exe. can give inv. priv. about corp. stock price
> - usu. illegal b/c of power abuse
> e.g. exe. sells bus. to 2nd corp. b/c he buys 2nd corp. stock to make profit

→ Insider trading occurs when an executive reveals private information about his corporation's stock and influences an investor. It's usually illegal because executives can manipulate corporate stock to make profits. For instance, insider trading would occur if a businessman sold his business to a corporation and told friends, who then invested in this corporation.

지문 해석 |
경제계에서 회사는 주식에 투자하는 사람들에 의해 세워질 수도 있고 무너질 수도 있다. 자, 이 회사의 한 임원이 어떤 투자자에게 주가에 영향을 미치는 회사 기밀 정보를 알려줌으로써 그에게 영향을 미칠 수 있다. 이를 내부 거래라고 한다. 내부 거래의 형태는 대부분 불법인데 왜냐하면 중역들이 그들의 권력을 남용할 수 있기 때문이다. 가령, 임원은 자신의 친구들에게 다른 회사의 주식에 투자하라고 말해줄 수 있는데, 왜냐하면 그는 자신의 기업을 이 두 번째 회사에 팔 계획이기 때문이다. 이러한 거래자들은 이득을 볼 것이지만 직원들은 일자리를 잃게 될 것이다.

Exercise 12. 노트 보고 요약하기(청취)   p. 186

A

1. If the earth suffered an asteroid impact, which many scientists believe killed the dinosaurs, the asteroid, regardless of size, would send massive dust clouds into the air. These would block out the sun and send the earth into a new ice age, killing everything.

Script |
Let's look at what would happen if an asteroid ever collided with the planet. Now, many scientists believe that this is actually what wiped out the dinosaurs, and research has given us a good idea of its effects. Depending on the size, the actual impact may or may not destroy all life on the planet, but even a relatively small asteroid could kick up enormous clouds of dust upon impact. If this were to occur, the dust would block out the sun, sending the earth into an ice age in which no life would survive.

Script 해석 |
만일 소행성이 지구와 충돌한다면 어떤 일이 일어날지 살펴봅시다. 오늘날 많은 과학자들은 이것이 실제로 공룡을 멸종시켰다고 믿고 있으며, 연구 결과는 우리에게 그 영향에 대해 잘 알려줍니다. 크기에 따라서 실제 충격은 지구의 모든 생명체를 파괴시킬 수도 그렇지 않을 수도 있습니다. 하지만 상대적으로 작은 소행성이라도 충격으로 거대한 먼지 구름을 일으킬 수 있습니다. 만일 이런 일이 발생하면 먼지가 태양을 막아서 지구에 빙하기를 일으킬 것이며, 그렇게 되면 어떤 생명체도 살아남지 못할 것입니다.

2. The United Nations was formed after World War II in order to avoid another war. Five important nations in this organization are America, Russia, Britain, China, and France, because they won World War II. Only these nations are permanent members of the Security Council, and they can veto any enforcement plans.

Script |

After the Second World War, most nations wanted to avoid another massive global battle. This led to the creation of the United Nations, which was intended to peacefully resolve international conflict. From the beginning, five countries have been instrumental in the United Nations. These are America, Russia, Britain, China, and France. See, only these five have permanent membership on the United Nations Security Council, because they were the victors in World War II. Thus, any one of them may veto any plans or proposals concerning policy enforcement that are brought up before the Security Council.

Script 해석 |

2차 세계 대전 이후, 대부분의 국가들은 이후 대규모 국제 전쟁을 피하고자 했습니다. 이는 국제연합의 창설로 이어졌는데 국제연합은 국제 분쟁을 평화적으로 해결하려는 목적으로 만들어졌습니다. 창설 단계부터 다섯 나라가 국제연합에서 중추적인 역할을 해 왔습니다. 이들 나라는 미국, 러시아, 영국, 중국, 프랑스입니다. 자, 이 다섯 나라만이 국제연합 안전보장이사회에서 영구적인 상임이사국의 지위를 갖고 있습니다. 왜냐하면 그들이 2차 세계 대전에서의 승전국이었기 때문입니다. 그래서 그들 중 어느 나라든 안보리에 제기된 정책 집행에 관한 어떤 안건에도 거부권을 행사할 수 있습니다.

B

1.

> Embezzlement: crime that can ruin career
> - use funds for stuff not int. for
> - done a lot w/ small stuff i.e. exp. lunch or pers. phone; these might help comp.
> - illegal when pur. is large & not related to business (e.g. a vac. home bought w/ dep. budg.)

→ Embezzlement is using company money to purchase things it was not intended for. Embezzlement usually involves purchasing small things that could help a company, like lunches or personal phone calls, but it is a serious, career-threatening crime when it is used for overly expensive personal purchases, like vacation homes.

Script |

In both business and government, there exists a very serious crime that can ruin a person's reputation and career. What I'm talking about is embezzlement. Embezzlement is when somebody uses company funds for something they were not intended for. Now, people do this a lot, especially with small purchases like expensive lunches or personal phone calls. However, these can still be written off as expenses that help the company. Illegal embezzlement usually involves a purchase that isn't at all related to business and involves an excessive amount of money, like buying a vacation home with a department's budget.

Script 해석 |

재계에서나 정계에서나 한 사람의 명성과 경력을 망쳐버릴 수 있는 매우 심각한 범죄가 있습니다. 제가 말하고 있는 것은 횡령입니다. 횡령은 어떤 사람이 회사 자금을 의도되지 않은 목적으로 사용하는 것입니다. 오늘날 사람들은 이것을 아주 많이 하는데, 특히 비싼 점심이나 개인 용무의 전화와 같은 소규모의 지출에서 그러합니다. 그러나 이러한 것들은 여전히 회사를 위한 비용으로 처리될 수 있습니다. 불법 횡령은 대개 사업과 전혀 관련이 없는 구입을 포함하고 엄청난 양의 돈을 포함합니다. 부처 예산으로 별장을 사는 것과 같은 행위가 그것이죠.

2.

> dr. must know if ill. is bac. or virus
> virus usu. won't have med. b/c virus rep. w/ h. cell → med. will dest. h. cell too

→ If a virus causes someone's illness, then there usually isn't any medicine that can effectively treat the virus. This is because viruses must infect host cells in order to reproduce, so medicine that could destroy the virus might destroy the host cell, too.

Script |

If you were to go to a doctor to get treated for an illness, he or she would first have to decide whether or not the illness was caused by bacteria or by a virus. If the illness is caused by a virus, then there usually isn't any medicine that the doctor can prescribe. One reason is that a virus does not reproduce on its own; it must infect a host cell in order to create more virus cells. This means that any chemical that could possibly destroy the virus would also destroy the host cell infected by the virus.

Script 해석 |

질병을 치료받기 위해 병원에 갈 것이라면, 의사는 우선 질병이 박테리아에 의한 것인지 혹은 바이러스에 의한 것인지 판단해야 합니다. 만일 질병이 바이러스에 의해 생긴 것이라면, 일반적으로 의사가 처방할 수 있는 약이 없습니다. 한 가지이유는 바이러스가 혼자서 재생하지 않는다는 것입니다. 바이러스는 더 많은 바이러스 세포들을 만들기 위해 숙주 세포를 감염시켜야 합니다. 이는 바이러스를 소멸할 수 있을 화학물질이면 바이러스에 의해 감염된 숙주 세포도 역시 파괴시킬 것을 의미합니다.

3.

> Calligraphy = art of writ. let. or sym. creat.
> - in Asia, nat. have cent. old trad. that teach call.
> - in west call. isn't used much b/c of print. press
> - used in west for comm. purp. i.e. comp. font or gift card

→ Calligraphy is the art of writing letters or symbols creatively, having a centuries-long tradition of being taught in Asian societies. In western tradition, it declined after the printing press was invented, but it has found commercial applications, like computer fonts or gift cards.

Script |

When we talk about calligraphy, or the art of creatively writing letters or symbols, we must look at how different societies view calligraphy. In many Asian countries, like China, India, and Iran, there is a centuries-old tradition of teaching everyone how to render that society's words in calligraphy. Now, in Western tradition, calligraphy hasn't been commonly used as an art form, mainly due to the creation of the printing press centuries ago. However, people have found uses for calligraphy in a lot of commercial applications, such as for computer fonts or gift cards.

Script 해석 |

캘리그래피, 다시 말해 창의적으로 글씨나 기호를 쓰는 예술에 대해 이야기할 때, 우리는 사회마다 어떤 관점으로 캘리그래피를 보는지 살펴보아야 합니다. 중국, 인도, 이란과 같은 많은 아시아 국가에서는 그 사회에서 사용되는 말을 서예로 표현하는 방법을 모든 사람에게 가르치는 수 세기의 전통이 내려오고 있습니다. 그러나 서양 전통에서는 캘리그래피가 예술의 한 형태로 보편적으로 사용되지 않았는데, 주된 이유는 수 세기 전에 인쇄기가 발명되었기 때문입니다. 하지만 사람들은 컴퓨터 글꼴이나 선물 카드와 같이 서예를 상업적으로 많이 응용할 수 있는 용도를 발견했습니다.

3. Pronunciation

Exercise 1. 자음 & 모음 p. 190

A
2. X 3. O 4. X 5. X 6. X
7. X 8. X 9. O 10. X

녹음 내용
1. bride, pride
2. advice, advise
3. lose, lose
4. pried, fried
5. through, true
6. thought, sought
7. this, these
8. thief, dip
9. dessert, dessert
10. base, vase

B
2. world 3. lay 4. bell
5. really 6. thighs 7. think
8. dad 9. some 10. soothe

C
silent ②   standing ②   television ③   vast ②
scared ②   conservative ②   neighbors ①   invasion ③
enormous ②   confusing ①   unusual ③   exasperate ②
answer ②   closed ①   closely ②   phase ①

D
1. great에서 g를 [k]로 발음 (옳은 발음은 [g])
2. for에서 f를 [p]로 발음 (옳은 발음은 [f])
3. written에서 r를 [l]로 발음 (옳은 발음은 [r])
4. nonsense에서 뒤의 s를 [z]로 발음 (옳은 발음은 [s])
5. village에서 v를 [b]로 발음 (옳은 발음은 [v])
6. thing에서 th를 [s]로 발음 (옳은 발음은 [θ])

E
2. lost 3. life 4. sport 5. wake 6. civilized
7. have 8. future 9. pleasant 10. thirsty

F

Asian ②	anthropology ①	ancient ②	calligraphy ③
Saturday ①	satellite ①	sacred ②	age ②
compatible ①	lateral ①	gravity ①	human ③
label ②	literature ③	narrative ③	narrator ②

G
1. written에서 i를 [ai]로 발음 (옳은 발음은 [i])
2. mold에서 o를 [au]로 발음 (옳은 발음은 [ou])
3. owl에서 ow를 [ou]로 발음 (옳은 발음은 [au])
4. valves에서 뒤의 a를 [ei]로 발음 (옳은 발음은 [æ])
5. ocean에서 ea를 [i:]로 발음 (옳은 발음은 [ə])

Exercise 2. 묵음 & 강조   p. 192

※ 아래 정답은 사람에 따라 다르게 발음할 수 있기 때문에 절대적인 기준은 아니며, 오디오 CD에 녹음된 성우의 발음에 준하여 표시된 것입니다. 일반적으로 d나 t는 뒤에 모음이나 h가 올때 연음되어 발음됩니다.

A
2. knight
3. fasten
4. chalk
5. doubt
6. debt
7. receipt
8. pneumonia
9. psychiatrist
10. climbing

B
2. ádvertising
3. evéntually
4. adjúst
5. photógrapher
6. indiréct
7. garáge
8. displáy
9. állies*
10. détail*

* allies와 detail도 가능하나 더 보편적인 강세를 답으로 표시하였음

C
2. récord (noun)
3. presént (verb)
4. addréss (verb)
5. díscharge (noun)
6. expórt (verb)

D
2. occúr, occúrrence
3. contribute, contribútion
4. arríive, arríval
5. pursúe, pursúit
6. hóstile, hostílity
7. desíre, desírable
8. emít, emíssion
9. ecólogy, ecológical
10. resólve, resolútion

E 2. Today we will **discúss** something that's always been a serious threat to **ágriculture**.
3. **Phýsical** barriers set up on farmland **absórb** or **defléct** natural **ágents** of **érosion**.
4. This is why many **agricúltural commúnities** reforest areas by planting new trees.
5. Even before **slávery** was **óutlawed**, there were several ways people could **defý** slavery.
6. The **rúnaway** slaves took long, **indiréct** routes through **désolate** areas.
7. Snakes can bite animals and **injéct** them with **vénom**.
8. It's the school's **responsibílity** to **repláce** them with louder **alárms**.
9. There are **situátions** in which a person's **proféssional** duties **conflíct** with his personal ones.

Exercise 3. 문장 강조 p. 194

※ 이 부분의 답은 사람에 따라 약간씩 다르게 들을 수 있기 때문에 절대적인 것은 아닙니다. 대체적으로 문장에서 강세를 받는 말은 명사, 동사, 형용사, 부사, 부정어 등이지만 반드시 그런 것은 아니며 문맥에 따라 달라질 수 있습니다. 또한 같은 문장이라도 사람에 따라 다르게 말할 수도 있습니다. 이 점을 참고하되, 대체로 어떤 단어에 강세가 오는지 유의하면서 문장을 잘 들어 봅시다.

A 2. kind, worried, housing, situation
3. working, lot, classes, next, year
4. think, which, rather, do
5. sounds, something, wrong
6. can't, find, research, materials, paper
7. You, won't, get, week, two
8. That, sounds, pretty, tough, situation
9. just, not, sure, what, do
10. wouldn't, school, summer

녹음 내용

1. What have you been up to lately?
2. I'm kind of worried about my housing situation.
3. I'll be working a lot on classes next year.
4. I'll think about which one I'd rather do.
5. It sounds like something's wrong.
6. I can't find any good research materials for my paper.
7. You won't get them for about a week or two.
8. That sounds like a pretty tough situation.
9. I'm just not sure what I'm going to do now.
10. You wouldn't have to go to school during the summer.

B 2. With the tag, at least a campus cop knows to check for it on your rear view mirror.
3. Sometimes animals will go extinct because they can't adapt to subtle habitat changes.
4. This would have dramatic effects on the animals that prey on these gazelles.
5. Without any animals to feed on, they too would become extinct.
6. Othello becomes passionately enraged when he mistakenly believes that she is unfaithful to him.
7. Before an entrepreneur can make his fortune, he must decide on what kind of business he'd like to start.

8. If they decide to build cars, then they probably won't be able to build house as well.
9. He will usually see which industry has the most customers at a certain place or time.
10. Humans, like most other animals, have a series of different organs, all used for different tasks.

C 1.
> I prefer to do activities on a holiday rather than just stay home and relax. One reason I prefer doing activities is that I have something to discuss with friends when I do an activity on a holiday. For example, I can tell stories about the time I went to the countryside for a picnic or rode my bicycle down a new trail. Moreover, I believe it is a waste of time to sit around and do nothing, because a holiday is such a good time to do things I want to do. I feel like I wasted a whole day when I just sit around and watch TV. In other words, it can be a more meaningful way of spending time if you do something worth doing.

2.
> I personally think that a person that has a great influence on people's lives today is Bill Gates. To start, he sells a lot of computer programs, more than anyone else. This means that people rely on him for their computers to work, and computers are needed for almost everything that we do. Next, Bill Gates donates lots of money to charity. He has given billions of dollars to help people in Africa. By using his money and power like this, he can influence others to give too, and this can help everyone. In conclusion, Bill Gates is someone who has a great influence on people's lives today.

4. Grammar

Exercise 1. 주어 동사 일치   p. 198

A
2. are   3. were   4. are   5. is   6. are
7. were   8. was   9. is   10. asks   11. live
12. have   13. were   14. show   15. are

B
2. One reason why I prefer doing outdoor activities ~~are~~ that I can breathe fresh air.
   is

3. OK

4. I have seen a lot of television programs that ~~shows~~ the suffering of children who have disabilities.
   show

5. OK

6. The newly elected president has certain characteristics that ~~is~~ seen among great leaders.
   are

7. One of the best ways to improve your writing skills ~~are~~ to write in a journal every day.
   is

8. OK

9. Some people say five years ~~are~~ not long enough to master a foreign language, but I think it depends on how much effort you put in.
   is

10. Both the reading passage and the lecture ~~discusses~~ the causes of the Iraq War.
    discuss

4. Grammar

Exercise 2. 자동사와 타동사   p. 200

A
2. X   3. X   4. to   5. to   6. X
7. X   8. X   9. X   10. X   11. with
12. on   13. with   14. to   15. X   16. X
17. on   18. X   19. X   20. X

B
2. Since Ben has never ~~traveled~~ Asia, he is planning to visit an Asian country this summer.
   traveled to
3. OK
4. I didn't note (at) any difference between the two pictures.
5. OK
6. I strongly oppose (to) the idea that she is a feminist writer.
7. My mom, who was very angry about my behavior, shouted at me and started to ~~talk~~ how rude I was.
   talk about
8. It contradicts (with) the fact that there were other European visitors at that time.
9. The professor does not discuss (about) Chinese traditions such as tea drinking and footbinding.
10. OK

Exercise 3. 사역동사   p. 202

A
2. do   3. recommended   4. forwarded
5. to do   6. styled   7. arranged
8. do   9. done   10. sent

B
2. A good sense of humor can help a leader ~~being~~ more effective in building harmony among group members.
   (to) be
3. Lowering taxes can create more jobs and ~~make~~ people live better lives.
   let / help
4. Indifference to elections can make the country ~~to~~ collapse.
5. Because I can't spare a moment right now, I'll ~~have~~ one of my co-workers to work on it.
   get
   또는 Because I can't spare a moment right now, I'll have one of my co-workers work on it.
6. OK
7. OK
8. Josh works so fast that he gets ~~done everything~~ and still has time left.
   everything done
9. You may make a request to have the book ~~return~~.
   returned
10. We hope to have this project ~~finishing~~ by this Thursday.
    finished

Workbook •• A75

Exercise 4. 감각을 표현하는 동사 p. 205

A
2. hear
3. have been seeing
4. look at
5. watch
6. feels
7. feels
8. hear
9. listen to
10. could smell

B
2. The anthropologist used some of the stories she ~~listened~~ from the local people.
   heard
3. The theory ~~isn't sounding~~ persuasive anymore because it has been opposed by many scholars.
   doesn't sound
4. These days, it's not unusual to ~~look at~~ a man wearing pink.
   see
5. A national leader must ~~hear~~ public opinions and share his ideas with people.
   listen to
6. The wound ~~is not looking~~ serious, but you'd better show it to a doctor.
   does not look
7. Ellen didn't know what the assignment was because she wasn't ~~hearing~~ what the teacher was saying.
   listening to
8. OK
9. This soup ~~is tasting~~ weird. Is it safe to eat?
   tastes
10. I wasn't really ~~listening to~~ the song clearly because of the noise from outside.
    hearing

Exercise 5. 동사의 시제 p. 206

A
2. gives
3. usually take
4. am taking
5. am going
6. walked
7. have hated
8. lost
9. has been
10. doesn't come
11. warms up
12. can't afford

B
2. OK
3. The horse ~~has run~~ away when he got scared.
   ran
4. We ~~ate~~ well ever since we hired a cook.
   have eaten
5. Alison ~~has given~~ me this scarf for my birthday.
   gave
6. OK
7. I won't go home before I ~~will~~ go out for the evening.
8. Tamara is going to call me while she ~~will be~~ on vacation.
   is
9. OK
10. Rob's going to work out before he ~~will go~~ to class.
    goes

4. Grammar

Exercise 6. 간접 의문문   p. 208

A
2. where I had been
3. what my favorite color was
4. where the elevator is
5. what you think of this poem
6. I could drive him home
7. how old Danielle is
8. how he could get downtown
9. if she could renew her passport
10. if you need anything

B
2. how to work
3. what to bring
4. where to go
5. when to call
6. how to bake
7. where to go
8. how to find
9. what to expect
10. whom to see

Exercise 7. To 부정사를 취하는 동사와 -ing를 취하는 동사   p. 210

A
2. to see
3. swimming
4. smoking
5. meditating
6. eating
7. the players to try
8. to count
9. to give
10. to tidy up

B
2. Holly stopped ~~to run~~ after she injured her knee.
   running
3. OK
4. Emma's essay is coherent and well-written, but she fails ~~reaching~~ a logical conclusion.
   to reach
5. OK
6. I miss ~~to stay~~ up late and ~~hang out~~ with my friends like I did when I was in school.
   staying   *hanging*
7. OK
8. I wished ~~having~~ an excellent birthday, but I was not able to do so because an exam fell on that day.
   to have
9. OK
10. Citizens want ~~improving~~ the quality of their lives in a more active way.
    to improve

Exercise 8. 울타리 표현 (Hedging)   p. 212

A
2. seem / appear
3. known / recognized
4. appears / seems
5. believed / known / recognized
6. known / recognized
7. doubt
8. proof
9. seem / appear
10. little

B
2. The airline appears to have lost your luggage.
3. It appears that this work will have to be redone by someone else.
4. My sister appears to be losing weight.
5. Greta seems to think nothing is ever her fault.
6. It is recognized that human activity is responsible for global warming.
7. It is believed that the economy will gradually improve.
8. It is known that eating a lot of fast food contributes to obesity.
9. There is some doubt that Michael is the most qualified person for the job.
10. There is little doubt that scientists will eventually discover a cure for cancer.

Exercise 9. 비교급과 최상급   p. 215

A
2. the oldest
3. less
4. biggest
5. as hot as
6. the most delicious
7. the busiest
8. yours
9. would rather
10. Rather than

B
2. OK
3. Today is the worst day of my life! It is even ~~more bad~~ *worse* than when I got lost in Japan last year.
4. My university science classes are ~~more hard~~ *harder* than I expected.
5. Many people consider that actress *the* most beautiful woman alive.
6. I will do it myself, *rather* than ask someone else.
7. Electric guitars are much louder ~~as~~ *than* acoustic ones.
8. A study shows that military veterans are twice as likely to commit suicide ~~than~~ *as* ordinary people.
9. That was ~~funny~~ *the funniest* movie I have ever seen.
10. OK

Exercise 10. 형용사의 쓰임 　　　　　　　　　　　　　　　　　　　　　　　　　p. 216

A
- **2.** about
- **3.** at
- **4.** at
- **5.** with
- **6.** in
- **7.** in
- **8.** of
- **9.** with
- **10.** to

B
- **2.** It's necessary for everyone to have an occasional break.
- **3.** It's annoying for her to clean up after the kids each day.
- **4.** It's boring (for me) to do the same thing every day.
- **5.** It was unpleasant for Jim to remember that time in his life.
- **6.** It's beneficial (for you) to have a good role model.
- **7.** It's unusual for the sun to shine so late into the day.
- **8.** The book was enjoyable to read.
- **9.** It is exciting for people who love traveling to visit new countries.
- **10.** It's stressful for Julie to work such long hours every day.

Notes

TOEFL® iBT books from LinguaForum

링구아포럼의 6단계별 토플 교재 eBasic-e-b-m-i-Hooked on

TOEFL® iBT 훅톤 시리즈 | Advanced Level
- New Edition Hooked On TOEFL (훅톤토플)
  Reading / Listening / Speaking / Writing
- 빈출 1순위 TOEFL VOCA / Frequency#1 TOEFL VOCA (영문판) / 빈출 1순위 TOEFL VOCA Workbook
- TOEFL® iBT INSIDER-The Super Guide (영문판) / TOEFL® iBT Test Book 1(영문판)

TOEFL® iBT i,m 시리즈 | High Intermediate ~ Intermediate Level
- New Edition TOEFL® iBT
  i-Reading / i-Listening / i-Speaking / i-Writing
- TOEFL® iBT Core Topic Guide (영문판·총 4권) / INTRO VOCA (한글판·영문판)
- TOEFL® iBT m-Reading / m-Listening / m-Grammar / m-Speaking / m-Writing

TOEFL® iBT b,e 시리즈 | Low Intermediate ~ High Beginner's Level
- TOEFL® iBT b-Reading / b-Listening / b-Grammar / b-Writing
- TOEFL® iBT Basic VOCA
- TOEFL® iBT e-Reading / e-Listening / e-Grammar

TOEFL® iBT eBasic 시리즈 | Beginner's Level
- TOEFL® iBT eBasic-Reading / eBasic-Listening

"세계가 신뢰하는 **Worldwide on-line iBT Test**"
www.linguaforum.com

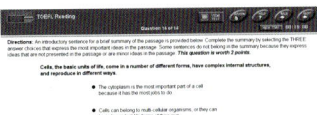

LinguaForum™

우153-792, 서울시 금천구 가산동 459-11 제이플라츠 빌딩 8F
교재주문 (02) 3480-6627 대표전화 (02) 3480-6614
● www.linguaforum.com ● www.finalibt.co.kr 회사 소개 / 도서 구매 / 온라인토플테스트
● linguaforum@timeholdings.co.kr 도서 문의 및 상담

글로벌 영어 교육 브랜드 링구아포럼이 개발한
TEPS 실전 종합서 STEP TEPS!

TEPS의 입문부터 실전까지 완벽 준비 가능한 STEP TEPS는 900점 이상을 목표로 하는 final 시리즈와 750점 이상을 목표로 하는 expert, 600점 이상을 목표로 하는 starter 시리즈로 레벨별 3단계로 구성되어 수험생의 실력에 맞게 선택할 수 있는 맞춤형 필수 TEPS 교재입니다.

900점 이상을 목표로 하는 실전 수험생들을 위한 STEP TEPS final 시리즈

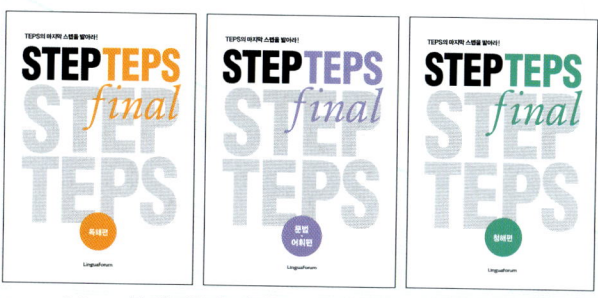

독해 / 청해 / 문법·어휘편

Point 1. Visual Mapping, Grammar Map, 독해, 청해 전략 풀이의 시각적 학습 자료를 제공하여 효과적인 학습 유도
Point 2. 독학과 강의 수업 모두에 적합한 구성 (별책 해답 / MP3 파일)
Point 3. 타 교재에 비해 월등히 많은 문항 수 (독해 약 300문항 / 청해 약 580문항 / 문법 약 1200문항 / 어휘 약 1200문항)
Point 4. 실전 시험과 동일한 수준과 형식의 진단고사와 Actual Test 4세트씩 수록

750점 이상을 목표로 하는 중급 학습자를 위한 STEP TEPS expert 시리즈

독해 / 청해 / 문법·어휘편

Point 1. 중급 학습자들의 영역별 취약 Point 전략 제시
  (문법 최신 기출 Point / Collocation 어휘 학습 / 빠른 독해 풀이 / 청해 파트별 오답 유형 분석)
Point 2. 중급용 교재 대비 최다 연습 문제와 실전 문제 수록 (별책 해답 / MP3 파일)
Point 3. 편리하고 친절한 해설서 제공
Point 4. 최신 기출 경향을 반영한 진단고사와 Actual Test 2세트씩 수록

600점 이상을 목표로 하는 초급 학습자를 위한 STEP TEPS starter 시리즈

독해·문법편 / 청해·어휘편

귀가 뚫리는 비법속으로
iNTO Listening
LinguaForum

[청취능력 향상과 영어듣기평가 및 영어 인증시험 완전 대비!]

▸ iNTO Listening 1
13,500원 (CD 1장 포함)

▸ iNTO Listening 2
13,500원 (CD 1장 포함)

▸ iNTO Listening 3
13,500원 (CD 1장 포함)

☑ **Catch two pigeons with one bean!**
Listening skill 완전정복을 통한 청취능력 향상과 각종 테스트 대비를 한번에!

- Listening skill 완전 분석 및 적용
- 주제별 유형별 풍부한 문제 수록
- 다양하고 현장감 넘치는 지문 제공
- 단어 암기에서 부터 Self-study까지 단계별 청취 마스터 시스템
- 수준별 총 3권 구성